FATE OF
THE STATES

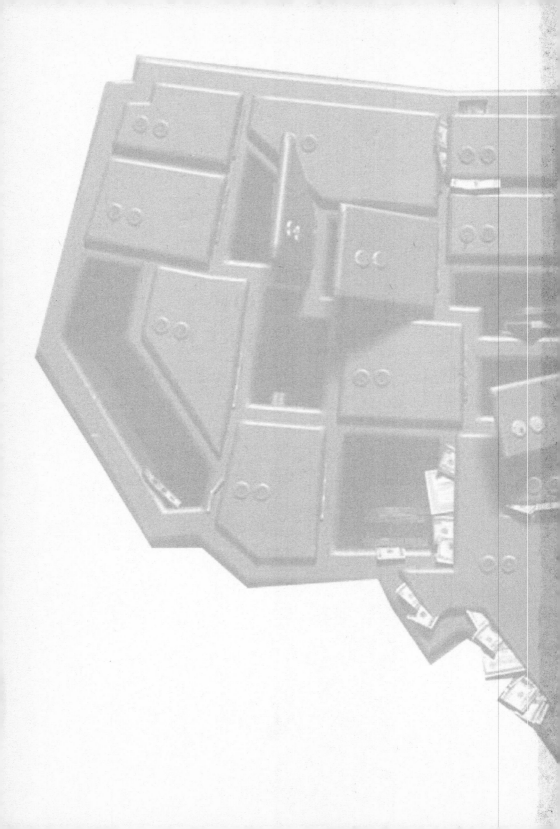

FATE OF THE STATES

THE NEW GEOGRAPHY OF AMERICAN PROSPERITY

MEREDITH WHITNEY

Portfolio / Penguin

PORTFOLIO / PENGUIN
Published by the Penguin Group
Penguin Group (USA) Inc., 375 Hudson Street,
New York, New York 10014, USA

USA | Canada | UK | Ireland | Australia | New Zealand | India | South Africa | China

Penguin Books Ltd, Registered Offices: 80 Strand, London WC2R 0RL, England
For more information about the Penguin Group visit penguin.com

Illustrations by Meredith Whitney Advisory Group unless otherwise indicated.

Library of Congress Cataloging-in-Publication Data

Whitney, Meredith.
Fate of the states : the new geography of American prosperity / Meredith Whitney.
pages cm
Includes bibliographical references and index.
ISBN 978-1-59184-570-6
1. United States—Economic conditions—2009–   2. U.S. states—Economic
conditions.   3. United States—Economic policy—2009–
4. U.S. states—Economic policy.   5. Recessions—United States.
6. Financial crises—United States.   I. Title.
HC106.84.W48 2013
330.973—dc23
2013006821

Printed in the United States of America
1   3   5   7   9   10   8   6   4   2
Book design by Alissa Amell
Set in Electra LT Std

ALWAYS LEARNING   PEARSON

For my grandfather, Kenneth W. Elvin, who raised me believing in the
original American Dream: that with hard work,
anything is possible.
And, of course, for John

Contents

Introduction   1

PART I   *The Fall*

Chapter 1

   It Starts at Home   17

Chapter 2

   Housing Revisited   31

Chapter 3

   States Gone Wild   53

Chapter 4

   Pensions: The Debt Bomb Nobody's Talking About   89

Chapter 5

   The Negative Feedback Loop from Hell   107

Chapter 6

   The New American Poverty   135

PART II   *The Rise*

Chapter 7

A New Map of Prosperity   155

Chapter 8

State Arbitrage   163

Chapter 9

David Takes On Goliath: New Political Precedents   183

Chapter 10

The Way Forward   195

Acknowledgments   207

Notes   209

Index   251

FATE OF
THE STATES

Introduction

I was a history major in college. Studying history is all about learning stories—stories about what led to seminal events and then sequels that explain what happened next and why. I love stories. My brain instinctively works to connect the dots in life, turning mosaics of information into narrative tales of how things came to be and what I think will happen as a result. I never look at any one data point or event in a vacuum. Rather I use a series of data points from myriad sources to tell the story of what is to come. Throughout my twenty-year career on Wall Street, the stories that have interested me most centered on the U.S. consumer. Not only does consumer spending account for 70 percent of U.S. gross domestic product, but it drives investment returns in almost every asset class, from stocks to commodities. Understanding the consumer and the direction of demographic trends means understanding where to invest.

For most of my career, I worked in equity research. In plain English, that means I immersed myself in one industry—in my case, the financial industry—and then informed clients about the latest trends in finance and about which companies were going to be the future winners and losers. You'd be surprised how many people on Wall Street don't know how to read company financial reports or interpret the underlying data. But delving into the numbers was always my favorite part of the job. With bank stocks, ensuring that a complex set of data isn't hiding something worrisome is crucial because a lot of the investors are mom-and-pop types who gravitate toward banks for their big dividends and their perceived safety.

I started my career covering one of the sketchier neighborhoods in the financial world—subprime consumer lenders. Companies like subprime auto-finance lenders, home-equity lenders, and credit-card lenders. During the 1990s, subprime loan volume soared, as did the profits of subprime lenders. I spent a lot of time visiting with the management teams of these firms. Most had no idea they were living on borrowed time. Their institutions' continued prosperity and survival hinged on their ability to access cheap credit—borrowing at low interest rates and then relending that money to subprime borrowers. One way they accessed this cheap credit was through securitization. That is, they would bundle the loans they'd made into newfangled bonds known as asset-backed or mortgage-backed securities. But securitization is like any other loan. Access to the market is tied to perceived ability to repay. In the late 1990s, investors started to lose faith. By the summer of 1998, the Russian credit crisis had stopped the global securitization market in its tracks. For many of the lenders I followed, that was the end.

Fast-forward ten years, and it wasn't just the ultratan guys with lots of gold jewelry making subprime loans. It was mainstream banks—New York–based financial giants—diving deep into subprime. This wasn't just what had been traditionally defined as subprime, a borrower with a dented credit record or no credit record; it was a whole new definition of subprime. It's a mistake to define "subprime" based upon the credit rating of the borrower. It needs to be defined by the type of loan and the borrower's ability to pay it back. For instance, if too much debt is loaded onto any borrower, no matter what their credit score may be, it becomes that much more difficult for the borrower to make good on that loan. And a lot of the mortgages that banks were underwriting—interest-only loans with deceptively low teaser rates, for example—were subprime loans even though the market didn't necessarily define them as subprime. For me, the summer of 2007 was déjà vu all over again. Banks were making bad loans, but the asset-backed and mortgage-backed securities markets kept buying them. As Citigroup CEO Chuck Prince famously pronounced in July 2007, "As long as the music is playing, you've got to get up and dance."[1] Well, the music seemed to stop almost immediately after Prince made that ill-advised remark. Investors pulled out of the securitization markets and, just as in the late 1990s, lenders started falling like dominoes. If they couldn't borrow, they couldn't stay in business.

I knew this story would end badly largely because I had lived through it once before. The fact that the protagonists were now the nation's leading banks and brokerage firms—not some lender-of-last-resort paying old ballplayers to hawk second mortgages on late-night TV—was irrelevant. It boiled down to math, and math doesn't play favorites based on pedigree. If a company cannot fund itself and cannot pay its obligations, the lights will ultimately go out (unless, of course, it gets a federal bailout). I saw early on what was happening, but at first a lot of people didn't want to hear what I had to say. Then I released an ominous report on Citigroup and, to my shock, it became the shot heard round the financial world.

The original, and now famous, call I made on October 31, 2007, tripped a wire in the markets. The report raised concerns about mortgage losses at Citigroup and warned that the megabank might be forced to cut its dividend. When the stock market reopened the next morning, Citigroup's stock plummeted, losing $17 billion in market value in one day. The S&P 500 dropped $374 billion.[2] The call that I made was similar to warnings I would make throughout 2008 about other banks. The reality was that Citigroup and the entire banking industry had amassed entirely too much debt and the all-night dance party of cheap and loose credit was over. Making matters worse, banks didn't even realize how much trouble they were in. A lot of the debt that they considered low risk was backed by residential real estate and other assets that were worth considerably less than they thought. Their financial statements were illusions—more like wishful thinking than clear-eyed accounting.

The problem with too much debt is that it narrows the margin of error for both the borrower and the lender. A bad quarter becomes a catastrophic one on the turn of a dime if a company has played too close to the edge and the mood of the market shifts quickly. That proved true for Bear Stearns in the summer of 2007, just as it did for

Citibank by the fall of 2007.[3] By 2008 the entire financial system was essentially felled by debt overload and an inability to access cheap money. By 2009 the industry had lost over $600 billion in write-downs and destroyed over half a trillion dollars in stock market valuation.[4]

How did this happen? And what might the sequel to this sad tale be? Looking for answers, I followed the money. Typically, the larger banks lend to the regions, businesses, and demographic groups demonstrating the highest rates of income growth. But during the housing boom, this approach became perversely self-fulfilling. By feeding the housing bubble, banks injected wads of new cash into local economies, generating new income for builders, decorators, real-estate agents, and hardware stores. Everyone felt a little richer—which led to ever-crazier bidding wars for homes on the market.

Easy money had big consequences. Banks borrowed more so they could make the loans that allowed consumers to borrow more. This destructive, codependent relationship allowed the financial services industry to expand rapidly, displacing manufacturing in economic importance after those jobs and production moved overseas beginning in the 1980s. This is why the system was so fragile. Consumer defaults would trigger banking defaults and vice versa, crippling the U.S. financial system for years to come. Five years after the beginning of the crisis, the U.S. lending system still hasn't recovered. Over $7 trillion has come out of the lending system, and more than 30 percent of Americans now have no access or limited access to credit.[5] People who need credit can't get it, and the housing market can't properly recover because mortgages are so much harder to come by. One key consequence: The unemployment rate has been high for longer than at any time since the Great Depression.

Over the course of 2007 and 2008, my name on Wall Street became synonymous with doom and gloom, which I found frustrating because for most of my career I had been a relentless seeker of growth and investment opportunity. By late 2008 I was more interested in figuring out where the next phase of American growth was going to come from than in dwelling on what part of the system still wasn't working. I wanted to figure out what the recovery from the worst financial crisis since the Great Depression might look like. What I knew for certain was that the road ahead would look nothing like the road we had been on for the past twenty-five years. The new economy would not resemble the old one. The numbers simply wouldn't allow it.

My grandfather grew up during the Great Depression. His father was a cop in Paterson, New Jersey. He grew up tough and close to broke. He saw how difficult it was to break the cycle of debt—how friends and neighbors who lived beyond their means would spend years digging out of debt. Witnessing such hardship turned my grandfather into the consummate debtophobe. When he bought a car, he paid in cash. When he bought a home, he paid in cash. "You can't make money," he'd often tell me, "if you owe money."

My grandfather's words kept coming back to me the deeper I dug into the latest economic data. It became clear that there were some regions of the country so burdened with debt that a muscular rebound in consumer spending would be virtually impossible. California,

Florida, Arizona, Nevada, Illinois, and New Jersey had some of the most highly indebted residents in the country—which I knew because I tracked the banks' geographic lending concentrations. During the housing bubble, banks had targeted these areas for their hot real-estate markets and for rising personal income levels. When the bubble finally burst, these states wound up with the nation's highest levels of negative equity (i.e., owing more on your mortgage than your house is worth) as well as some of the highest unemployment rates. They were also where banks had cut back credit lines most dramatically. Anyone in these areas living paycheck to paycheck had gotten a sobering margin call over the past few years. Without equity to borrow against—a key source of funding for small businesses—new-business creation, along with new-business job creation, plummeted and unemployment soared. Choked off from credit, consumers cut back on spending, digging the economic hole even deeper.

The recovery in those states would be plodding at best. But the story was very different in the states that had never been targeted by the banks during the boom years. In the central corridor of the country—sometimes referred to as the "flyover" states—the boom years were less exuberant. In Ames, Iowa, for instance, home prices went up a mere 5 percent in 2005, compared with 20 percent in Jacksonville and 41 percent in Phoenix.[6] Banks weren't offering folks in Iowa or Texas unlimited access to credit, and thus homeowners never got in over their heads. Because housing didn't boom, it didn't bust there either. Consumer spending was more closely correlated with employment and wage growth than with availability of credit. Since jobs in the central corridor weren't dependent upon housing, these states didn't see huge spikes in unemployment after the bust. What's more, manufacturing jobs are now coming back to these areas in a big way, as more and more companies locate there to take advantage of less expensive real estate and incredibly cheap and plentiful U.S. energy.

But there was something else I discovered that made these fly-over states so attractive to employers and job seekers. Their state and local governments hadn't piled on scads of debt during the boom times. As a result, there was no pressure to hike tax rates. And because they didn't have crippling debts, they had money to invest in education, roads, airports, job training, and other public services. To be sure, energy production is a big part of the story in some locales. There's no doubt, for example, that North Dakota's oil patch would still be booming even if, back in the 2000s, there'd been a housing bubble on the prairie. Nevertheless, more companies were starting to pay close attention to which states offered the lowest tax rates, boasted the best and most sustainable infrastructure, and were the most pro-business as measured by right-to-work laws and workers' compensation rules. Since 2008 these central corridor states have had unemployment rates well below the national average, as well as rising consumer spending and robust tax receipts—the exact opposite of what's happened in the housing-bust states.[7]

Talk about a shocking reversal of fortunes. California, New Jersey, and Illinois were economic powerhouses. Postrecession, not only are their citizens eyeball deep in debt, but their state and local governments are awash in red ink too. Today these states can't help but have outsized tax rates because their government budgets are so out of control. They've been forced to cut deeply into education, infrastructure, and other public services. And in an unhappy coincidence, these states also happen to be three of the most politically and bureaucratically gridlocked in the nation, making reform incredibly difficult. California, notoriously unfriendly to business, raised the marginal state tax rate on those making over $250,000 to the highest rate in the country in 2012.[8] The result: a rush to the door by many of those high earners. In 2011, Illinois hiked its income tax rates by 66 percent.[9] The governor was then forced to try to strike side deals with large businesses that threatened to leave the state. Even after the tax hikes, these states still have enormous budget gaps that require even deeper cuts to education and other public services. State and local government spending cuts combined with severely weakened consumers don't exactly help the job market either. Unemployment in these former boom states has been consistently above the national average since 2008.[10]

Last decade's housing boom and bust may have been a national story, but until I pored through the numbers, I didn't realize how distinctively local some of the fallout truly was. It wasn't just the consumers or banks whose fates were tied to housing; state and local governments were deeply connected in ways I had never imagined. In fact, many state and local governments had made the same types of gambles on housing that banks and consumers had: They bet that home prices (and thus property-tax revenues) would never, could never decline—and then borrowed and spent accordingly. Too many government budgets baked in overly optimistic assumptions about property-tax receipts. Even the worst-case scenarios anticipated only a temporary 5 percent to 10 percent decline in real-estate prices. When the bust did occur, governments had no backup plans other than piling on more debt while they waited for revenues to rebound. This created a negative feedback loop from hell: Higher debt (including unfunded pension obligations—more on those later) required higher taxes to meet debt service, which indirectly added to the indebtedness of taxpayers already struggling with their own mortgage and credit-card debt. When the states were forced to cut costs, public services deteriorated, thus pressuring home prices and effectively eliminating the home-equity lines of credit some consumers had once used as safety nets. The only thing that could break this cycle would be employment and income growth, but local businesses and state and local governments were all cutting back, dampening the job market. There would be more existing jobs lost than new ones created.

The consequences for homeowners in housing-bust states have extended beyond the loss of home equity. Everyone knows neighborhoods can deteriorate, yet nobody expects the town where they've put down stakes to be the one singled out in the newspaper for fiscal dysfunction. The typical home buyer thinks he's getting a good deal—due to the neighborhood, the schools, proximity to a metropolitan center, or the fact that (until recently, at least) the value of their house seemed to go up every year. They take for granted all the things that keep a neighborhood and a city and a real-estate market humming, such as smooth roads on the interstate or trash collection right at the curbside every Monday and Thursday. These are basic services everyone expects in an attractive, functioning community. They expect them for good reasons: Property taxes are high, and for most Americans, the home is the largest purchase they'll make as well as the biggest debt they'll incur. Life savings hang in the balance, and there ought to be some dividend from this massive investment, right? What homeowners forget is that many of the services they take for granted are not mandatory but discretionary. The only thing more shocking than seeing trash collection curtailed or parks closed is clicking over to Zillow and discovering that the value of their homes has declined another 5 percent.

None of this was inevitable, as we'll see in the pages that follow. Some local leaders identified the risks early and acted accordingly. Far too many politicians either ignored the risks or assumed they'd be gone from office before the you-know-what ever hit the fan. Just as reckless consumers piled on mounds of household debt during the real-estate boom, reckless local leaders mindlessly larded on billions of dollars of new municipal and state debt to fund pet projects or to give crazy contracts to politically influential unions—like the 16-plus percent pay raise New York City gave its eighty thousand teachers back in 2002.[11] What too few voters appreciated at the time was that they would be just as liable for the pension and municipal debt approved by their elected officials as the mortgage or credit-card debt they had incurred on their own. Whether the bill comes in the form of a monthly mortgage payment or higher taxes, it's still the consumer/voter who pays it. And just as with credit cards, it's the compounding that kills. A little more debt piled on today translates into a much higher bill tomorrow. Not at all coincidentally, the states and municipalities where consumers are drowning in debt are the same ones where governments are drowning in debt. Consequently, the financial gap between the strongest and weakest states in the United States has rarely been wider.

There are any number of ways to tell the story of all that's gone wrong economically and what the future now holds. My focus is on the states—some whose futures have been clouded by shocking amounts of leverage and overspending but also others now enjoying an upsurge in economic growth and job creation because they didn't spend or borrow themselves into oblivion during the housing boom. With clean balance sheets, probusiness governors, and proximity to cheap energy and labor, these states are growing as fast as or faster than some emerging markets like Brazil, Russia, India, and China.

America is moving forward, but there are badly battered states that are holding back the overall growth of the U.S. economy. I have never been more optimistic about growth inside some parts of the United States; however, I have also never been more pessimistic about other areas that seem doomed by structural unemployment and sky-rocketing poverty rates. This book addresses the boom and bust reshaping America, how they happened, and what can be done to narrow the gap between America's new have and have-not states. The first half of the book explains how we got into this mess. Economic cycles are nothing new, of course. What's different about this latest boom and bust is the fact that there were no inevitable external forces at play. This wasn't the New England whaling industry of the 1800s, whose fate seemed sealed the moment Edwin Drake drilled the world's first commercial oil well outside Titusville, Pennsylvania, back in 1859.[12] The housing boom and bust did not have to happen. They were a by-product of flawed public policy on the federal level combined with terrible strategic planning by the banks. For a while the housing mania enriched not only banks and homeowners but also state and local governments. Awash in new tax revenues, cities and states borrowed and spent as if the good times would never end. Unfortunately, they did.

The second half of the book focuses on a lesser-understood element of the Great Recession—the states that were ignored by the banks during the boom and are recovering more quickly as a result of that benign neglect. In the central corridor states, government finances are healthier, taxes lower, and government services and infrastructure more robust. Shrewd local leaders are beginning to leverage those advantages in order to lure employers and employees away from the coasts. Not all hope is lost for the housing-bust states, but in order to remain competitive in an economy in which production, labor, and capital have never been more mobile, state leaders must make tough and potentially unpopular decisions on everything from energy policy to taxes to pay and benefits for public workers. The fixes are certainly doable, but they are not necessarily likely to be done—which is why the smart money is already betting on the central corridor emerging as the new driver of the U.S. economy.

■ PART I ■

The Fall

Chapter 1

■

It Starts at Home

Forget everything you think you know about the direction of the American economy, about our growing need for foreign oil, about the rise of the service economy and the decline of American manufacturing. The story of the next thirty years will not be a repeat of the last thirty. Growth in America is going to come from making things— and not Big Macs or e-cards but important stuff like fuel and chemicals and cars. We are now close to producing more oil than Saudi Arabia. We are the single greatest natural gas producer in the world. We are the largest agricultural exporter in the world.[1] What's more, manufacturing is bouncing back in the United States almost as quickly as it once left. Honda, Toyota, BMW, Toshiba, and Airbus are all building new U.S. plants or already are producing goods here.[2] The "all in" cost differential between producing goods in China and the United States has narrowed dramatically. On the global stage, the United States looks competitive relative to other countries and regions. America offers one common language, one common currency, a stable inflation environment, relatively unequaled political and social stability, and developed legal and capital-markets systems.

Despite these common strengths, the rebound is not occurring everywhere in the United States. It's happening mainly in central corridor states not bogged down economically by foreclosures and budget chaos. They have the money to retrain workers and offer tax incentives to relocating companies—flexibilities not found in housing-bust country. Economic power in the United States is shifting away from longtime coastal strongholds toward the interior. What's going on today is tangibly different from any other time in American economic history because shifting geographic fortunes are not being driven by external factors such as new technology or even immigration—things local leaders could never have controlled or anticipated. In the past, cities and towns lived and died with the industries that dominated them. This is familiar. What is unfamiliar is communities being gutted by government ineptitude. Here we are in uncharted territory. Never before have industry and population been more mobile. Americans and global business alike can choose where to produce, where to locate, and where to invest, and they are voting with their feet. Everything is cheaper today. Moving is cheaper. Communication is cheaper. Technology is cheaper. Relocating a business is cheaper.

The housing industry that drove growth in America for the past thirty years is a perfect example of the new velocity of capital. Banks and home builders do not stay the course. When home prices start dropping, they pick up stakes and search for new markets. There is no loyalty in housing because everybody understands that housing demand is fickle. The market is built entirely on perception—the perceived attraction, for example, of retiring in a warm, sunny climate where you could buy a $300,000 condo today and watch its value double in a few years. The real estate market was never built on need. Home prices in Las Vegas, Arizona, Florida, and California didn't skyrocket because people *had* to move there. They rose because speculators and second-home buyers *believed* more people *would* move there.

Of course, changing geographic fortunes are nothing new in U. S. history. New economic winners and losers emerge every couple decades. Technology changes, demography shifts, and consumer tastes evolve. Yes, the cycle is spinning faster this time around—change is occurring over years instead of decades—but it's important to understand how this process has played out in eras past because the spoils for the winners and penalties for the losers are much the same today as they were a hundred years ago. Drive across the United States and you will encounter your share of abandoned mills, dilapidated housing, overgrown railroad tracks, and other telltale signs of the American ghost town—communities that once swelled with people and industry but are now beset by decay and neglect. Many grew up around single industries like coal production or manufacturing and attracted newcomers thanks to plentiful job opportunities. As long as the industry did well, so too did the towns. Jobs and personal-income growth enabled company towns to build and improve upon public services like schools, parks, and libraries. However, once the industries began to decline or move on, employment and personal income often declined with them. Over time, municipal governments struggled to pay for services they could afford when tax bases were healthier. Towns were forced to cut back, and with those cuts the towns became less and less attractive places to live. This is how boomtowns become ghost towns.

With roots in a core agrarian economy, the U.S. population was once spread across the country, with big rural populations in the South. Cotton production in the South gave birth to industry along the Mississippi River and created boomtowns like Jackson and New Orleans. With highly fertile soil, proximity to great waterways, and—shamefully—an abundance of slave labor, Mississippi became one of the United States' biggest exporters and wealth creators. After the invention of the cotton gin in 1793, annual cotton production in Mississippi soared to 535 million pounds in 1859 from zero in 1800. Big Northeast real-estate concerns like the American Land Company and the New York Land Company rushed to buy up valuable Mississippi farmland. "Cotton provoked a 'gold rush,'" writes cotton historian Eugene Dattel, "by attracting thousands of white men from the North and from older slave states along the Atlantic coast who came to make a quick fortune." The Civil War and the end of slavery brought an end to that gold rush, and now Mississippi ranks the poorest state in the country.[3]

By 1850 the textile mills of Lowell, Massachusetts, had emerged as a new epicenter of American industry and population growth. Among young people, Lowell is probably best known as the city featured in the based-on-a-true-story movie *The Fighter*, in which Mark Wahlberg portrays the poor kid who makes good in the big league of the boxing circuit. But back in the midnineteenth century, there were ten thousand textile workers in Lowell producing fifty thousand miles of fabric every year—their looms powered by mills and waterwheels built alongside the Merrimack River. Lowell became the first large-scale factory town in America. Some called it the "cradle of the American Industrial Revolution,"[4] as raw cotton could be turned into cloth all in one centralized location. But just as new technology created Lowell, it played a part in Lowell's decline too, as rail lines made canals obsolete and steam power and turbines improved on Merrimack River waterwheels. Electric streetcars also enabled workers to live farther away from company towns, foreshadowing the suburbanization to follow.

Industrial Revolution (1750–1850)

Agriculture, manufacturing, mining, transportation, and technology. Migration from the UK to New England/Mid-Atlantic.

Economic development regionally limited as the power source was water based.

By the late 1800s, New Bedford and other New England cities with their own seaports began to eclipse Lowell. By the 1900s, the textile industry started to abandon the Northeast altogether for the South—particularly the Carolinas—as steam-powered mills and cheaper labor made production there more profitable. Some New England mills were closed outright or forced into bankruptcy. (Others stayed open but barely, allowed to wither on the vine by absentee owners who refused to make the necessary but costly improvements required to keep the old mills competitive.) Lowell became a shell of

Power Revolution (1850–1920)

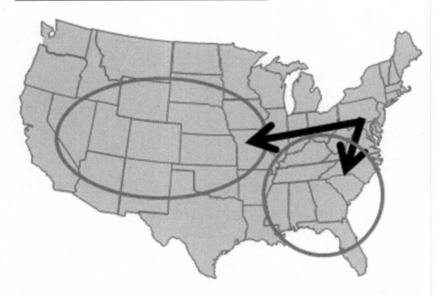

Steel production, railroads, chemicals, petroleum, electricity, early auto/ mass production.

The Southeast and West opened up as the power source switched to the steam engine, then to electricity.

its former self in the second half of the 1900s. Some even claimed it resembled Europe after World War II.[5] Today some of the mills and canals have been turned into national parks and museums—a sure sign of a place whose glory days have come and gone.

Central and western Pennsylvania is another example of a one-time economic hotbed whose fortunes faded. Coal-mining towns like Bethlehem, Easton, and Allentown embodied the power revolution and economic boom of the 1860s through to the 1920s. Thanks to plentiful supplies of coke—a coal by-product used to make steel—Bethlehem and its eponymous steel company grew into the second-largest steelmaking town in the country, behind only Pittsburgh and its big employer, U.S. Steel. As steel production began to shift overseas in search of lower labor costs, however, Bethlehem Steel fell on hard times, going out of business for good in 2001. Its old plant is now home to a casino and shopping mall operated by Las Vegas Sands. Sadly, this has become the fate of many of these once-vibrant towns. Hospitals and universities have replaced I beam producers and steelmakers as Pennsylvania's largest employers.

The best modern-day example of the rise and fall of an American city is probably Detroit. As the home of the U.S. auto world and headquarters to Ford, GM, and Chrysler, Detroit embodies the devolution of the Factory Belt into the Rust Belt. From the 1920s to the early 1980s, Detroit and its surrounding cities were iconic symbols of U.S. auto production. The automobile industry was born in the United States, but by the 1970s the industry had overpromised and overspent on pension and benefit obligations for its employees. Sure, there were

Manufacturing Revolution (1920–1980)

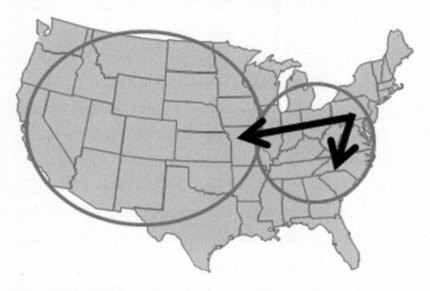

Automobiles, assembly line, etc.

Areas like Detroit, Cleveland, etc., became iconic manufacturing cities.

other contributing factors to Detroit's decline—such as the arrival of Japanese imports sporting better gas mileage—but none had more impact than the uncompetitive labor costs, which drove millions of jobs overseas. In 1978 GM employed over 500,000 hourly workers. By 2009, when GM was ultimately forced to file for bankruptcy, it had 54,000 hourly workers. It is telling that even as GM had only 54,000 hourly employees in 2009, the company was still supporting 450,000 retirees who were receiving GM pensions and health benefits.[6]

Once the bastion of manufacturing wealth in the United States, in the past ten years Detroit has lost half of its population, and some

residential areas are so decrepit—so littered with abandoned homes—
that the city has embarked on a municipal razing project to remove
them. The city is struggling to make a comeback, but that comeback
will hinge on its ability to get people to move back to the city. It is the
ultimate chicken-and-egg scenario: In order to attract more people,
Detroit needs to spend big bucks getting its infrastructure and services up to snuff, but it needs more people paying taxes to be able to
pay for better infrastructure and services.

The U.S. economy is constantly transforming itself. Today cheap
energy in the form of natural gas is creating a manufacturing revival
in the United States, onshoring job that had once been lost and creating many new jobs within the central corridor, close to production.
In the past, industry caused job and population shifts toward the
South, the Northeast, and, more recently during the real-estate
boom, the coasts. These changes are slow and steady, but before you
know it, the country has been transformed.

Economic booms and busts have painful repercussions. Industries die, and towns and regions slowly die with them. Ghost towns
materialize as drive-by relics of a region's lost glory. With no jobs to
be had, people moved on. In 1810, for example, Salem, Massachusetts, was the sixth-largest city in the country and one of its most important ports; today it's not even the sixth-largest city in Massachusetts.

Boom-and-bust cycles used to play out over multiple decades.
This time around, it's happening faster. Back in the 1990s, all the
ingredients existed for America's next economic thrust into housing:
Baby boomers were getting ready to retire, borrowing costs were lower

than they'd been in a long time, and the government was actively pushing a housing policy that explicitly encouraged homeownership. States like California, Arizona, Nevada, and Florida all boomed with retiree and second-home buying. Speculators drove prices even higher. Communities were born and expanded around real estate, not industry. People didn't need to move there; they chose to buy homes in these areas. Thus, when the sand hit the fan in the housing bust, the people who could move on did, and local property-tax bases lost value with every departure. A city or town is only as vibrant as its

Leverage/Housing Revolution (1994–2008)

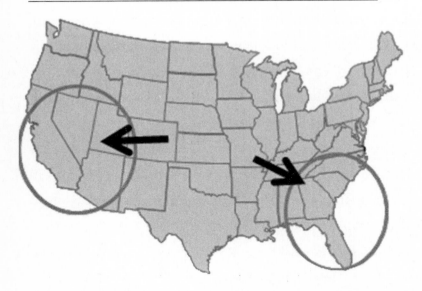

Real-estate assets inflate, cash-out refis, high homeownership, securitization, housing bubble.

States closer to the coasts, such as California, Arizona, and Nevada, in the West, and Florida, Georgia, and North Carolina, in the East, rose to prominence.

housing market. When the tax base weakens, so too do the public services that property taxes underwrite. Lower services translate into lower home values, and the cycle goes on and on.

Today it isn't technology or geography driving regional booms and busts. Cities and states are determining their own fates. Those that decide to borrow against future tax receipts in order to overspend are dimming their future economic prospects. Businesses and home-owners can almost always move to escape the final bill, gutting the tax base in the process. Federal taxes may be inescapable, but a California taxpayer or business can fairly easily pick up and move halfway across the country to avoid paying ever-rising California state and local taxes. In the world of telecommuting, some white-collar emigrants might not even have to leave their old jobs.

Human capital is as important to a tax base as equity capital is to a corporation. Each acts as a primary source of tax receipts or cash flow. So think about what an exodus can mean. California—the most populous state in the country, with 12 percent of the population—contributes 13 percent of the overall U.S. GDP and generates over $100 billion in state and local tax receipts per year.[7] From 2008 to 2010, California's tax receipts fell from $118 billion to $105 billion, while overall state and local tax receipts dropped from $781 billion to $702 billion. In Riverside, California, sales-tax revenue declined by an incredible 17 percent in 2009 alone.[8] It's a decline that can be explained almost entirely by population shifts. In 2004 Riverside had the highest domestic net migration of any metro area in the country, gaining 95,000 new residents in one year, according to a Brookings study. Four years later, Riverside ranked 350th in net migration (out of 363 metro areas), with more than 7,000 people leaving for greener pastures.[9]

The problem isn't just the lost population and tax receipts. It's who exactly is leaving. According to demographer Wendell Cox, California has been hemorrhaging high-income, well-educated residents, even though the net outflow has been masked to some degree by strong international immigration to the Golden State. Between 2000 and 2009, 1.9 million Californians left for other states, and based on demographic trends, a disproportionate number of those leaving appear to be well educated. Consider that California ranks 5th nationally in share of population 64 or older holding college degrees but only 23rd in college degrees among those ages 25 to 34. Between 2000 and 2008, California lost 370,000 jobs paying wages 25 percent or more above the state average. By comparison, the state gained 65,000 of those high-paying jobs between 1992 and 2000. California is even losing its status as the high-tech leader. Between 2000 and 2011, the state had zero employment growth in science, technology, engineering, and mathematics versus 5 percent growth in those fields nationally and 14 percent growth in Texas.[10]

The point is that wealthier people have the means to move on, and their exodus hastens the demise of the cities and towns they leave behind—which prompts even more people to leave. It's what I call the negative feedback loop from hell. The coastal and Sun Belt states that lived through the housing bust can no longer afford to spend as much on schools, police, and other services as when times were flush.

Some residents are relocating to central corridor states, where business is booming and so too are tax receipts and spending on core services. These states are growing their economies at high-single-digit annualized rates, while the housing-heavy states have shown little growth or negative growth. A new American demographic shift is happening right before our eyes.

Chapter 2

■

Housing Revisited

Give me your tired, your poor,

Your huddled masses yearning to breathe free,

The wretched refuse of your teeming shore,

Send these, the homeless, tempest-tost to me:

I lift my lamp beside the golden door.

—EMMA LAZARUS, "THE NEW COLOSSUS,"

INSCRIBED ON THE STATUE OF LIBERTY

Rewind the clock one hundred, two hundred, three hundred years. When immigrants risked their lives to come to America, what drew them here was not the possibility of owning their own home. And it certainly wasn't taking out a mortgage. They dreamed of a country that offered religious and political freedom and the opportunity to earn a better living. To have a better life in a new country where anything seemed to be possible. That was the original American dream. Fast-forward to today, and some immigrants are still risking their lives to make the trip, coming to this country for a chance at a better life. Once again, their American dream is not about homeownership.

Some just want to earn a higher wage and send money back to their families. Others come here for political freedom or to provide a better life for their children. Whether they wind up renters or homeowners is not a pressing concern. And still today in pursuit of that dream, they are some of the hardest-working people who live in this country. Their dream has never necessarily been to own a home but simply to prosper from religious and political freedom, find a better-paying job, and have the opportunity to give their children a better existence than they have.

Sometime in the twentieth century, the American dream was redefined in a way that made homeownership an essential part of the American experience. This didn't happen by chance. The federal government explicitly promoted homeownership. The first step down this road was the Homestead Act of 1862, which enabled the federal government to give away land free of charge in an effort to entice people to move west of the Mississippi. The Homestead Act was rooted in the politics of the day, as its backers aimed to isolate the Southern slave states by spreading free, "yeoman" farming to the Western territories.[1]

This wouldn't be the last time leaders in Washington promoted homeownership for reasons that had little to do with the financial merits of owning property. On paper, lawmakers' motivations were straightforward—to make the housing market safer for lenders and make mortgages more affordable for borrowers—but their ultimate goals were rooted in social engineering. "A family that owns its own home . . . has a more wholesome, healthful and happier atmosphere in which to bring up children," President Herbert Hoover once said. His White House successor, Franklin D. Roosevelt, ratcheted up the pro–homeownership rhetoric another notch during World War II. "A nation of homeowners," said Roosevelt, "is unconquerable." I would argue a lot has changed since those days. Today, Roosevelt's motto might be similar—just replace homeowners with employed citizens. After all, it doesn't much matter whether you own a home if you can't make the mortgage payment. But back then, homeownership became a bona fide national aspiration.[2]

Before the 1930s, buying a home in the United States was prohibitively expensive, especially if you had to borrow money to do it. Mortgages back then were predominantly sold and underwritten by insurance companies, not banks. They required at least a 50 percent down payment, and borrowers had to pay off the loan in five years. These mortgages worked as "balloon payment" loans in which principal is paid off in one large balloon payment at the end of the loan, rather than amortized over its full length. When the Great Depression hit, this balloon structure of home loans practically invited defaults—in much the same way interest-only mortgages, option ARMs, and other teaser-rate products doomed homeowners during the last housing bust.[3]

In 1940 the home-ownership rate in the United States was a modest 44 percent, much below the current 65 percent.[4] Many prospective homeowners were simply unable to get a loan. They didn't feel deprived, rather motivated by the goal of moving up the ladder of financial stability. But the mortgage market started to change in the

1930s. The U.S. government enacted policies aimed at making home-ownership a more realistic goal for U.S. consumers. Congress began encouraging savings-and-loan banks—think Bailey Building & Loan from *It's a Wonderful Life*—to extend the length of mortgages and therefore allow for lower borrower monthly payments. Also, by guaranteeing S&L deposits, the government effectively gave home lenders more money to lend out. This practice actually began in 1933 with the creation of the Home Owners' Loan Corporation, which was a New Deal agency that kept people in their homes by allowing borrowers to refinance variable-rate, short-term, nonamortizing mortgages into fixed-rate, fully-amortizing, long-term ones. It was America's first loan-modification program—a policy that, much like the post-2008 version, kept people in homes regardless of whether that was their best financial option.

The establishment of the Federal Housing Authority (FHA) a year later expanded the role of S&Ls, also known as thrifts, in underwriting these new, borrower-friendly mortgages. For first-time home buyers seeking loans, these new mortgages initially had twenty-year structures, but by 1948 the maximum term was extended to thirty years, a structure that has since become standard in the American mortgage market. The rise of the thirty-year mortgage opened up the housing market to a segment of Americans who had never before considered the possibility of homeownership. The net effect was not unlike that of those cheap T-shirts imported from China and sold at Walmart—which encourage people to buy a three-pack instead of the single shirt they actually need. The fixed-rate, long-duration, self-amortizing structure of the thirty-year mortgage allowed borrowers to spread principal re-payment over a long period of time and eliminated the payment shock of the previous balloon structure. It also inherently lowered the monthly cost of a mortgage, sometimes at the expense of taxpayers, who were subsidizing the loan through FHA mortgage insurance. Borrowers knew that the size of their mortgage payment would not change over the life of their loans and that they could keep up with the new lower-monthly-payment structure, which made homeownership less daunt-ing. Soon the mortgage-interest tax deduction that had been part of the federal tax code since 1913 became a home-buying carrot not just for wealthy Americans but for average ones too.[5] The thirty-year mortgage was here to stay.

By comparison, homeownership has never been so aggressively promoted in other countries. France, the Netherlands, Denmark, and Germany all have home-ownership rates below 55 percent, and their housing systems seem to work fine and are arguably more stable than those of countries like Spain and the United States, which have much higher home-ownership rates.[6] There's nothing inherently bad about homeownership, obviously. Problems arise when government encourages and promotes home buying, enabling citizens to take on a big slug of debt and all the risk that entails.

The contrast between mortgage finance in the United States and Canada is particularly striking. Canada has a tradition of high-down-payment, variable-rate, short-term mortgage lending. The typi-cal mortgage term is only five years, and mortgage interest is not tax deductible. Also, there isn't much of a secondary market for non-government-guaranteed mortgages that have been bundled into mortgage-backed securities. Why is that important? Canadian lenders must hold mortgages on their own books, which constrains their ability to make additional home loans. They better feel highly confident in their borrowers' ability to pay them back. Another key difference between U.S. and Canadian mortgages: Canadian banks have full recourse to a borrower's personal assets. Default on a Canadian mortgage, and the bank can take not just your house but also your car, your jewelry, and your savings. The Canadian system even makes selling a home more onerous. Canadians who refinance or pay off their mortgages early not only have to repay principal but also owe some of the interest that would have accrued over the remaining life of the loan.[7] The entire thought process of a home buyer in Canada has to be different.

Of course, there is no "Canadian dream" comparable to the twentieth-century version of the American dream of homeownership, which is why a government role in promoting homeownership has been such a uniquely American phenomenon. The FHA provided mortgage insurance, giving banks the confidence to make home loans. The Veterans Administration gave returning soldiers insured loans with low down payments. The Federal Deposit Insurance Corporation guaranteed Americans' bank deposits, allowing banks to raise money for mortgages more easily and inexpensively. (With a government guarantee, banks didn't have to offer high interest rates to attract deposits.) Last but definitely not least, the establishment of Fannie Mae in 1938 provided a resale market for FHA-insured loans—and later for VA loans too—which freed up lender capital for even more new mortgage underwriting.[8]

The homeownership push of the post–Great Depression/World War II era was effective, and home prices began rising year after year along with homeownership. By 1960 the home-ownership rate had climbed to 62 percent, a level at which it stayed until the mid-1990s (when it began to climb again, peaking at 69 percent in 2006).[9] Fannie Mae had grown so large that in 1968, Congress spun it off into a semiprivate company. This new half-governmental, half-private market creation was known as a government-sponsored enterprise, or GSE. It was the ultimate "heads I win, tails you lose" setup. Ostensibly, Fannie was a company owned by stockholders, but its government charter meant taxpayers were implicitly on the hook for its debt. Shareholders wanted rapid growth, and the implicit government backstop made it a seemingly low-risk investment. Two years later it was joined by Freddie Mac, a competitor the government created to end Fannie's monopoly in the secondary mortgage market. Together these two GSEs began to usurp the role—and the mortgage-lending profits—of the S&Ls.[10]

The S&L industry collapse hardly slowed the growth of the housing industry. S&Ls were quickly eclipsed by Fannie and Freddie, which by 2001 controlled 50 percent of the mortgage market. Additionally, a new crop of subprime mortgage lenders emerged, eager to expand the business. By the 2000s, not only were the government and lenders aggressively marketing homeownership, but investors were also getting in on the action. After the dot-com crash in March 2000, investors were turned off from the stock market and now looked to real estate for returns. If the subject around the retirement-home bingo table during the late nineties had been the latest dot-com stock investment, the investment pastime of the 2000s became real estate. And everyone thought they were an expert.

Even the actual experts made blunders. In 2000 and 2001, then–Federal Reserve chairman Alan Greenspan responded to the double economic whammy of the dot-com crash and 9/11 by engineering an unusually steep yield curve that stimulated the economy by encouraging banks to make more home loans. He cut short-term rates to 1.75 percent, a level considerably lower than the 5 percent yield on ten-year Treasury bonds.[11] The mortgage market typically takes its interest-rate cues from Fed and Treasury rates, which meant that the rate on a traditional thirty-year mortgage was now far less attractive than the rate of a shorter-term, adjustable-rate mortgage. Greenspan himself was on record criticizing the growth of the GSEs, and in a 2004 speech to a meeting of the Credit Union National Association, the Fed chairman went so far as to encourage homeowners to take out adjustable-rate mortgages (ARMs) instead of thirty-year mortgages. Greenspan argued that many Americans would have saved "tens of thousands of dollars" by financing their homes with an ARM instead of a thirty-year fixed mortgage. "The traditional fixed-rate mortgage," Greenspan said, "may be an expensive method of financing a home."[12] Of course, if thirty-year mortgages were in fact excessively expensive, that was due in large part to the steep yield curve Greenspan himself had helped manufacture. Moreover, those "tens of thousands of dollars" in savings he cited hinged on one of two assumptions: mortgage rates not going up after the teaser rates expired or homeowners being able to sell their houses for profit if the stepped-up interest rates proved unaffordable. Three years later, both of those assumptions would prove fatally flawed.

By pushing more home buyers toward ARMs, Greenspan increased the role of securitization in fueling the housing bubble. Wall Street firms were making record fees from packaging mortgages as mortgage-backed securities, which were then sold as pseudo-high-grade bonds to yield-hungry investors. The problem was, there was a finite supply of traditional, qualified borrowers. In order to keep the volumes pumping, lenders had to go down the credit curve into subprime lending. In the 1980s and early 1990s, subprime mortgage lending was a relatively small portion of the overall securitization market. But between 2003 and 2005 sales, or "originations," of subprime mortgages and near-subprime mortgages increased 135 percent. Adjustable-rate mortgages' share of the total mortgage market soared from 26 percent to 48 percent.[13]

Just think about how nonsensical this was. Rates were rising in 2004, and adjustable-rate mortgages were becoming more popular.[14] Typically, in a rising-rate environment, the borrower would try to lock in a lower-rate mortgage in order to protect himself from the possibility of his mortgage payment rising over time. Anyone taking out this type of mathematically unsound financing product had to be doing so for one of two reasons: Either they couldn't qualify for a traditional thirty-year mortgage or the only mortgage payment they could afford was an interest-only mortgage or some other initial-low-cost, teaser-rate product. The net effect was to upend the traditional hierarchy of the housing finance business, shifting market share away from the GSEs and toward mortgage-lending upstarts like Countrywide and Golden West Financial. Accelerating the growth of the ARM market was strong demand for higher-yielding bonds; this allowed banks and investment banks to repackage exotic mortgages into even more exotic mortgage-backed securities and collateralized debt obligations—products that would then be resold to investors, with the proceeds used to fund still more new mortgages. Uninsured by Fannie or Freddie, these new mortgage-backed securities were so complicated, so sliced and diced, that investors knew little about what they were buying beyond the credit ratings assigned to these securities by the credit-rating agencies. (Those ratings proved flawed.) Underscoring how incredibly opaque these securities were, Sheila Bair, the then-chairwoman of the FDIC—ostensibly one of lenders' regulators—admitted in a 2008 interview with *Fortune* magazine that FDIC economists had failed at what seemingly should have been a simple enough exercise: identifying the underlying loans in CDOs held by banks.[15]

The dramatic increase in subprime mortgage lending did not cause the housing bust, but it was the classic canary in the coal mine. The reason: Over 75 percent of the new subprime mortgages underwritten were ARMs. With the steep yield curve drawing more banks into the mortgage business—specifically into ARMs—competition heated up. Banks and other lenders started moving down the credit spectrum in order to get more business and feed the securitization beast. Between 2001 and 2006, the interest-rate gap between prime and subprime mortgages narrowed dramatically, from 3.5 percentage points to 2 percentage points.[16] This in turn made home loans more affordable—at least during the teaser-rate period—for people who would not have qualified for a home loan just a few years earlier. Not only were the teaser rates low, but banks started competing over loan terms too, allowing people of all credit stripes to get mortgages with no down payment or no monthly principal payments (the infamous "interest-only ARM") during the teaser-rate period. There were also the infamous NINJA loans: no income, no job, no problem. If my grandfather had lived to see this, he would have been horrified.

Underwriting mortgages that homeowners could only temporarily afford was not only unethical, and in some instances illegal, but also terrible business. More than half of the largest originators from the second quarter of 2007 wound up either bankrupt or acquired in a distressed-situation deal.[17] Wachovia was swallowed up by Wells Fargo. (Wachovia's fate had been sealed in 2006 by its $25 billion acquisition of Golden West Financial, the largest thrift in the subprime mortgage capital of the world, California.[18]) Washington Mutual, the nation's largest S&L, went bankrupt and was eventually taken over by JPMorgan Chase.[19] Colonial BancGroup was shuttered in 2009, its assets taken over by BB&T.[20] And Countrywide was bought by Bank of America for $4.5 billion. (This price was a fraction of Countrywide's onetime $26 billion stock-market valuation, yet buying Countrywide still proved crushingly expensive for BofA. Countrywide saddled it with $40 billion in real-estate losses. "The worst deal in the history of American finance," is how Tony Plath, a finance professor at University of North Carolina at Charlotte, described the BofA-Countrywide deal to the *Wall Street Journal*.)[21]

While Greenspan's rate cuts certainly encouraged the switch to more aggressive mortgages, changes in federal housing policy played a role too. In 1994 President Bill Clinton and Fannie Mae CEO Frank Raines—Clinton's former budget director—embarked on a new push to increase the rate of homeownership in the United States. Clinton believed homeownership was "the realization of the American dream," and his stated goal was "to develop a plan to boost homeownership in America to an all-time high by the end of this century." The strategy was unveiled in a 1995 policy paper published by the U.S. Department of Housing and Urban Development and endorsed by the president himself in an introductory note. As Drexel University finance professor Joseph R. Mason pointed out in a 2008 report penned for Criterion Economics, the strategy put forward by the Clinton administration explicitly encouraged the kind of no-skin-in-the-game, borrow-now-pay-later mortgages that would ultimately sink the housing market. For example, the strategy paper praised the "great strides [that] have been made by the lending community in recent years to reduce down payment requirements, particularly for low- and moderate-income homebuyers." It called for "financing strategies, fueled by the creativity of the private and public sectors," that might make homeownership possible for "households [that] do not have sufficient available income to make the monthly payments on mortgages financed at market interest rates for standard loan terms."[22] In 1994 the Clinton administration pushed through revisions to the Community Reinvestment Act that incentivized loans to low-income borrowers by making such loan making a prerequisite for approval of bank mergers or acquisitions. Also in 1994 Fannie Mae reduced from 5 percent to 3 percent the minimum down payment required to qualify for a Fannie mortgage. Five years later, Fannie tiptoed further into subprime by easing income requirements for lower-income borrowers.

The Housing Boom: The Ownership Society and Securitization

Unprecedented access to home loans opened up possibilities that had never existed before for many Americans. During the housing boom, eighteen million new homeowners were created and $8 trillion in additional mortgage capital was injected into the economy.[23] This made the impossible possible. More homes were built. More furniture and appliances were purchased. Home-equity lines of credit were tapped for vacations and other discretionary spending. The impact on the job market was massive. According to the Bureau of Labor Statistics, the housing bubble created 1.2 million real estate–related jobs between 2002 and 2005. Unemployment dropped to its lowest level on record. Best of all, jobs in home building and construction couldn't be outsourced or offshored. The work had to be done locally, which had an incredible multiplier effect on local economies.[24]

However, in the same ways America's manufacturing boom in the post–World War II era was not shared equally by all Americans, the economic boom of the last twenty-five years was not experienced equally among all Americans either. The real-estate boom shifted economic power from industrial states like Michigan, Ohio, and Indiana—where real-estate markets were softer—to states like California, Arizona, Florida, and Nevada. The country shifted in one generation from a manufacturing-based economy to an economy whose growth came from housing, consumer leverage, and, to a lesser extent, technology.

The homeownership rate climbed from 64 percent to close to 70 percent in just twelve years.[25] The problem was, the unprecedented demand for homes stimulated an equally unprecedented rise in home prices. What followed was a period of hyperinflation of real-estate assets, leading to a period marked by cash-out refinancings, peak homeownership, go-go securitization, and eventually the piercing of the housing bubble and the onset of the Great Recession. The housing-related riches that had accrued to states like California, Arizona, and Nevada in the West and to Florida, North Carolina, and Connecticut in the East simply vanished.

From 1994 to 2006, average home prices in California and Florida increased 482 percent and 463 percent respectively, which was more than 2.4 times and 2.3 times the national average. Sure, housing prices rose 199 percent nationally during that time, but the gains were disproportionately weighted to coastal and Sun Belt states.[26] Homeownership rates in these states soared by 12 percentage points. The economies in these states thrived. More than 5.1 million jobs were created during that period, 21 percent of all job creation in the country, and the overall contribution of these states to total U.S. GDP stood at 20 percent by 2006, the peak year in housing. The good times seemed like they would never end.[27]

Not coincidentally, consumers started to borrow more as the values of their homes appreciated. This was a variation on the stock-market wealth effect. But with real estate, unlike with stocks, consumers tapped their winnings by borrowing rather than by selling. Consumers piled on debt, further boosting the economy in the short term, though not all consumers piled on debt equally. In California, Nevada, Florida, Arizona, New Jersey, and New York, debt per capita ballooned by over 100 percent in just one decade. Feeling flush from their real-estate gains, American consumers grew addicted to their credit cards as a cash-flow-management vehicle. This access to credit allowed consumers to continuously spend beyond their means and gave small businesses the ability to hire more people. Most of the debt pile was tied to real estate. In California 88 percent of consumer debt per capita was related to the value of homes. In Nevada the figure was 85 percent; in New Jersey, Florida, and Arizona, 83 percent, 85 percent, and 78 percent respectively.[28]

Politicians in these boom states had never had it so good. There was more money to go around, and the notion that home prices could ever decline seemed absurd. Few things are more dangerous in government than an elected official with an open checkbook, and too many elected officials chose to solidify their political bases by directing surplus tax dollars wherever they pleased. The school system in Montgomery County, Maryland, for instance, chose to spend a $32 million budget surplus not on reducing class sizes but on increasing take-home pay for teachers.[29] In Nevada state spending almost doubled over the past decade. Arizona was close behind, with spending growing 93 percent. Spending in California grew 70 percent from already-high levels. The problem was, the rising standard of living in places like Las Vegas and Phoenix was grounded not in something truly sustainable like wage growth but in one-time withdrawals of home equity.[30] People literally started using their homes like ATMs. The prevailing mind-set: "The value of my house is up ten thousand dollars. Well, then, there's no harm in taking out a ten-thousand-dollar home-equity loan. Even if I can't afford to repay, I can always just sell the house and still turn a profit. Right?"

This kind of myopic thinking would prove painful not only for homeowners but also for the communities in which they lived—communities whose economies had grown dependent upon the housing boom. The pockets of highest unemployment and slowest economic growth began shifting from historically poor Southern states like Mississippi and Louisiana to the nouveau riche–turned–nouveau pauvre states like Arizona, Nevada, and Florida—those most affected by the housing bust. In 2006 those three states had below-average unemployment as well as the highest GDP growth in the nation, at 6.6 percent, 7 percent, and 6.7 percent respectively, according to the U.S. Bureau of Economic Analysis. Just four years later, Arizona, Nevada, and Florida ranked forty-eighth, forty-ninth, and fortieth in GDP growth, while Nevada had the highest unemployment rate in the country at 14 percent. (California was second worst at 12 percent.)[31]

The Housing Bust

In 2006 home prices in America peaked, and the rest is history. That very same year, subprime mortgage lenders began to go out of business due to rising losses. By 2007 more than twenty-five subprime lenders had declared bankruptcy.[32] By 2008 the tidal wave of losses was no longer limited to subprime. Iconic firms like Bear Stearns and Lehman Brothers collapsed under the weight of the housing-bust carnage. From their peak, home prices declined over 30 percent in the top ten cities across the country. In Las Vegas home prices dropped 60 percent. In Phoenix home prices declined 49 percent. Miami, Tampa, Los Angeles, and Chicago were all hit with their own crippling declines.[33] Today home prices have rebounded slightly off the bottom, but given the sorry state of the economy, it's far-fetched to think prices will quickly rebound to break-even levels for those homeowners who bought at or near the peak of the market.

While the housing market appears to have stabilized and pockets are improving, or stabilizing, off the bottom, prices are still way off their peaks. In many states, such as California, Florida, Arizona, and Nevada, home prices would have to more than double just to get back to even.[34] Making normalization of the housing market even more challenging is the completely dysfunctional condition of the current mortgage market. We still have no U.S. housing policy. The Federal Reserve has distorted mortgage pricing to such an extent that the entire market is effectively mispriced. Most mortgage activity today relates more to refinancing activity than to new home sales, so those that have good credit are paying less for it and those with less-than-good credit are renting, unable to buy homes. For many want-to-be homeowners, low rates have almost nothing to do with being able to buy a home if they can't access a loan in the first place.

In the near term, the economic gap between the have and have-not states cannot be closed without rapid reinflation of the housing market, and that seems unlikely given the current state of mortgage finance in the United States. Lenders are much more cautious about underwriting non-GSE-backed mortgages, which hurts affordability. Since the U.S. mortgage-backed-securities (MBS) market collapsed in 2008, lenders have begun to raise down-payment requirements and mortgage fees again, as the option to churn mortgages into MBS has all but disappeared. In other words, with banks' ability to unload credit risk and generate revenue via MBS securitization now cut off, borrowers are faced with a more expensive mortgage product at a time when home loans are already harder to obtain. This is perhaps why Federal Reserve chairman Ben Bernanke shares my housing-market caution. Said Bernanke in November 2012: "Overly tight lending standards may now be preventing creditworthy borrowers from buying homes, thereby slowing the revival in housing and impeding the economy recovery."[35]

It's going to be a difficult cycle to break. States and municipalities are strained financially by weak tax receipts resulting from declining home prices. They respond by raising taxes, cutting programs, or both. Higher taxes and reduced social services create new downward pressure on home values, which in turn takes another bite out of property-tax revenues. Of course, scenarios like this have played out before in the United States, and the afflicted cities and states did recover within a few years. But in prior cycles, the holes they were digging out from were not nearly so deep. Consider what happened to New Hampshire in the early 1990s. New Hampshire was arguably the state hardest hit by the savings-and-loan crisis. Seven of the state's seven largest banks went belly up, New Hampshire's unemployment rate reached 8 percent, and average home prices fell 20 percent.[36] Yet not a single New Hampshire municipality filed for bankruptcy. Why not? New Hampshire's state and local spending as a percentage of state GDP was 17 percent in 1992 versus a national average of 18 percent. In 2009 the national average was 21 percent, and four of the country's most populous states—California, Michigan, New York, and Ohio—topped 23 percent. Whatever policy mistakes New Hampshire politicians made back then, overspending was not one of them.[37]

Even for those who are not underwater on their mortgages, access to credit has been severely impinged on. Since the peak, almost $2 trillion in available credit-card and home-equity lines have been cut from the system.[38] With so much credit taken out of the system, consumer spending has declined. The steady erosion of basic social services at the state level is creating more out-of-pocket expenses for middle- and low-end consumers who must compensate for reduced public services such as transportation, health care, and education.

Owning a home would become a core component of the American experience, and by the second half of the twentieth century, both business and the government were intent upon turning more Americans into homeowners—whether they could ultimately afford it or not. For a while, it was good business. An economy and a country with a high homeownership rate enjoy an economic multiplier effect. Very little related to home buying or home ownership can be outsourced to India or China. The vast majority of costs associated with building homes are labor related, and people who broker, build, fix, and clean homes are always local. When a family buys a home, they pay a real-estate agent and a home inspector. They buy furniture for the home and perhaps hire a contractor or handyman to upgrade the kitchen before moving in. And if they were city dwellers before relocating to the burbs, maybe they even buy a new car. The government figured out that promoting housing promoted both jobs and consumption, boosting the overall economy. If company towns used to be built around industries, the government discovered that it could create "housing towns" simply by loosening the rules around owning a home and qualifying for a mortgage. What the government failed to appreciate, however, was that this housing boom was built on mortgages too many buyers simply could not afford. And as my grandfather used to tell me, the more debt you take on, the smaller the margin of error you leave yourself should anything go wrong.

Chapter 3

■

States Gone Wild

Almost all states are required to have balanced budgets. Almost all have caps on how much municipal bond debt they can issue. Yet over the past few decades, elected officials have figured out ways around these well-intended restrictions. Gaming the system wasn't even particularly hard, and it was impossible for the average person to track what was happening because information and disclosure were all but nonexistent. But all of this changed in 2009 when states were forced to open their proverbial kimonos and disclose the magnitude of unfunded pension and health-insurance obligations tied to state workers and retirees—as was now required under new Governmental Accounting Standards Board rules.[1] And 2012 disclosure requirements were even greater, further breaking down the entrenched system of opaque and misleading state and local financial disclosure. The problem essentially boils down to rich promises made to state and local government employees that governments could never afford.

Since 1960, state and local workforces have grown one and a half times faster than the private sector. Current taxpayers fund the rising salary costs associated with all of those new hires, and future taxpayers are also on the hook for the retirement benefits of all of those hires. Add this to the amount of debt owed by the federal government and the amount of debt the average American has amassed over the past decade, and the obvious question arises: "Who's going to pay for all of this?"

Cities and states never questioned where the money was going to come from to pay for the new sports stadiums or generous union contracts. Local spending decisions were based on assumptions that property-tax revenues would keep on rising. State expenditures assumed ever-increasing income from sales and income taxes. And if the tax revenue wasn't there? Cities just assumed that their states would be there to bail them out, just as the states figured that the federal government would be their fiscal safety net.

The U.S. government system was designed so that the federal government takes responsibility for national issues like defense and immigration. Generally, it is up to the state and local governments to provide the public services that we rely on at an everyday level. How safe is the drinking water? How often is the trash collected? How good are the public schools? How safe are the streets? This is what defines the quality of life in our communities. The deal we make with our states and municipalities is a straightforward one: They provide us with basic services and a social safety net, and we pay for those services—either with current tax dollars or with future ones we'll owe to repay principal and interest payments to bondholders. The cost of services rendered is supposed to align with the revenues collected.

That's the idea, anyway. Because forty-nine states have constitutional requirements to balance their budgets every year or two, whenever tax revenues fall short of expectations, states are supposed to either hike tax rates or attack expenses by cutting spending and programs. Thirty-six states have already raised taxes, layering on special levies or one-time taxes, causing a brief uptick in tax receipts.[2] But receipts have since leveled off, and in many states they're trending down. The outcome is inevitable: more budget cuts. Since 2008 Nevada has cut $80 million from mental-health programs. New York State has cut $1 billion from its state college and university system. And Washington State has cut $2.6 billion from K-12 funding.[3]

The reality is that over the past decade, states haven't had the money to pay for all of their programs, projects, and promises, forcing them to seek significant spending cuts. Over the past five years, states have cut over a quarter of a trillion dollars out of their budgets—the equivalent of 13 percent of 2010 total spending and 17 percent of 2010 tax receipts.[4] Education and public safety have been frequent targets for cutbacks at the state level, but state aid to cities and counties has suffered most. Local governments traditionally rely on state transfers for over 40 percent of their funding, but with state budgets now being slashed, there is less money trickling down.[5] After decades of expanding social services, refurbishing schools, doling out generous raises to cops and teachers, and building new parks and sporting venues, the local-government machine has had to pull back dramatically and begin a long and seemingly endless series of cuts to programs and services.

% Change in State Expenditures from 2000 to 2010

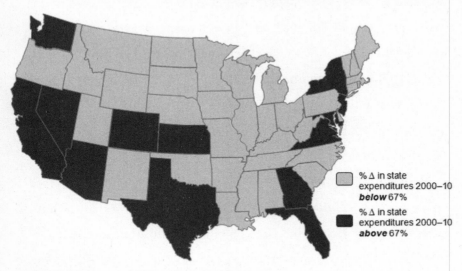

% Δ in state
expenditures 2000–10
below 67%

% Δ in state
expenditures 2000–10
above 67%

SOURCES: BEA, U.S. CENSUS, AND MWAG

From 2000 to 2010, state spending grew by 72 percent in California, 98 percent in Texas, and 114 percent in Nevada. That new spending totaled $107 billion, $59 billion, and $7 billion respectively. State and local government spending as a percentage of each state's gross domestic product (GDP) also rose dramatically. In 2009 it accounted for over 25 percent of Michigan's GDP; the figure for California was 25.3 percent, for New York over 28.1 percent. California alone spent $431 billion in 2009, according to the U.S. Census Bureau. Add together New York's expenditures of $276 billion and Michigan's $86 billion, and the sum exceeds Turkey's entire GDP, which is the eighteenth largest in the world. Many states have essentially become dependent on their own spending to prop up their economies. There is, of course, great discrepancy from state to state. In 2009 Texas government spending accounted for a relatively low 9.7 percent of GDP. But it's not that Texas has been frugal. In fact, its expenses have been growing at a fairly torrid pace—up 98 percent from 2000 to 2010—but it has a larger revenue stream due to the thriving oil and gas industries.[6]

Budgets are bloated with pet projects of lawmakers wanting to pump money into their districts and into constituents' pockets. Taken individually, many of these projects seem well intentioned, reason-able, and even beneficial—the Boys & Girls Club facility in the Lacoochee section of Tampa Bay receiving $1 million out of Florida's $70 billion budget or the Government House in St. Johns County, Florida, receiving $2.5 million to create an "Interpretive Film & Ex-hibit and Government Museum."[7] But the cumulative effect is devas-tating. Padding of budgets with fluff spending has been going on for so long that it has become a difficult habit to break.

For years nobody seemed particularly worried. For the same rea-son so many people believed home prices could never decline, states never foresaw a decline in tax receipts—and certainly never foresaw a prolonged one. They spent as if the good times would never end and made big promises to state and local government employees based upon the deliberate bet that they wouldn't. Total state tax collections peaked in the second quarter of 2008 at around $241 billion, accord-ing to the U.S. Census Bureau. Individual tax receipts collected by the states topped out in the same quarter at $99 billion.[8]

Then came the bust. Within a year, the bottom fell out of real estate and states were caught shorthanded. Those states with the greatest exposure were left with the largest budget gaps. Foreclosures skyrocketed, and states and cities saw their tax rolls shrink at a time when they needed more cash, not less, to pay for the expensive benefits, pensions, and infrastructure and other projects (which invariably run over budget) they had just approved. The school district in Newton, Massachusetts, for example, spent $197 million on a new, bond-financed high school—a veritable superschool boasting an Olympic-size pool, indoor track, climbing wall, dance studio, arts wing, and electronic music center. Construction costs ran $50 million over budget, and when the new high school finally opened in 2010, the district was suddenly faced with a $6 million budget gap—which it closed by laying off teachers, increasing class size (one Advanced Placement math class had forty-six students), and eliminating classes in Latin and Russian.[9] Of course, Newton wasn't alone in its foolish excess: Many states and municipalities borrowed billions, willfully deluding themselves that the money would materialize from ever-increasing property-tax revenues.

The severity of the recessionary storm was fully revealed in 2009, when second-quarter tax receipts plunged by $40 billion—a record 16.4 percent decline from the previous year.[10] Thirty-six states posted double-digit revenue losses, the largest declines in history. The slump continued quarter after quarter with only modest gains, prompting Lucy Dadayan, a senior policy analyst at the Rockefeller Institute of Government, to warn that "state tax revenues will continue to be insufficient to support current spending commitments" and that more spending cuts and tax increases were most likely on the way for many states.[11]

In fiscal year 2013, which began in July 2012, the Center on Budget and Policy Priorities (CBPP) expected 350,000 more K-12 students in our public schools and another 1.7 million college and university students, many of whom receive state aid. With more employers doing away with health coverage and an increase in the number of unemployed workers lacking any benefits, the CBPP projected that 5.6 million more people would seek Medicaid coverage, which is jointly financed by states and the federal government.[12] Where will the additional funds needed to meet these obligations come from? Many states have already made deep cuts in health and education spending. Florida, for instance, slashed assistance to state colleges, and North Carolina took an ax to education spending, lopping $2.6 billion from its fiscal 2013 budget. That comes on top of the nearly $1.5 billion North Carolina schools have been forced to give back to the state in so-called discretionary reductions.[13] In other words, faced with its own shortfall, North Carolina took back monies it had already appropriated to counties, cities, and school districts. But this is what happens when states put together budgets based on overly rosy revenue projections.

The state of California has been the worst transgressor when it comes to foolish government spending. The state was in relatively good fiscal shape until 2000, when it fell victim to the implosion of the dot-com boom. With revenues shrinking and cost-of-living increases mandated for current and retired state employees, a budget gap opened; as the downturn dragged on, the gap widened into a chasm and then an abyss. One of the key reasons for the record deficits was that during the good years public sector unions negotiated some astoundingly rich contracts. In 2011 the *Wall Street Journal* cheekily advised young people seeking high-paying jobs to forgo Harvard and become California prison guards. Training, the piece pointed out, took four months instead of four years, and the state paid you while you learned, with starting salaries that ranged from $45,000 to $65,000 and went up—way up—from there. In 2010 one sergeant with a base salary of $81,683 collected $114,334 in overtime and $8,648 in bonuses. And he was eligible for an annual $1,560 "fitness" bonus for getting a checkup. The capper: He could retire at fifty-five with 85 percent of his salary and medical care for life.[14] Thus the prison guard with thirty years of service, whose highest level of compensation was $100,000 a year, would be eligible to retire at age fifty-five with an $85,000 annual pension. According to the annuity calculator on CNNMoney.com, a fifty-five-year-old male employed in the private sector would need $1.63 million in retirement savings in order to purchase an annuity with a comparable yield.[15]

The city of Stockton, in California's Central Valley, offers another example. Stockton is flat broke and in 2012 became the largest U.S. city to ever go bankrupt. City officials admit they approved outsized benefits for city workers without having any understanding of the eventual cost. Writing in the *Wall Street Journal*, Steven Malanga, a senior fellow at the Manhattan Institute, quoted the city manager likening Stockton's fiscal history to a Ponzi scheme in which employees were promised "huge—and unfunded—salaries and benefits," whose costs the city didn't calculate and couldn't afford. Citing "a lack of transparency" as Stockton's biggest problem, officials now admit that the union contracts allowed for the insertion of hidden costs—a hundred different ways in which employees could quietly boost their pay. One egregious example: Stipends for a fire captain's uniform, needed or not, could add $35,000 to a $101,000 base salary.[16]

Even before the housing collapse in 2007, Stockton couldn't afford its generous benefits, so it turned to risky investments. Using $125 million of borrowed funds, it invested in the California Public Employees' Retirement System (CalPERS), California's pension fund, hoping to earn returns higher than the interest rates it was paying on its debt. Instead, the city lost nearly a quarter of its original investment—money that it had borrowed in the first place![17] As Stockton's fiscal situation deteriorates, residents are paying the penalty. There are now 25 percent fewer police officers, which translates into dangerously long waits for emergency assistance. If a house is burglarized and no one is hurt, chances are the police won't show up at all. California municipalities like Stockton find themselves boxed in fiscally by a constitutional amendment California passed in 1978 called Proposition 13. Prop 13 capped property-tax assessments at the 1975 value of residents' homes, limited rate increases, and, for good measure, required a two-thirds vote of the state legislature to increase income taxes (which now makes it harder for politicians to make up for lost property-tax revenues).[18] No reassessments were allowed under this law unless properties changed ownership. So in spite of California more than doubling its home values during the better part of the last decade, little new revenue was collected from properties that hadn't changed hands.

Some of the gimmicks that chronic overspenders like New Jersey and Illinois have used to balance their budgets amount to little more than rearranging the deck chairs on a sinking ship. In 1991 New Jersey closed its budget gap by having the Turnpike Authority buy just over four miles of toll roadway from the state. New Jersey governors of both parties borrowed from the state's pension fund to close gaps. In 1997 the governor invested state money in the stock market; you can probably guess how badly that worked out. In 2009 an amnesty plan for tax evaders netted New Jersey $725 million in delinquent taxes. Did the governor use the windfall to shore up the pension fund? No, he handed out property-tax rebates to citizens earning less than $75,000.[19] The problems of New Jersey are so deep that even current governor Chris Christie—who came into office as an outspoken budget hawk—now appears to have been overly optimistic about what he could actually achieve as governor given the mess the state is in. Revenue expectations continue to disappoint, forcing Christie to cut infrastructure spending and back off a tax cut he once vigorously lobbied for.

Unfortunately, when revenues don't cover costs, you have a sure prescription for disaster, and when there is too much debt, there is little, if any, margin for error. In fiscal year 2009 California's spending outpaced revenues by 224 percent (in 2010 it was 92 percent), while New York's spending outpaced revenues by 177 percent (89 percent in 2010). For Texas that same year the number was 136 percent (99 percent in 2010), and for Florida 166 percent (89 percent in 2010). A rebound in state revenues improved those numbers, but the core problem remained: Tax collections were still woefully below spending, rebounding only back to 2006 levels in 2010. During this same year, Florida was the only one of the twenty-five largest states (by GDP) to lower its spending.[20]

The economies of Florida, Arizona, and Nevada mirror that of California in that their GDPs are all lower than they were in 2007, with Florida down over 7 percent, Arizona 7 percent, and Nevada 9 percent.[21] When nominal GDP is declining and fixed costs keep rising, states get caught in a vortex of spending cuts and layoffs, which put even more pressure on their economies. These states suffer lower tax receipts. (Tax receipts have gone up recently only because actual rates have been hiked. Repeated rate hikes are not only often counterproductive but also certainly unsustainable.) Lower tax receipts lead to wider budget gaps, more spending cuts, reduced consumer spending, and new job losses. This is a difficult cycle to break. The less desirable the economic opportunities are within a state—due to lack of jobs, education, training, or some other social services—the higher the probability that businesses and people will leave the state. In 2011 alone, pharma company Biogen Idec relocated three hundred R & D jobs from San Diego to Research Triangle Park, North Carolina; chip maker Intel decided to build a $3 billion research center in Hillsboro, Oregon, instead of at its Santa Clara, California, headquarters; and health-care company Medtronic announced the relocation of three hundred customer-service jobs from Los Angeles, California, to San Antonio, Texas. "They are going to save 30% to 40% on all factors versus Los Angeles," said San Antonio Economic Development Foundation president Mario Hernandez of Medtronic's move. "And [workers] can live very comfortably very near the facility." According to a study by business relocation expert Joseph Vranich, the number of business relocations from California increased fivefold between 2009 and 2011.[22]

State finances are more or less a zero-sum game. Imagine a fixed pie of tax receipts that pay for the provision and upkeep of education, health care, roads and bridges, sanitation, public safety, debt service, pension payments, health care insurance, etc. So when more money goes to one program, less is left for another. If the federal government is at the top of the food chain—the ultimate "rich uncle" willing to lend states a hand when times are tough—the local government is at the bottom of the food chain, with the states somewhere in the middle. One of the first things a state can do, after asking for a federal money infusion, is to reduce monies to the local governments. This is where it really smarts for the local governments. In 2010, which is the most recent data available, 41 percent of local-government money came from state transfers, the rest by and large from property taxes. By comparison, 36 percent of the states' monies came from the federal government.[23]

The process on the surface seems simple enough, but it has become far from simple over the past sixty years. Take fiscal year 2010, for example. States took in just over $700 billion in tax receipts but spent over two and a half times that amount, or $1.9 trillion. Cut another way, states spent $1.2 trillion more than they took in. In 2000, by way of comparison, states spent twice their tax receipts and spent $540 billion more than the tax dollars they took in. Needless to say, the trend has been going in the wrong direction. Some of this is explained by the increased demand for Medicaid and welfare assistance, programs subsidized by the federal government and administered by the states. In fiscal year 2010 states received roughly $585 billion from the federal government for these programs.[24]

If states want to raise money so they don't have to take from one project to fund another, they have three options: raise taxes, increase taxes, or sell assets. Over the past decade, states have been more inclined to plunge further into debt and/or raise taxes than to sell assets. States have papered over the disconnect between tax revenues and spending by issuing unprecedented amounts of debt—some secured by taxes, some by specific revenue (like highway tolls)—and by looting the pensions of their current and future retired state employees. Between 2000 and 2010, states doubled the amount of municipal debt outstanding and took mostly fully funded pension plans and other benefit obligations into a deficit of close to $1 trillion.[25]

Although this kind of public-sector overspending was irresponsible and unsustainable, on one level it's understandable, especially when the economy was robust. States and cities wanted to make capital improvements, and low interest rates made it inexpensive to borrow money. Officials in Jefferson County, Alabama, borrowed $3.2 billion from JPMorgan Chase and other lenders to finance a sewer system.

Harrisburg, Pennsylvania, got burned by a trash-to-energy incinerator project that left the town $310 million in debt.[26] "It was easy to borrow the money . . . too easy," said political consultant Jeffrey Bell.[27] What politicians so conveniently forgot is that borrowed money, no matter how low the interest rate, eventually has to be paid back.

Budgeting should be a simple process, but it's not. The basic structure is supposed to work as follows: States collect income taxes or sales taxes in exchange for public services such as transportation, state agency services, higher education, and other locally administered programs. Local governments' revenues are generated primarily through property taxes and nontax revenues such as transfers from states. For example, in 2008 local governments derived 33 percent of their revenues/funding from such transfers; by 2010 that number had risen to 40 percent. Local governments collect primarily property taxes in exchange for services largely related to K-12 education and police and fire service. Theoretically, states try to tie their budget projections to what they think their tax receipts and other revenues will be, but there is no requirement that they do so. In fact, today state expenditures have very little correlation to revenues. States' expenditures are more closely linked to cost-of-living or inflation-growth projections. These numbers don't always line up when times are good, so you can imagine what the past five years have been like. Local governments have increased property taxes and states have increased income-tax rates, but these efforts have failed to keep up with expenses. Even after laying off nearly 700,000 state and local employees, expenses are still rising, and revenues are not keeping up.

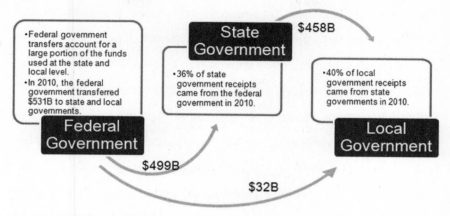

SOURCES: BEA AND MWAG

Originally, current taxes were supposed to cover current expenses. Over the years, however, the system has become more convoluted and incestuous. Today a dangerous system of dependency exists whereby states rely on the federal government for over a third of their spending, while local governments depend on states for 40 percent of their budget dollars.[28] If either the federal government or the state gets into a financial bind, it always has the option to reduce monies flowing down the food chain. No one is lower down the food chain than the local governments.

In 2011 the single largest federal-to-state transfer in history ended with the expiration of the American Recovery and Reinvestment Act (ARRA). When ARRA was being debated in Congress, White House economist Christina Romer argued that unemployment would decline to 7.0 percent by 2011 if it was passed but soar to 8.8 percent if it wasn't. Well, over the entire term of the ARRA program (from 2009 to 2011), states received over $480 billion in assistance in the form of contracts, grants, loans, and retirement benefits, and by the end of 2011 the unemployment rate stood at 8.9 percent.[29]

The ARRA money was supposed to go toward creating jobs, investing in infrastructure, saving schools, and generally stimulating a flailing economy. However, more than 37 percent of this money was simply used to cover state budget shortfalls, effectively "kicking the can" of tough cutbacks a few years forward.[30] In other words, a number of states, both large and small, managed to ignore their reckless spending over most of the 2000s and then, handed extra money by the federal government, decided to use those funds to cover budget deficits instead of using it for its intended purpose: providing for residents. This was simply unprecedented.

Aside from piling on more federal debt, the real risk of this one-time stimulus was the enormous "cliff effect" it created for the states that received the monies. Rather than address the clear structural problems that had created the states' fiscal mess, the federal government determined it was better to buy time for the states to recover. Ironically, this merely accelerated the time bomb. In fiscal year 2009 these monies cushioned 28 percent of the states' shortfalls, and by fiscal year 2011, states were using these monies to pad 37 percent of their budget shortfalls. This ultimately did little for California, for example, which received the lion's share of the ARRA funds at over $40 billion.[31] As recently as May 2012, California faced a deficit of over $16 billion. Needless to say, the state's unemployment rate is near the highest in the country. Much like the bailout of the banks, the money spent did little to fix the underlying problems.

The end of the ARRA stimulus money eventually forced states' hands. In fiscal year 2011, Connecticut, Illinois, Maryland, and Nevada raised taxes at the state level, and in Illinois the hike was a whopping 66 percent increase. Meanwhile, cities and towns started to raise property-tax rates in order to offset declining assessments. But these tax hikes haven't been enough to offset lower transfers from the states. Admittedly, tax receipts have rebounded from the lows of 2010, but they are still only tracking at 2007 levels.

States and local governments have already gone beyond increasing income and property taxes to increasing transportation and sales taxes, increasing taxes on luxury items, and increasing even further taxes on cigarettes and liquor. Some states and local communities have begun considering things that have been simply off the table until now: legalizing state gambling and allowing the sale of liquor in formerly dry counties. Politicians who once declared passionately, "We will never sell booze in this county" or "We will never allow gambling in this state," soon were backpedaling, offering to "sell just beer and wine" or "allow a lottery and one slot machine." In fiscal year 2011 Georgia, Florida, and Pennsylvania all voted to expand their gambling and gaming laws. Arizona, Michigan, New Jersey, and New York all voted to expand their lottery laws.

Even once-taboo options like privatization are suddenly on the table.

Confronted with the prospect of closing 70 of its 278 state parks, California elected to outsource the day-to-day operations of at least six parks. Arizona, also faced with the prospect of closing 13 of its 30 state parks, is considering auctioning off the day-to-day management of its parks to private companies. The fact is that current park fees are not covering the cost of upkeep, and states no longer have the resources to make up the difference. As an example, California's Brannan Island State Recreation Area, near Rio Vista, cost California roughly $740,000 a year to operate, more than double what it took in from fees and concessions revenues. Rather than fight new management, most park goers are just happy their parks are still open. "We're not talking about a private company putting up billboards," a spokesman for the nonprofit California State Parks Foundation commented.[32]

In fiscal year 2010 the federal government transferred just over $500 billion to the states, with states receiving over $700 billion in tax receipts, over $450 billion from insurance trust revenue (employee retirement systems, unemployment, and workers' compensation programs), and over $300 billion from other revenues to account for their $1.9 trillion in expenditures.[33] In order to balance their budgets, states have increased their borrowing over the past decade. How was this possible when so many states must balance their budgets under the law? The undeniable answer: debt. In fiscal year 2010, states issued $147 billion in new general-obligation bonds (municipal bonds backed by the credit and taxing power of the state rather than by a specific source of revenue, such as highway tolls) and increased their unfunded pension liabilities (the difference between what a state is required to pay into a pension plan and what it has actually paid) by $225 billion. Record-low interest rates have made debt accumulation appear at least manageable, even harmless. As a result, states have amassed close to $1.5 trillion in additional municipal debt since 2000, almost doubling their total municipal-debt load.[34] While some states have limitations on how much debt they can have outstanding, the rules typically apply only to general-obligation bonds and specifically to the debt service on those bonds—not to the actual amount of debt amassed. Clearly in a low-rate environment like the one we have been in for the past fifteen-plus years, these "debt limits" encourage the same type of easy-money-mortgage mentality that too many American consumers adopted during the housing bubble. Yes, teaser-rate mortgages may be affordable in the short term, just as issuing $100 billion in five-year general-obligation bonds may be relatively inexpensive. But what happens if you have to refinance your mortgage or roll over your municipal-bond debt at a time when rates are much higher?

Finances should never be that complicated. "Don't spend what you don't have" is a simple adage most individuals take to heart but one never fully embraced by politicians. Governments see themselves as providers of last resort for basic social services. For years, states and municipalities could afford to be generous and spend more than they took in. Federal funding helped out the states, state funding supported the cities, and a growing economy supported tax revenues at all three levels. Then came the Great Recession. There was so much demand for unemployment benefits, states had to take loans out from the federal government just to keep the programs going. Now the states are struggling to find ways to pay those loans back. States that borrowed too much or funded their pensions too little are caught in a budgetary vise. It's even worse for the cities and counties. The feds are sending less to the states, the states are cutting back on aid to cities, and cities are being forced to accept spending cuts and austerity budgets that just a few years ago would have been unimaginable.

Forty-nine states are bound by their own constitutions to maintain balanced budgets, yet for five of the past ten years, the states have run $590 billion in shortfalls. As states issue more debt in order to balance budgets and avoid spending cuts, the size of state debt grows and so does the annual cost of all that debt. Growing debt-service costs have been camouflaged over the past decade by low interest rates, but that game is coming to an end. Even low rates cannot cover up the sheer weight of the debt loads being amassed. Over the past few years, tax receipts have not been growing fast enough to keep pace with rising debt service, forcing states to cut back elsewhere.

As any consumer knows, spending what you don't have is unsustainable. For states, excessive spending is coming to an abrupt end with bruising consequences—much like what happens to the consumer who runs up way too much credit-card debt. Sooner or later, even the minimum payment on the credit-card bill becomes too large and there isn't enough money left over to pay for everyday expenses. That's the predicament far too many states now find themselves in. In six of the past ten years, states have had to cut back or eliminate programs, and in some cases raise taxes, to balance their budgets, but there is less and less wiggle room as the costs of minimum service payments on debt keep growing into a larger portion of the overall pie. Over thirty states have cut public health assistance. Twenty-nine states have cut elderly and disabled assistance. Over thirty states have cut K-12 education programs. Over forty states have cut payroll or imposed furloughs on state workers.[35] For some it's only going to get worse—in part because many of their taxpayers are in deep trouble too.

The Wrong Bet and the Worse Outcome

One fall day in 2001, I visited with the management team at MBNA, the largest independent credit-card company at the time, now owned by Bank of America. The country was in a recession, and the conversation revolved around credit. Were people paying their bills on time? Were delinquencies becoming more or less frequent? For a lender a loan is only as good as the borrower's willingness to honor it, so judging the risk qualities of a customer is critical. The folks at MBNA told me something important: As far as credit goes, 80 percent of losses came from 20 percent of customers. And what was the commonality of that 20 percent? They were the customers least likely to own a home.

Turns out that it wasn't just MBNA that believed this. It was the entire lending industry. But back in the fall of 2001, roughly 65 percent of Americans owned homes. That was the way it had been for several decades, so there was a long precedent to support that underwriting mentality and discipline. However, from 2002 on, it became an entirely new playing field. By 2006 homeownership had shot up to almost 70 percent in the United States.[36] Did the 80/20 logic still apply? Turns out, lenders didn't adjust to the new reality of homeown-ership and consumer credit as homeownership skyrocketed. If people owned homes, they were deemed more creditworthy. Therefore, as more and more people qualified for homeownership, they were plied with more and more debt. From 2000 to 2008 mortgage debt grew by over 150 percent, revolving home-equity lines grew by over 500 per-cent, and standard credit-card debt grew by almost 60 percent.[37] Be-cause rates were near record lows, the monthly payments, or carrying costs, were low too. The clear problem was, there was no guarantee those carrying costs would stay low. Because so much of this new debt was priced on an adjustable-rate basis, it made once-unthinkable debt levels seem manageable to many new or first-time borrowers.

By 2009 the U.S. consumer owed over $14 trillion, mostly in mortgage loans to banks and other consumer finance companies. The situation was especially bleak in the housing-bust states. In Cali-fornia, for instance, consumer debt per capita reached $74,950 in 2010, and the ratio of debt-to-income per capita soared to 174 percent in 2010. Nevada followed closely behind at $57,660 and 156 percent respectively.[38] Homeowners had been on a borrowing bonanza. At the peak of the cycle, homeowners took over $300 billion out of their homes and borrowed another $700 billion in home-equity lines of credit. More often than not, that was in addition to their first mort-gages. "Skin in the game," or equity in homes, dropped to under 45 percent by 2008 from well over 65 percent in the 1980s. Heading into 2008, banks were prepared to let homeowners take on even more debt. On top of the over $700 billion in drawn home-equity lines of credit in 2008, there was an additional $700 billion in unused lines extended and ready to be drawn upon. The numbers on credit cards are even more astounding. In 2008 there was over $800 billion in credit-card debt outstanding, but there was also an additional $4.7 trillion in untapped credit-card lines available and ready to be tapped.[39]

When the housing bust and credit crisis hit, home prices nationally were hit hard, but in some areas they were truly devastated. If a consumer got to the housing party late, as so many did between 2003 and 2006, they found themselves underwater in debt by late 2008, owing more on their mortgage than their underlying home was worth. The ripple effect on local communities where home values were hit the hardest was profound. There consumers had suffered the greatest wealth destruction, and suddenly unemployment was rising too. That's not all. Consumers in areas that had once been overbanked— where getting a loan had once been easy—were suddenly cut off from new credit. According to the *Wall Street Journal,* loan volume was plunging in the coastal states: "The largest drops were in cities scattered across California and Florida, the states hit hardest by the U.S. housing bust. New lending in Merced, California, which experienced one of the worst housing collapses in the United States, ended last year 81 percent below the peak of 2006. The three largest U.S. cities—New York, Chicago and Los Angeles—experienced decreases of 38 percent, 44 percent and 55 percent, respectively."[40] Conversely, states in the middle of the country have done a better job of keeping consumer debt in check. Residents there have better employment opportunities and more disposable income, and thus lenders are willing to extend them credit. In Cedar Rapids, Iowa, for instance, consumer loan volume in the fourth quarter of 2011 was 52 percent higher than in the same period of 2006, according to the *Wall Street Journal.*

There's a popular expression in the banking industry: "A rolling loan gathers no loss." What it means is that as long as there is liquidity in the market, losses are not meaningful. Once it becomes difficult to refinance a loan, roll debt over, or even get a new loan, all bets are off. Some borrowers need more time to pay off the principal, whereas others cannot afford the higher interest payments that kick in after the teaser rates expire. That's when the losses come. By late 2008 the banks were painfully aware of how dangerously aggressive they had been in handing out loans during the boom. In order to protect themselves, they quickly cut back any excess credit lines they had remaining in the system. What that translated into was $4.7 trillion of unused credit-card lines being cut back to $3.2 trillion by early 2010, a more than 30 percent cut of $1.5 trillion from the entire U.S. credit-card system. Given that credit-card lines had truly become a cash-management vehicle for some consumers and small-business owners, these cuts were especially disruptive. At that point, at least 50 percent of credit-card customers were revolving their credit-card debt every month, meaning they did not or could not pay their monthly payment in full each month. Home-equity lines of credit were going in the same direction. From mid-2008 to mid-2010, home-equity lines of credit were cut back from over $700 billion to $514 billion, almost $200 billion less.[41] The lending party was officially over. Unused credit lines that had once given consumers a sense of security (albeit elusive and unjustified) for unforeseen events like a sudden car repair, a child needing braces, a spouse suddenly losing a job, etc. were gone. There was no emergency credit available, no new credit offers; it was just the bills that remained.

As people began to emerge from the haze of the housing bust, they were served with not one but two rude awakenings. Not only did they owe $14 trillion in consumer loans, but they owed another $6 trillion that had been run up on their tab in the form of state and local government obligations.[42] Because much of this state debt was guaranteed by future tax dollars, state governments had effectively doubled down on an already debt-burdened consumer. It is bad enough losing money you have in the bank or stock market; it is a whole different matter to lose borrowed money, which is effectively what has happened to residents of states that piled on the most debt over the past decade.

Most people understand that when a state issues municipal-bond debt—specifically debt that carries the guarantee of the taxing authority—residents of the state are collectively bound to pay it back. Such a notion is so well understood that almost every state has a cap on this kind of debt so that the total debt load never gets out of control—never jeopardizes the financial health of the states and their residents. But if the cap only applies to the debt service, not to the total amount of debt, state and local governments can too easily talk themselves into taking on debt that could be much more expensive to service down the road. The low-interest-rate environment in the United States enabled, if not encouraged, states to pile record amounts of debt onto their balance sheets while safely remaining below their "caps." The same "monthly payment" mentality that lured many consumers to take on mortgages that they couldn't afford enticed states to load up on debt obligations they couldn't afford either. The cost ends up being borne by all taxpayers, frugal and spendthrift alike. Let's say, for example, the Fitzgibbon family resisted the temptation of taking on excessive debt or too big a mortgage, but their neighbors, the Gradys, took a huge chunk of equity out of their already highly leveraged home and racked up mounds of credit-card debt to boot. For a while the Gradys enjoyed a far more lavish lifestyle than the more frugal Fitzgibbons—spending on cars, fifty-inch flat-screen TVs, expensive vacations, and the like. When the housing bust hit, the Gradys were faced with bills they just couldn't afford. The Fitzgibbons might have been sympathetic, but nobody expected them to be on the hook for their neighbors' debts. But things worked differently for the neighbors when it came to the debts their state and local governments racked up on their behalf. Both neighbors had to pay equally for the excessive government spending of the past decade.

Making matters worse was the 30-plus percent decline in home prices that left nearly a quarter of all people with mortgages owing more on their mortgage than their homes were worth. So imagine your home value declines by 30 percent, but your property taxes actually rise—a familiar story all across the country. The first option used by many local politicians to offset lower tax revenues was simply to hike tax rates. This had the unintended result of actually further depressing home values—and thus property taxes—because the higher taxes did not come with better services. Imagine you're a prospective home buyer looking at two similar and similarly priced homes in neighboring towns. The school systems are equivalent, as are town recreation programs and the fire and police departments. But one house carries a $5,000 property-tax bill, while the other's is $10,000. Which house are you going to buy?

From 1993 to 2007, 64 percent of all jobs in the United States—over fifteen million total—were created by small businesses.[43] Credit was easy to come by, making it that much easier to start a small business. Banks rarely want to make uncollateralized loans to start-up businesses, given that the failure rate of such businesses within the first year after opening their doors is over 70 percent. What made starting a business so easy from 1993 to 2007 was the fact that small-business funding was available to entrepreneurs in the form of home equity. Soaring real-estate values were like free money. In California home prices tripled, and in 2006 over half of all nonfarm jobs in California were with small businesses.[44] Six years later, California had a higher percentage of negative equity—of mortgages that were underwater—than any other state in the country. The funding spigot for small business ran dry. Throw in relatively high taxes and a generally difficult business-operating environment—in 2012 California had the third-highest cost of doing business, according to a CNBC survey—and it's exceedingly unlikely small business will be what pulls California out of its unemployment crisis.[45]

Since 2008 home prices in California have fallen almost 40 percent, and almost 30 percent of California mortgages are underwater. Credit has declined radically throughout the state, businesses have gone bust, and the unemployment rate remains the third highest in the country at over 10 percent. California has had one of the highest unemployment rates in the country for going on five years. New-business formation is next to impossible without credit, as is self-funded job training or buying a new home (which has the economic multiplier effect of job creation). The entrepreneur who ten years ago might have funded a start-up business on her MasterCard—or perhaps even on three MasterCards and a Visa, given banks' liberal lending policies at the time—no longer has the same access to credit. The most direct impact has been on construction companies. At 25 percent, construction has the highest unemployment rate of any industry in the United States.[46]

An insatiable appetite to spend put both states and consumers in the very same place: heavily in debt. California, which is home to some of the most indebted consumers in America, also has one of the most indebted state governments in the country. The problem for anyone who lives in California is that they get both bills. On an average per-capita basis, this translates into $73,000 in consumer debt and an additional $11,000 in tax-supported state obligations. New Jersey isn't much better, with $61,000 in average consumer debt per capita and another $16,000 in tax-supported state obligations.[47] Some other debt-soaked states, along with their residing consumers, are Illinois, Nevada, Michigan, and Ohio.

Debt-to-Income per Capita (2011)

SOURCES: NY FED, BEA, INSIDE MORTGAGE FINANCE, AND MWAG

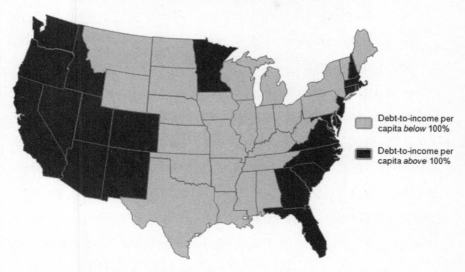

Debt-to-income per capita *below* 100%

Debt-to-income per capita *above* 100%

Much of the trouble states are in today is linked to overexposure to real estate. During the boom years, the affected states—chiefly in the Sun Belt, the Northeast, and the West—saw tax revenues soar along with real-estate prices. The numbers are striking: From 2000 to 2010, real-estate sales, rentals, and leasing provided 21 percent of GDP growth in Florida, 18 percent in California, and 22 percent in New Jersey.[48] These revenues came from transaction and annual real-estate taxes, of course, as well as growth in ancillary industries such as construction and mortgage lending, which, in turn, paid taxes. Unfortunately, the states spent real estate–related revenues as quickly as they came in. Public-sector unions saw these bulging coffers as leverage to negotiate generous pay and benefits packages, many of which included automatic cost-of-living increases. Not until I studied the various pension funds of each state (more on pensions later) did I understand how public-employee pay packages constricted states' financial flexibility. Expensive infrastructure and education projects were undertaken, each with a politically powerful interest group clamoring for its piece of the pie. The banks and bond investors financing the excess seemed unperturbed—convinced that home prices, and therefore property-tax receipts, would go up in perpetuity.

As I have said, the pain has not been felt equally across the country. The states with the biggest real-estate booms, namely Arizona, California, Florida, and Nevada, took the biggest hit. Ironically, they were victims of their own success in luring new residents. There was a great migratory wave of Americans moving to the Sand States. Arizona, for instance, added 1.3 million people between 2000 and 2010, a 26 percent population growth.[49] With all the new arrivals, a mind-set of perpetual growth took hold. Builders overbuilt, mortgages were granted to people who couldn't afford them, and, among home buyers and real-estate investors, the proverbial and preternaturally dangerous irrational exuberance took hold. Then the delinquent mortgages grew, foreclosures followed, and the housing market collapsed.

The birthplace of subprime lending, California was responsible for 20 percent of all mortgages underwritten in the United States, and Florida was right there behind it.[50] Through the growth of securitization, small lenders made loans, large lenders made loans, and tens of millions of Americans could suddenly afford to buy a house. With credit so readily available, consumer spending increased, employment increased, and overall economic output increased. The coasts truly were driving economic growth in the United States, and loose credit was responsible for most of it.

The positive effect of abundant credit, investment, job creation, income growth, more investment, higher tax receipts, more government spending, etc., made for mini booms all across California and other Sand States like Nevada and Florida. Retailers flooded markets with new stores, built to support burgeoning suburbs. Chains like Costco, Home Depot, and Best Buy did their biggest business in California. The music was playing loudly, and Californians couldn't help but get up and dance. But in 2007, when the music officially stopped, it was Californians who would be hit the hardest. The debt binge so many Californians had been on for over twenty years was about to end painfully.

By 2010—the last year for which data is available—consumer debt per capita in California hit $74,950—a debt-to-income ratio of 174 percent. By comparison, the average debt per capita in Texas was $36,000, which translates to a debt-to-income ratio of 89 percent. Even with low interest rates, a 174 percent debt-to-income ratio leaves little margin for error. It is harder to qualify for a new loan, it is certainly harder to make payments on the debt already being carried, and there are no unused credit lines that can be tapped in case of an emergency.[51] This is a big deal, considering that over 50 percent of Americans use their credit-card lines to manage their monthly cash flows. Unused credit lines represent a "what if" safety net for many. What if my spouse loses his job, what if my child needs braces, what if I get sick, etc. With no credit lines, "what if" quickly becomes "what now?"

In sharp contrast to the debt-laden coasts and Sun Belt, things look very different in the center of the country—where credit was more scarce during the boom and therefore debt loads are more benign now. Consumer debt per capita throughout the central corridor of the United States is less than $35,000, half that of California. Per capita debt-to-income levels tell the same story with dramatically lower numbers in the center of the country.[52]

Because so many of the subprime lenders went belly up between

Consumer Debt per Capita (2000–2010)

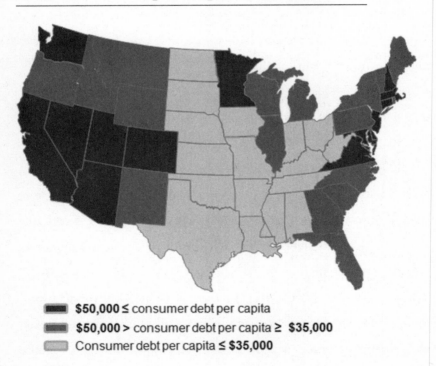

- $50,000 ≤ consumer debt per capita
- $50,000 > consumer debt per capita ≥ $35,000
- Consumer debt per capita ≤ $35,000

SOURCES: FEDERAL RESERVE BANK OF NEW YORK, U.S. CENSUS BUREAU, AND MWAG

Consumer Debt-to-Income per Capita (2010)

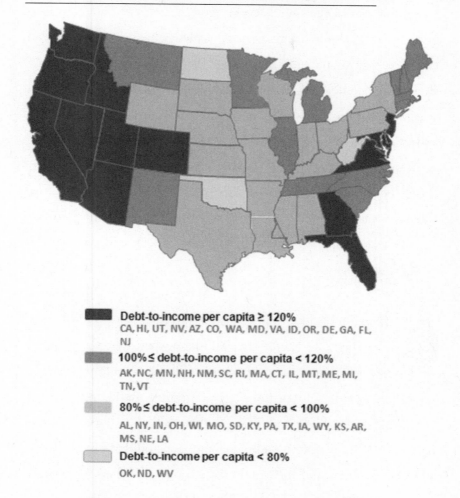

Debt-to-income per capita ≥ 120%
CA, HI, UT, NV, AZ, CO, WA, MD, VA, ID, OR, DE, GA, FL, NJ

100% ≤ debt-to-income per capita < 120%
AK, NC, MN, NH, NM, SC, RI, MA, CT, IL, MT, ME, MI, TN, VT

80% ≤ debt-to-income per capita < 100%
AL, NY, IN, OH, WI, MO, SD, KY, PA, TX, IA, WY, KS, AR, MS, NE, LA

Debt-to-income per capita < 80%
OK, ND, WV

SOURCES: FEDERAL RESERVE BANK OF NEW YORK, U.S. CENSUS BUREAU, AND MWAG

2006 and 2010, a new breed of pseudolenders has filled the lending vacuum for the credit challenged. Check cashers, payday lenders, and pawn shops have emerged as sources of quick credit, but the associated costs for borrowers are far higher than those of the more traditional banks that once served these customers. Factor in fees, and the annual interest charges associated with borrowing from a payday lender shop can range between 50 percent and 250 percent.[53] Perhaps not coincidentally, the hit pawn-shop reality show *Pawn Stars* is filmed in a city, Las Vegas, that had the highest concentration of subprime loans during the housing boom and in a state, Nevada, that is the only one in the country in which mortgage debt owed on single-family homes exceeds the homes' total valuations. Nationwide, since 2008 over $2 trillion in credit has been pulled from the housing-finance system, and the bulk of that credit has been pulled from areas now experiencing the greatest financial hardship. The city of North Las Vegas, for example, declared a state of emergency in June, blaming a 37 percent decline in property-tax revenue.[54] In America's *nouveau pauvre* states, it's becoming a lot more expensive to be poor.

When a community loses access to credit, it puts pressure on almost all aspects of life within that community. Remember the saying "It is harder to have had money and lost it than to have never had it at all"? Well, substitute "debt" for "money," and that's basically the situation many coastal and Sun Belt states now find themselves in. In just five years' time, mortgage credit to California, Florida, Arizona, and Nevada declined by three quarters of a trillion dollars, or 10 percent, from its peak in 2006. From 2008 to 2011 mortgage credit in California collapsed by over 18 percent, and in Nevada mortgage credit collapsed by 30 percent during the same time period. With so much credit coming out of those states, it is no wonder home prices there have plummeted, posting the sharpest declines in the country.[55]

States in the Midwest, which were struggling with the decline in their manufacturing base, felt the real-estate bust much less acutely. Of course, many of these states were already in recession. Wealthier regions with fewer new out-of-state residents than the Sand States, such as New England and the Northwest, saw real estate contract but not collapse.

Then there were states that fell somewhere in the middle. In Atlanta's exurbs, for example, weed-choked lots sit where new shopping centers and subdivisions were once planned. Dan Chapman and Jeffry Scott, writing in the *Atlanta Journal-Constitution* in 2010, noted that "the downturn all but killed residential development—the economic lifeblood—across Atlanta's northern exurbs. . . . Barrow, Bartow, Cherokee, Forsyth, Hall and Jackson counties." As recently as 2008, those counties had "notched some of the highest growth rates in the nation. . . . Property tax revenue poured into these counties."[56]

In the spring of 2012, Georgia State University's Rajeev Dhawan forecast no net growth in Georgia employment and only 0.8 percent in 2013. "Gains in growing sectors, such as professional and business services, manufacturing and health-care services, have not been great enough to offset losses in lagging sectors such as construction, local government, and banking," Dhawan explained. Real estate, in effect, was proving a stubborn drag on Georgia's economy.[57]

The overdependence on real estate had a profound impact on

state revenues, sometimes in indirect ways. When the value of a family's house declines—even if that family has no intention of selling and the breadwinners are gainfully employed—there is still an emotional and psychological toll. Call it the reverse wealth effect. They are less inclined to splurge on big-ticket items, they put off renovation projects, and they just generally spend less. All this leads to even further declines in tax revenue. States then have to increase taxes, cut spending, or both, which results in less discretionary income for those who are employed and the loss of all income for some with government-funded jobs. So the debt hangover is a double whammy for everyone—a gruel diet of reduced spending with a side order of higher taxes.

Chapter 4

■

Pensions: The Debt Bomb Nobody's Talking About

Back in the early 2000s—when Silicon Valley was still flush and the California real-estate market was soaring—Lou Paulson, then head of the Contra Costa County, California, firefighters' union, negotiated a sweet new contract for his members. Veteran firefighters could now retire at age fifty with an annual pension equivalent to 90 percent of their final salary. "There was plenty of money around," said Paulson. "To go back to that time, things were really good."

That was about to change. After the housing bust, Contra Costa's tax revenues plummeted. In order to avoid the closure of six fire stations, the firefighters' union proposed a November 2012 ballot initiative that, if approved, would levy a new $75-a-year tax on every county homeowner. Kris Hunt, director of the Contra Costa Taxpayers Association, was outraged that the firefighters would ask more from taxpayers when it was the spiraling cost of firefighters' own pensions forcing the county to shutter stations. Hunt's group responded by publishing the names of every retired Contra Costa County employee with a pension of $100,000 a year or more. As it turned out, there were 665 members of this $100K club, including 24 whose pensions exceeded $200,000. Of the 665, 268 were firefighters—which meant there were more retired firefighters with a $100,000 pension than there were current firefighters on the job (261).

One of the $100K club members was a fifty-five-year-old retired fire captain named Jaad Ajlouny. Ajlouny said he was blindsided by the catcalls from angry voters—folks who not so long ago had gone out of their way to thank him for his service. "Just sitting around in a bar, you know, minding my own business," Ajlouny recalled in a radio interview, "and a guy yells over: Hey, Jaad, come on over here and buy me a drink with that retirement I paid for."

The Contra Costa ballot measure failed. Everybody might still love firefighters, but what they did not like was retired fifty-five-year-olds taking home $100K a year at a time when many taxpayers were out of work and could not afford to put any money aside for their own retirements. One such no voter—Matt Heavy, a construction worker who had gone through a tough period—told NPR in an interview that the firefighters were being unfair: "I felt hostage . . . either pay the extra money or we're going to start shutting down stations. And the bottom line is the reason that they're asking for the money is because the pensions are just skyrocketing."[1]

A ballot measure that was intended to save six firehouses had morphed into a local referendum on pension reform. "After 10 years of being driven by pension costs," said Dan Borenstein, a columnist for the Contra Costa Times who opposed the measure, "[the prevailing view was] we're not going to let you put the cart before the horse. You've got to show us you're serious about controlling costs before we're willing to go along with the tax increase." Stories like Contra Costa's are sure to play out again and again and again simply because state and local governments don't have the money to pay for the retirement packages they once promised public employees. In 2009 new Governmental Accounting Standards Board (GASB) rules finally exposed how much pension debt elected officials had incurred on our behalf. The numbers were two years old, but it was disclosure nonetheless. As of June 2008, states were on the hook for over $452 billion in unfunded pension debt on top of what they owed by way of traditional municipal debt (note, both guaranteed by the future taxes of their residents). Even scarier, those numbers were before the worst of the credit crisis—and each state seemed to have its own unique way of crunching the numbers. Indeed, the next year's financial disclosures revealed that these unfunded pension obligations had grown 50 percent in just one year's time, from $452 billion to $678 billion.[2] Adding the amount of heath-care and other benefits states owed, and that number ballooned to $1.3 trillion in 2009. As of 2011, that number was $1.4 trillion, and that is not counting municipal-bond obligations.[3]

With not nearly enough money to go around, the impending war over public-employee pensions threatens to be one of the more vicious political debates this country has seen, pitting Americans against Americans, neighbor against neighbor. On one side there's the public-sector employee, who worked an entire career—sometimes at a pay level below what she could have earned in the private sector— under the assumption that her job would provide a secure (and perhaps early) retirement with few financial worries. Until now, she hasn't had to worry much about retirement. After all, a great retirement package, generous vacation days, and a better work-life balance are part of what attracted her to public-sector work in the first place. On the other side of the debate there's the guy in the private sector who lost large chunks of his 401(k) savings in the stock market and perhaps even had to tap those savings for living expenses after losing a job. Now he's being hit with higher taxes and continued cutbacks to basic public services. The fight is not just political but constitutional too: Courts are now deciding whether municipalities can use ballot measures and bankruptcy laws to void or change public-employee pensions.

At the heart of the problem is a difficult truth: There's not enough money to pay for everything, and by law, pension payments trump most other types of spending. Tax revenues are down, bills keep rising, and spending keeps growing. But based on the official pecking order, pension obligations and municipal-bond debt service must be honored before any money can be funneled to everyday expenses for education, police protection, road repair, and other essential services. Because so many baby-boomer teachers are now retiring, taxpayers are being called on to pay more but are actually getting less in return. Pension and health-care costs are increasingly crowding out other line items in state and municipal budgets. The number of retirees drawing a pension is growing, but the number of workers contributing to the pension plan is declining (which is the same scenario that led to GM's demise). Back when overall tax receipts were rising, this disconnect went largely unnoticed. But with revenues as strained as they have been for the past five-plus years, crowding out has become a real hot button in communities across the country. "I went toe to toe with the public unions looking out for the kids of Rhode Island because if we didn't fix those pensions, there would be no good public schools," says Gina Raimondo, treasurer of Rhode Island.[4]

Taxpayers are asking some very pointed questions. "Why is my neighbor's pension payment more important than my daughter's right to a good education in a class with a low student-teacher ratio?" "Why are we laying off police officers and letting crime rates spike to pay pensions for retired cops who now live out of state and don't even pay local taxes?" Public employees have a reasonable response: If taxpayers don't like the terms of their union contracts, then they shouldn't have elected the mayors, school boards, and city council members who approved them. Of course, mortgage lenders had a similar type of response—if you don't like the terms of your adjustable-rate mortgage, why did you sign the papers?—but their argument was overwhelmed by financial realities. In the aftermath of the housing bubble, the priority of payments got flipped. Consumers who had once paid their mortgage bills before anything else—they couldn't risk losing the equity in their homes, after all—suddenly started giving precedence to car and credit-card payments over their mortgages since they no longer had any home equity to protect. The priority of payments for taxpayers is about to undergo a similarly dramatic shift.

Years from now, 2008 will prove to be a turning point in

American history. In just one year the Dow lost 33.8 percent and the S&P lost a staggering 37 percent. For many Americans this meant huge portions of their retirement nest eggs; their IRA and 401(k) savings suddenly evaporated after years of scrupulous saving. Factor in job losses and destroyed home values, and the retirement hopes of many Americans faced some serious downgrading. No more beach houses. No more summer homes on the lake. The dream now is just having enough money to live comfortably.

But not all retirement dreams have been downgraded—certainly not those of state and local government employees and retirees. Not only didn't they have to contribute much money, if any, to their retirement plans, but the payments they receive postretirement are guaranteed by tax dollars. The ups and downs of the stock market had little bearing on their retirement plans. As their neighbors wept over their year-end 401(k) statements, public employees barely even looked at theirs. Their retirement was money in the bank.

For decades this divide wasn't something broadly discussed because the trade-off seemed reasonable. Even as the private market largely abandoned pension funds in exchange for employee-driven and paid-for retirement plans, the fact that the public sector was still sticking to the same old system got little attention. Rather, most understood that there was a fair trade-off between working for the private sector, where benefits might be less generous but salaries were higher, and working in the public sector, where lower pay was offset by a more secure retirement. Moreover, being a police officer or a garbage collector can be dangerous, unpleasant work, so it makes sense to offer some incentives to get people into those jobs. After all, the work-related fatality rate for police officers (nineteen deaths per hundred thousand people) is four times higher than that of the average American worker.[5] The problem is, the size and cost of those incentives seemed to grow exponentially. In 2012 the Bureau of Labor Statistics compared compensation (both salary and benefits) for state and local government employees with that of the private sector, and the differential was a staggering 34 percent—in favor of the government employees! Today, "pensions" are almost uniformly associated with the public sector and never discussed in the private sector—unless the topic is reducing or eliminating them.

Generally, in the private sector an employee is on his own when it comes to retirement savings. Ironically, however, that same employee is on the hook for the public sector's retirement savings. In other words, a dry cleaner working for himself is responsible not only for his own unguaranteed retirement but also for the retirement of his next-door neighbor, the county judicial clerk. The outrageousness of this guarantee became clear when, in 2009, under directives from the Government Accounting Standards Board, states first disclosed both the size of the pension obligations and how much elected officials had looted from pension funds—usually by borrowing money from pension funds and promising with IOUs to repay it in the future.[6]

Aside from suffering dramatic declines from the equity markets over the past decade, pensions have also been the secret slush fund of elected officials. Monies from pension funds are not withdrawn all at once; it's an ongoing payout as employees retire. Therefore, as long as the retiree is getting his or her check on time, nobody worries about where the money is coming from. By design, officials can offer grand promises of future benefits with little sacrifice today. For example, rather than give a public-employee union a pay raise, which could affect a city's ability to balance next year's budget, mayors can offer future cost-of-living adjustments on employees' retirement plan. These COLAs are effectively built-in annual raises on pension benefits. Over the past decade, while real wage inflation has been just 2 percent annually and closer to 1 percent more recently, many retirees have gotten annual increases of 3 percent or more from their pension payouts. So in reality, pensioners have done a whole lot better than workers. But at some point, when those future promises become current-day realities, there won't be enough money. That time may be upon us sooner than you think. Josh Rauh, of Northwestern's Kellogg School of Management, believes that by 2025, over half of states' pension funds will run out of money.[7]

There are other examples of abuse in the pension system that I will describe later, but first here's a quick primer on how pension accounting works. Today states owe nearly $3 trillion between bonded debt, unfunded pensions, unfunded health insurance, and other benefits. Over half of this relates to benefits for past and current state and local government employees. But even among neighboring states conditions vary greatly. For example, in Illinois the total tax-supported debt per capita is $20,000, but next door in Indiana, that number is a mere $2,000—one-tenth of the pension debt Illinois taxpayers are on the hook for.[8]

Under most private-sector retirement plans in the United States, postretirement payouts depend upon how much an employee has put into the plan—usually a 401(k)—how long the employee has been contributing to the fund, and how well the underlying investments have performed. Weakness in any of those three variables reduces the ultimate payout. Of course, how much an employee contributes to a fund and for how many years are factors under the employee's control, depending upon how much money he can afford to put aside. And as we have learned over the past "lost decade" of zero market returns, investment results are highly volatile. The market crash of 2008 wiped out a decade's worth of gains for some employees. There are no guarantees under these plans; the employee bears all the risk. How well the fund performs and how much the employee puts in are often the only determinants of how much money will be left at retirement.

Government pension plans work very differently from private-sector 401(k)s and IRAs. Under government pension plans, the employee contributes little, typically less than 10 percent of the total contribution. The taxpayer is responsible for the rest, and those contributions start on the very first day of employment, whether there is money available or not.[9] There are imbedded annual COLAs meant to be buffers against inflation, yet those adjustments are not tied to any particular inflation metric. In a low-inflation environment, they're akin to pay hikes. The average COLA is around 3 percent per annum. Note that average wage growth has been 2 percent for most of the past decade—and 1 percent more recently.[10]

Maybe the most outrageous difference, however, is the fact that unlike the market-dependent results of private retirement plans, government pensions set return assumptions that are guaranteed by the taxpayer. Particularly outrageous are return assumptions that fly in the face of the actual performance of the market over the trailing ten or twenty years. The average annual-return assumption used by government pension funds today is 8 percent, despite the fact that the actual returns of many pensions funds over the past decade have been closer to zero.[11] Understanding this makes it easier to see why unfunded pension liabilities have been growing at such a meteoric pace. For a $30 billion state pension fund, the gap between 8 percent and 0 percent represents $2.4 billion per year that has to be made up by taxpayers. No wonder that inside of just one decade, government pension funds went from being fully funded to being underfunded by nearly $1 trillion.

Compounding the problems of lower-than-expected returns, imbedded COLA increases, and low employee contributions are irresponsible politicians who too often treat the funding of pensions as a choice rather than an obligation. By not funding pensions in one year, a state could save money for another program, effectively robbing Peter to pay Paul. All this really accomplishes, of course, is adding to taxpayer debt down the road. Failing to make a payment or an actuarially recommended contribution is often justified as a temporary solution to a shortfall in tax revenues, one that will be made good in the following years. However, a state like New Jersey has been inadequately funding its pensions for over a decade and today is under-reserved to the tune of $42 billion.[12]

Over the years, some states have been playing the equivalent of credit-card roulette with their pension funds. They pay the minimum owed—some shirk even that—hoping to outrun the debt being accumulated. If only they can get one great year of stock-market returns, perhaps their pensions can recoup some lost or withheld funds. If only there's a pickup in their economies, then a tax-revenue surplus can be tapped to replenish their depleted pension funds. The worst kind of rationalization may be this one: If only we can get a market-thumping return on money borrowed through pension-obligation bonds—the equivalent of taking out a margin loan to buy stocks—then maybe we can make up for the shortfalls in what we owe. In Vegas they call this problem gambling. In state capitals it's everyday accounting.

How could all of this happen in plain sight? Just consider the incentives behind sustaining a broken system to the bitter end. When it comes to pensions, politicians are like the guy at the party who orders pizza but then disappears when the doorbell rings and someone has to pay. Many of the pension guarantees were negotiated by elected officials who knew they would be long gone from office before anyone realized that the promises they had made were completely unaffordable for their constituents. Contractually negotiated pension benefits tend to grow during the good times, when the presumption is that the good times will last forever. They don't, of course. But by the time that's apparent, there's usually a new mayor or new governor who has to deal with the consequences. It's not unlike what happened in the financial industry: Few of the CEOs responsible for feeding the housing bubble are still in charge. "It is much easier for them to use a temporary solution and let the next set of government leaders tackle the problem," said Edward Mangano, county executive for Nassau County, New York. "This 'kick the can down the road' policy has to stop."[13]

There's also a huge incentive for politicians to make aggressive, unrealistic assumptions about pension investment returns. After all, the more aggressive the accounting assumptions, the smaller the unfunded pension liability appears to be. Pension funds use gimmicks like averaging actual returns over several years so that the real status of the funds doesn't look so bad. Additionally, by using high-return assumptions—remember, the average today is 8 percent—states hide or understate unfunded liabilities. Simply by assuming high, 8 percent compound rates of return on pension investments, the state can lower the amount of money it is required to contribute to the pension fund. The market does all of the hard work—at least on paper—and those cost-of-living adjustments suddenly become more affordable. States like Connecticut, Louisiana, and Massachusetts have investment-return assumptions of at least 8.25 percent, the highest in the nation. When a fund can assume its returns will be higher, its contributions, naturally, can be lower. In the case of Rhode Island, the state estimated that the contribution, or cost, for a state employee would be over 50 percent higher if the government were to move from an 8.25 percent investment-return assumption to a 6.2 percent investment-return assumption. The actual returns over the period in question turned out to be just 2.28 percent a year. And the lower the return, the higher the required contribution. It's completely absurd, yet this is not a problem unique to Rhode Island. These games are played all across the country.[14]

State and local governments have underfunded—even nonfunded—their pension funds for years now, and they can't seem to break the habit. As a result, taxpayers are now waking up to unfunded pension liabilities whose size rivals that of their municipal bond debt. When combined with the cost of health insurance promised to current and former state employees, the total obligation is almost 40 percent higher than the bonded debt. In other words, a muni investor or concerned taxpayer poring over state budget documents will end up grossly underestimating the amount of debt the state truly owes if all he's looking at is bonds. In New Jersey actual debt is at least four times greater than bonds outstanding.[15]

But again, not all states are created equal. Collectively, as of 2011, the states are on the hook for nearly $800 billion of unfunded pensions, and when combined with other debts secured by tax receipts, total future obligations exceed $2.5 trillion. Drill down into the numbers and what you find is that some states have been especially reckless, whereas others have actually been strong fiduciary stewards for their taxpayers. So let's review the good, the bad, and the ugly when it comes to pension policies and how those track records will shape the future of those states.

In 2000 seventeen states did not meet the "recommended" funding contribution of 80 percent; by 2010 that number had grown to twenty-nine states. If you entered the millennium underfunded, odds are that you are in bad shape today. However, for states that got hit hard by both high exposure to the housing downturn and the 2008 market crash, refilling pension coffers will be a huge challenge. Further tax hikes and budget cuts are political nonstarters in states like Arizona (73 percent funded, with a $10.3 billion unfunded liability), California (79 percent and $104 billion), and Connecticut (53 percent and $21 billion). Nevada began the millennium with a funded ratio of about 85 percent; today that ratio is just over 70 percent, with a $10 billion unfunded pension liability. Which states have managed pensions most responsibly, even in the face of declining tax revenues and weak investment returns? Leaders include Delaware (92 percent, $1 billion), Nebraska (83 percent, $2 billion), Oregon (86 percent, $8 billion), and Washington (92 percent, $5 billion). But the standard setter is clearly New York, which has the only fully funded pension plan in the nation.[16] In a state known for political dysfunction, New York has been surprisingly proactive when it comes to pensions. Reforms New York has enacted include raising the retirement age from fifty-five to sixty-two for state workers and from fifty-five to fifty-seven for teachers; requiring higher pension contributions for some public workers; and capping the impact of overtime on pension payouts.[17]

As if not contributing to their pensions weren't bad enough, some states have essentially doubled down on their unfunded liabilities—taking out margin loans, via issuance of pension-obligation bonds, in the hopes of turbocharging their investment returns. Pension-obligation bonds work like this: If a state doesn't have the money to contribute to its pension funds but doesn't want to cut money from other spending projects to get it, it has the option of issuing pension-obligation bonds. The idea is that the proceeds of these bond sales can plug big holes in the state's pensions, so long as the investment returns earned on the bond proceeds exceed the coupon payments to bondholders. The biggest and best example of this "logic" was in 2003, when Illinois issued $10 billion in pension obligation bonds.[18] The governor at the time, Rod Blagojevich, sold the bonds as "no-risk, no-new-debt"[19] and likened the transaction to a mortgage refinancing. In reality, it was high risk, and it was new debt. It was just a transfer of debt in the form of unfunded pension obligations to the bonded debt of the state. The arbitrage didn't work: At a staggeringly low 45 percent, Illinois's funded ratio is 9 percent lower today than it was before the issuance of the $10 billion in pension bonds, and the state's bonded debt has tripled from $8.4 billion at the end of 2002 to over $28 billion in 2011—$17 billion of which stems from pension bonds.[20] Today Illinois has a staggering $160 billion in unfunded pensions and bonded debt. It also owes an additional $44 billion in unfunded health-care and related benefits.[21] This works out to almost $13,000 per capita, the fifth highest in the country but the fourth highest as a percentage of gross domestic product. Add up all the various obligations—pension-bond debt, unfunded pension liabilities, and unfunded retiree health-care costs—and Illinois finds itself in the deepest pension hole in the country.

Illinois is one of a handful of states that owe more to their pension funds than they do on their tax-supported municipal bond debt. Ohio and New Jersey owe more than twice their tax-supported municipal debt in unfunded pension obligations. Neither has adequately contributed into its pensions for over a decade, so the hole has gotten deeper with each passing year. All three states are in desperate need of pension reform. In fact, the recent teachers' strike in Chicago seemed to reflect a go-for-broke, get-it-while-you-can negotiating approach by the Chicago Teachers Union. The union had to know that a day of reckoning was coming for its retirement plan—only 60 percent funded and saddled with $10 billion in unfunded pension and health-care liabilities. Rather than pick a fight over pensions, Chicago's 30,000 teachers went on strike early in the 2012–13 school year to demand huge pay hikes and to protest teacher evaluations and provisions dealing with jobs for laid-off teachers. The strike closed over 400 of the city's 578 schools, put about 350,000 students in limbo with no supervision and no place to go, and left parents desperate to find some type of accommodation. With the average public-school teacher salary in Chicago at $74,839—versus $56,069 nationally— striking for a 16 percent salary increase over four years seemed outrageous to many Chicago parents, particularly when general wage growth had been barely 1 percent per year.[22] But perhaps Chicago teachers felt they needed to get what they could now, knowing that they'd have to give back on pensions later.[23]

The biggest problem for state and local governments is how pension costs are crowding out other budget items. Consider the

California cities of San Diego and San Jose. In San Diego expenses for the city's retirement fund increased from $43 million in 1999 to $231 million in 2012 and now comprise the equivalent of 20 percent of the general-fund budget. However, even as the city budget grows, San Diego is actually lowering its current payroll, with the total city workforce down 14 percent since 2005.[24] In San Jose the city's pension expense increased from $73 million in 2001 to $245 million in 2012.[25] The latest payment is equal to 27 percent of the city's general-fund budget, which is the same percentage by which San Jose has downsized its workforce over the past decade. As both of these cities work through a tough economy and an even worse housing market, the retirement-benefits problem looms larger, even for traditionally prounion Democrat lawmakers. San Jose mayor Chuck Reed, a Democrat, called reforming pensions "my number one priority because it's the biggest problem we face. It's a problem that threatens our ability to remain a city and provide services to our people."[26] San Diego's Republican mayor Jerry Sanders took a similar tack: "If we continued to have hugely escalating pension costs every year," he told *Governing* magazine, "we simply could not sustain any level of service in the city of San Diego." The people agreed, and with two historic ballot measures, voters approved trimming retirement benefits for government workers in both cities so that more dollars could be allocated to productive means rather than for pensions and retiree health-care costs.[27]

Again, what this all this boils down to is the simple fact that there is not enough money to go around. All sides need to give. If compromises cannot be reached, the only alternative may be bankruptcy, and as alternatives go, bankruptcy has pitfalls for everyone involved. In government bankruptcy proceedings, coupon payments to muni investors and pension payments to former state employees have "senior" status. That is, they take priority over funding of basic social services like education, police protection, and road and bridge maintenance. In other words, municipal bondholders and pensioners have equal and first claim on tax receipts, and all other spending is subordinate to those payments. Something often forgotten is that the deal on the table is often better than the one determined by the courts. Consider Central Falls, Rhode Island. When the unions couldn't agree on appropriate concessions, the town was forced to declare bankruptcy. The ultimate pensions granted to the unions were far worse than the ones the city of Central Falls had been offering during negotiations, so much so, in fact, that other cities and towns in Rhode Island were scared enough to fall in line on one of the most sweeping pension reforms yet in this country. Rhode Island's state treasurer, Gina Raimondo, is now the go-to adviser on pension reform to politicians across the country.

Chapter 5

■

The Negative Feedback Loop from Hell

In 2006 Nevada was the envy of the nation. Today it's an economic calamity—a victim of runaway spending and borrowing during better times.

Fueled by tourism and roaring demand for real estate, Nevada's economy in the mid-2000s was truly electric. The state's gross domestic product was growing at a pace more common to up-and-coming third-world nations than parts of the United States. According to the U.S. Bureau of Economic Analysis, the Nevada economy grew an average of 9 percent a year in 2004 and 2005—three times the growth rate of the U.S. GDP. What was happening in the city of Las Vegas was especially breathtaking: Personal income in the Las Vegas metropolitan area increased 10 percent in 2005.[1] The city had morphed into a supercharged jobs magnet, with metro-area population expanding 42 percent during the 2000s—the fastest population growth in the country. "I think we're at the crossroads, whether we want to be the entertainment capital of the world or a great American city," Las Vegas mayor Oscar Goodman gushed in 2005. "Things are so wonderful in Las Vegas, and it's time to move to the next level."[2]

Fast-forward six years, and suffice it to say that things in Las Vegas are no longer so wonderful. Mayor Goodman and other government leaders never appreciated just how much of their windfall derived from a housing bubble that was sure to end badly. Home prices in the state had doubled between 2001 and 2006, funneling huge sums of new tax dollars into state and local coffers. State tax revenue had doubled over that period as well, and the legislature seemed intent on spending every last dime.

Then came the real-estate crash. Las Vegas home prices fell 60 percent. Statewide, the decline was 56 percent, and now 57 percent of Nevada mortgages have negative equity—that is, homeowners owe more on their homes than the properties are worth. By 2011 Nevada's onetime state budget surplus had evaporated into the widest budget deficit in the country—$1.2 billion, equivalent to 54 percent of the total state budget. Schoolchildren and college kids bore the brunt of the inevitable budget cuts. In-state tuition at the University of Nevada at Las Vegas soared from $6,600 to $10,700 a year, and the legislature cut K-12 school funding by $270 per student.[3]

The timing could not have been much worse for local school systems like Las Vegas's Clark County School District, which experienced a 33 percent decline in property-tax collections between 2008 and 2012. Pushed to the fiscal brink and its teachers unwilling to accept cuts to pay or benefits, the school district announced in May 2012 that it had to lay off 1,015 teachers and reading specialists in order to close a $64 million budget shortfall.[4] Average class size in the school district soared from thirty to thirty-five pupils for grades four and five and from thirty-two to thirty-nine for grades six through twelve. One kindergarten teacher was told to expect thirty-seven students in her class for the 2012–13 school year. "With 37 kids, how are we supposed to teach anything?" Griffith Elementary School teacher Christie Rodriguez complained to the *Las Vegas Sun*. Rodriguez's own daughter was set to begin school the following year. "It's terrifying," she said, "to think [my daughter] will be in a class with that many kids."[5] So terrifying, in fact, that many Clark County parents have been voting with their feet. Once the fastest-growing school district in the country, Clark County has seen its enrollment drop for four consecutive years.[6]

This is not an isolated story. In Nevada and all across the United States, cities and states that were once flush with cash are running out of money needed to pay for libraries, safe streets, clean drinking water, and, yes, schools. Even worse, the debts they've rung up in order to close budget gaps are threatening governments' ability to deliver these basic services not just today but also in the future. Meanwhile, new economic epicenters are emerging in some of the unlikeliest places. Booms in American agriculture and energy production have turned states like Iowa and North Dakota into hot job markets while also ushering in a new era of U.S. manufacturing. In these areas, governments are struggling to keep up with the demand for housing and for infrastructure like roads, bridges, and schools. The good news is that these governments have the money to pay for all this, and they are spending and investing like crazy. North Dakota, a state with virtually no debt and some of the fastest-growing oil fields in the world, is working hard to keep pace with all the new population growth and industrial development: Roads are being graded, temporary housing is being erected, and schools are being built. From 2011 to 2012 North Dakota's spending per pupil shot up over 8 percent to $12,225, versus $8,363 in Nevada, according to the National Kids Count Program.[7]

The reversal of fortune started off quietly, but each year the cutbacks in public services take more of a toll on communities that not so long ago were swimming in cash. Things so many used to take for granted—new textbooks for classrooms, low student-teacher ratios, open libraries, adequately staffed police stations and fire houses, regular trash collection—have been meaningfully reduced or done away with entirely. Since 2008 nearly seven hundred thousand state and local government jobs have been eliminated.

The crisis would be more manageable if the only problem were declining tax revenues. Cutbacks in state spending have exacerbated the local tax-revenue decline. During the 2012 and 2013 fiscal years alone, states cut payouts to local governments by a total of $1 billion.[8] At the same time, municipalities are being hammered by the rising costs associated with mountains of debt and public-employee pension obligations accumulated when times were more flush. It's certainly possible that elected officials in North Dakota would have wildly overspent in the mid-2000s if the money had been available. But regardless of whether the fiscal prudence of central corridor states was the result of serendipity or good planning, the reality is that these states don't have the financial burdens now crushing the housing-boom states. They are free to spend money on actual improvements and services, rather than on old debt and excessive retirement benefits. A tale of two Americas is emerging: one weighed down by debt and facing de minimis economic growth and another brimming with opportunity and nimble to invest in the future.

Over just the past decade, state spending has spiked 67 percent while tax receipts have increased a mere 30 percent. States racked up a stunning $2 trillion in additional debt, all while leaning more and more on handouts from the federal government. But not all states. Some took on little debt, while others took on staggering amounts.[9]

Total Liabilities / GSP, FY2011

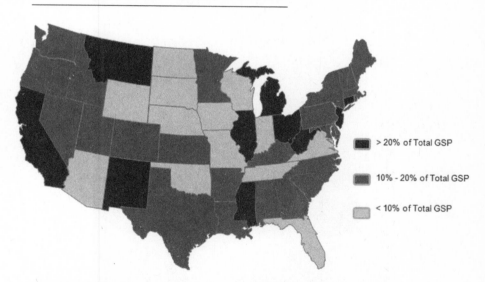

Note: Total liabilities include GO debt, unfunded pension liabilities, and unfunded OPEB liabilities.

SOURCES: STATE CAFRS, COMPTROLLERS, PEW CENTER, MOODY'S, AND MWAG

Despite all the public focus on the fiscal cliff and the need to reduce the federal debt, there has been relatively little attention paid to reducing the debt incurred by the states and backed by their taxing authority. From 2009 to 2011 that debt grew by over $400 billion, or by over one-fifth. And that still wasn't enough for spending-addicted states. Rather than dealing with the root cause of this mess—too much spending on too many of the wrong things—states have papered over their budget gaps by taking more from the feds, by borrowing more from the bond market, and by shirking their responsibility to fully fund the pensions of government employees. The federal government's outlays to states have risen more than 130 percent. They

% Change in State Expenditures from 2000 to 2010

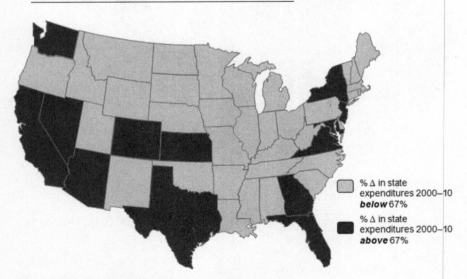

% Δ in state expenditures 2000–10 *below* 67%

% Δ in state expenditures 2000–10 *above* 67%

SOURCES: BEA, U.S. CENSUS, AND MWAG

now stand at their highest levels ever and are expected to reach over $700 billion by 2016.[10] State politicians should have treated the post-2008 increase in federal aid as a bridge loan—one designed to help states avoid drastic cutbacks while they worked to close their budget gaps. Instead, they just kept on spending.

The mismanagement of states' finances was until recently a well-kept, dirty little secret, as politicians and budget makers disclosed precious little about their actual debt loads. Rising tax receipts from a booming housing environment and a prolonged low-interest-rate environment, which motivated states to borrow more and investors to demand more municipal bonds, led to a "there are no calories in chocolate cake" style delusion for many cities and states. In San Bernardino, California, which filed for bankruptcy protection in 2012, the city attorney has alleged that the mayor and the city council didn't know how deep a fiscal hole the city was in until it was too late. "We haven't had good, solid information over the last 16 years," one city councilman told the local paper. "Why? That's up for determination. I don't believe they're falsified. I believe there's maybe some incompetency or ineptness or trying to stretch the truth, trying to make things look better."[11]

Until 2009 when regulators started requiring fuller disclosure, investors and taxpayers had no way of knowing that 75 percent of state and local debt was off the balance sheet, in the forms of unfunded pension and health-care benefits. Because this information was not widely available, states and cities maintained easy access to the debt markets without raising questions about the added cost of new borrowings. Most "experts" looking at municipal affairs have focused on debt-service levels and on some caps on that debt. They have stated unequivocally that there's nothing to worry about. They're quick to point out that states have never defaulted and that bond defaults by cities and other muni bond issuers have been almost as rare. The reality is that just because something has not happened in the past does not mean it won't happen in the future. That was one of the more painful lessons from the housing bust. Far too many lenders, home buyers, and real-estate investors refused to believe home prices could decline significantly because there had not been a decline in the average U.S. home price since the Great Depression.

The first cracks in the there's-nothing-to-worry-about facade are now appearing. In 2012 the California cities of San Bernardino, Stockton, and Mammoth Lakes all filed for bankruptcy protection, and many cities throughout Michigan have been taken over by state-appointed emergency managers. The credit-rating agencies have begun telling bond investors to expect more defaults. In September 2012 Fitch Ratings cautioned investors that it "anticipates an increase in defaults and bankruptcies."[12] Moody's Investors Service has already warned that the California bankruptcy filings "could signify not only a lack of ability, but a lack of willingness to pay debt service at the expense of other financial obligations."[13] There surely would have been even more defaults by now had interest rates not dropped to historic lows. The average yield on the Bond Buyer Go 20-Bond Municipal Bond Index (WSLB20) has plummeted from 6 percent in October 2008 to 3.7 percent in January 2013, and the near halving of interest rates has allowed states and municipalities teetering on the brink of fiscal crisis to borrow more money without paying more in finance costs.[14]

Piling on debt at a low interest rate may allow a state to remain below a "debt cap" that limits monthly or yearly debt payments. But it is a short-term fix. Any spike in interest rates—obviously rates cannot stay low forever—would push some state and local budgets over the brink. When borrowing costs do finally rise, the pricey pensions and other generous benefits promised to state and local government workers will go from a theoretical worry for taxpayers to a painfully real one. If those obligations are already starting to crowd out money needed for basic public services in places like Las Vegas, just imagine what happens when more baby boomer–age civil servants start retiring en masse. Taxpayers will learn that by law debt and pension payments actually take priority over all other state spending, including that for education and public safety. For some municipalities, bankruptcy might actually be the only way out.

There's a reason politicians put off making hard decisions. After all, why alienate key constituencies in order to solve a problem that might not come to a head until after they've left office? But with this budget crisis, ignoring and procrastinating may not work. The mayor who turns a blind eye risks his city sliding into Detroit-like despair and disrepair. The governor who does not act risks letting his state become America's Greece—subjecting her citizens to all the privations associated with austerity budgeting. He risks sinking his state or city into an economic feedback loop from hell—one in which budget deficits beget tax hikes and spending cuts, which drive away jobs, further eroding the tax base and deepening the budget crisis that the hikes and cuts were intended to fix. Look at what's happened in the actual Greece. The *bottom* income-tax rate there has increased from 5 percent in 2000 to 18 percent in 2010.[15] Greece's unemployment now exceeds 24 percent, and the GDP has declined 6 percent per year for two consecutive years.[16] Alexandros Adamidis, a business-relocation expert in Bulgaria, recently told a Greek newspaper that he receives "10 phone calls a day" from Greek businesses seeking to relocate.[17] The *Financial Post* reported that between April 2011 and April 2012, some seven thousand Greeks left Greece for Germany in search of jobs and lower taxes.[18] This is the fate elected officials in housing-bust states are tempting if they fail to fix their finances.

American consumers love their credit cards—sometimes too much. Politicians like to buy on credit too. But while consumers know there's a downside to revolving credit-card debt, politicians actually have little incentive to do anything but revolve because they'll be gone before the bigger bill comes due. Plus the new spending facilitated by increased borrowing is good politics. While some of the increased state spending has gone to fund vital projects and services, a disproportionate amount has gone to state employees—hiring more people (1.4 million) and, more often, increasing existing employees' pay and benefits. Given the tremendous escalation in pay, pension, and other benefits over the past decade, it is hard to imagine that any mayor, school-board member, or city councilman actually believed these deals would be affordable in the future. But because these increases are contractual, they are difficult to abrogate or trim. The actual amount of "discretionary spending" in most budgets is quite low. The Las Vegas school system tried to close its budget gap by suspending contractually negotiated teacher pay raises, a solution vehemently opposed by the teachers' union; an arbitrator wound up ruling in favor of the union, forcing districtwide layoffs. Indeed, what ends up being the most discretionary are the expenditures that have the most tangible impact on everyday life—social services, road repairs, new textbooks for classrooms, additional teachers to reduce class sizes, school buses, police and fire-safety vehicles, parks, libraries, and all the other services individuals and families depend upon. Over the past five years, $290 billion has been cut from such core services. But the real pain will be felt over the years to come, as "emergency" money that was meant to cushion the blow eventually runs out. In the past four years, the money saved through spending cuts at the state level accounted for less than half of the dollars used to close budget gaps. Until now, states have been able to bridge budget gaps by tapping rainy-day funds, accessing federal stimulus money, increasing taxes, or borrowing more money via the bond market. But these levers have all already been pulled.

We have reached a breaking point for some states. There is no more money. There are no more stimulus dollars. There are no more rainy-day funds to raid. The emergency options have all been tapped. From 2008 to 2012 states squeezed just under $600 billion from one-time measures to close budget gaps.[19] Spending on schools, public safety, and other vital services still got slashed. What will be next? And how bad will things get?

Cumulative Measures Used to Close Budget Gaps (FY08–12)

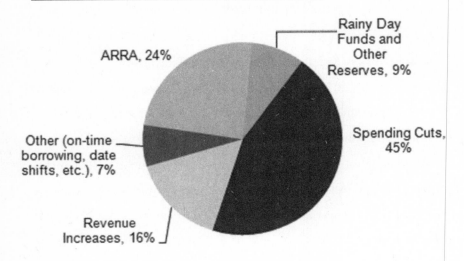

ARRA, 24%

Rainy Day Funds and Other Reserves, 9%

Spending Cuts, 45%

Other (on-time borrowing, date shifts, etc.), 7%

Revenue Increases, 16%

SOURCES: BLS AND MWAG

Politically it is far easier to increase than decrease spending, and elected officials have gone to great lengths to avoid the politically painful steps required to rein in spending. More often than not, rather than align expenses with current tax receipts, elected officials have just borrowed more—taking from the till of future tax dollars—to pay for current government spending on projects and goodies. Because tax receipts have little bearing on state spending, spending has outpaced tax receipts by a factor of two since 2000. Now the inevitable spending cuts have finally arrived, and the most vital government services are the ones bearing the brunt.

Education

For most states, the biggest budget expenditure is education, both K-12 education and higher education. K-12 accounts for 20 percent of spending, whereas higher education accounts for 10 percent, on average.[20] The next-largest state expense is Medicaid, which is growing two or three times faster than most state budgets. Clearly the explosion in Medicaid expenses has left less of the budget available for education and infrastructure projects. While a pothole or two may not be a game-changing risk in the near term, cuts to education are serious near-, medium-, and long-term threats to the quality of life within a state.

According to the Center on Budget and Policy Priorities, thirty-seven states reduced per-student funding to their school districts in 2011, and seventeen states cut per-student education funding to a level below where it was prerecession. Higher education has been hit especially hard: Funding for public colleges and universities has been reduced by an average of 11 percent since 2010, to the lowest levels since the 1980s, according to the State Higher Education Executive Officers Association. Higher education is discretionary, and discretionary items are always most vulnerable. Consider that from fiscal year 2011 to fiscal year 2012, while state general-fund spending on Medicaid increased by $16 billion, general funds cut more than $5 billion from higher education and $2.5 billion from K-12 education. Remember, most K-12 spending comes from municipal monies, and cuts to K-12 education are far more damaging to the quality of teaching, since funding cuts cannot be offset with tuition hikes, as has been the case with public colleges and universities.[21]

Other than moving, families have few ways to protect their children from the corrosive impact of shrinking school budgets. Sure, private schools are an option for those who can afford them, as are charter schools for families fortunate enough to get a slot. In 2011 Tanya Moton pulled her daughter out of a public school in order to enroll her in a nearby charter school. "The classes were too big, the kids were unruly and didn't pay attention to teachers," she told the *New York Times* of the former school.[22] But Tanya Moton is one of the lucky ones. Nationally, only 13 percent of public-school students attend charter schools.[23] Moreover, charter schools are not immune to budget cuts. In 2012 the Philadelphia school district cut its payout to city charter schools by $700 per pupil, a 7 percent reduction in funding. "Charter schools are going to have to . . . be more efficient and find ways to serve [students] in a leaner and more creative way," said Lawrence Jones, president of the Pennsylvania Coalition of Public Charter Schools.[24]

States walloped by the real-estate bust, such as California, have had to make the deepest cuts. From 2007 to 2011 California's GDP contracted by over $28 billion. In other words, after a five-year period in which the state issued $397 billion of debt and increased the size of its unfunded pension liability by almost $80 billion, its economy still wound up worse off.[25] California used to be the gold standard for public education. From universities to grade schools, its education standards were the top in the nation. Since 2008, however, California has cut more than $6 billion from education spending.[26] There's less money for textbooks, teachers, and arts and sports programs. With fewer teachers, "virtual classrooms" are sprouting up in which a live teacher is telecast into a classroom but without any actual physical classroom presence. In 1990 California had a 1.3 percent lead over the United States as a whole in the share of its population that had graduated from high school. By 2008 California's population had 6 percent fewer high-school graduates than the national average. In many school systems it's the arts and music programs that are cut first. Art teachers who survive layoffs are often reduced to going classroom to classroom offering "art on a cart" like hot-dog vendors. In 2008 the Los Angeles Unified School District had to suspend one of its key arts programs because of a spending freeze. In 2011 San Diego Unified School District's visual- and performing-arts program faced a $2.8 million cut—from a $3 million budget. This was part of an effort to plug a $120 million hole in the school district's $1.2 billion budget. That $2.8 million in cuts amounted to just 0.23 percent of the budget.[27] In wealthier communities, raffles, bake sales, and other fundraisers sometimes help save arts and music programs on the verge of being axed, preserving parents' dreams of watching a son or daughter play violin in a school orchestra. In poorer communities such dreams die without proper funding.

Cuts are also coming out of basic programs such as busing. Last year Illinois cut $89 million from its school-transportation budget. In Lake Elsinore, California, school-bus service was scrapped entirely, forcing students to find their own way to school. "There are enough crosses on the side of the road. We don't need more," Salvador Sepulveda beseeched the Lake Elsinore school board before it voted to end bus service. Sepulveda believed it was simply too dangerous for his grandson—a first grader—to walk to school. Yes, some kids can get a ride to school with parents, but for some of those parents the added cost of gas is a burden. Others risk being late for work.[28]

After doing what they could to raise revenues through higher property taxes, school systems have had to cut and cut deeply in order to balance their budgets. K-12 public education is free, of course, so raising tuition rates was never an option. But higher education is a different story. State universities have the ability to collect—and raise—tuition. Recall the protests in Oakland and Davis, a town just outside Sacramento, during the spring of 2010. Hundreds of college students tried to block interstate highways in protest of spending cuts for education.[29] They knew these cuts were simply a prelude to tuition hikes in 2011. Not surprisingly, the states hit hardest by the housing bust and large budget deficits have seen the sharpest spikes in the cost of tuition for four-year colleges. Arizona, California, and Nevada saw tuition costs rise by 94 percent, 80 percent, and 76 percent respectively between the 2004–5 and 2011–12 school years. Nationally, only Maryland and Ohio saw state tuition actually decline over the same time periods.[30]

Which states have the highest tuitions? Three of the five—Illinois, Michigan, and New Jersey—are states with faltering economies and massive state budget shortfalls. Cuts to higher education have been so deep in these states that their public colleges and universities have been forced to charge tuitions 50 percent above the national average. In Illinois, Michigan, and New Jersey, average tuitions for four-year public colleges were $10,975, $10,170, and $11,667 respectively, according to the College Board, versus the national average of $7,506.[31] Since 2007 California has cut $2 billion from higher-education spending. These cuts caused an 80 percent spike in tuition costs, and now only 18 percent of California high-school graduates are enrolled in state colleges or universities, versus 22 percent prior to 2007. And it's not just the four-year colleges that are affected: In-state enrollment in community colleges has shrunk from 2.9 to 2.4 million.[32] In 1990 California's population had 15 percent more college graduates than the national average. Twenty years later, that big advantage has been halved to just 7 percent.[33]

In case you're wondering, Wyoming boasts the lowest public-university tuition, at $3,917, even as the state's overall per-capita spending on higher education is third highest in the country.[34] Perhaps not coincidentally, Wyoming now boasts the fifth-highest per-capita income in the country, making it the only rural state among the top five. Of course, massive tuition hikes serve to exacerbate the student-loan crisis, a $1 trillion problem sure to end badly if the job market for twentysomethings doesn't improve. According to the

Economic Policy Institute, 9.4 percent of college graduates ages twenty-one to twenty-four were unemployed in 2011 and another 19.1 percent were underemployed—and thus unlikely to be earning enough to repay their student loans.[35]

It's not just college students getting the shaft. State education dollars also go toward job-training and retraining programs, and those monies are getting cut too. According to the *Wall Street Journal*, funding for local job-training centers in California is 2 percent lower than it was in 2007, even though the number of unemployed Californians has more than doubled to nearly two million. No wonder California is saddled with one of the highest rates of long-term structural unemployment in the country.[36]

Libraries

Libraries have also been budget-cut casualties. Nationally, the American Library Association reports that 60 percent of libraries had flat or decreased budgets last year. Forty percent of all libraries have had three consecutive years of revenue shortfalls. For library patrons, the timing of the cuts couldn't be much worse. Library usage is countercyclical. When times are good, people buy books and magazines. When times are tough, they go the library. So even as demand for libraries has surged, libraries have had to cut hours, trim staff, and eliminate or significantly reduce programs in order to stay open at all.

The free, taxpayer-supported, public library is as uniquely

American as hot dogs and hip-hop. The first free public library in the world was built in Peterborough, New Hampshire, in 1833. Over the decades, public libraries' role in American life has expanded and evolved. Libraries have always been a safe and quiet place to study—an epicenter of autonomous learning. Kids grew up with their library cards as their only identification—good for five books at a time. Nowadays libraries' role in the economy and in our lives is different. Some might say bigger. With computers and Internet access, libraries are now used by job hunters to help them connect with potential employers. An American Library Association survey reveals that "more than 70% of libraries report that staff helped users complete online job applications. But the majority of libraries do not have enough staff to assist job-seekers with their vital efforts to get back into the workplace." Worse, the librarians who still have jobs may lack the proper training to help job seekers navigate the technology. So for now, many libraries have to settle for being just another Wi-Fi hot spot.[37]

In late 2011 Detroit closed four out of its remaining twenty-three library branches. This came after the city had already fired eighty-two library staff earlier in the year.[38] But it's not just poor cities gutting their library systems. Troy, Michigan, which in 2008 *Money* magazine voted the twenty-second-best place to live in the United States, is a relatively affluent city with a median household income from 2006 to 2010 of over $87,000. J.D. Power and Associates and DuPont Automotive have offices there. But due to lack of funding, even Troy's library was closed down, leaving behind a sobering Web site FAQ section for confused residents. Residents wondering where to gain access to books or other library materials were directed to other local libraries' help desks in order to see whether their Troy library cards would be accepted.

Libraries are vulnerable because bean counters don't see the benefits of funding them. "We have invested in full-time librarians for the last three or four years and we haven't seen the kind of payoff we'd like," Washington, D.C., school chancellor Kaya Henderson announced at a 2012 meeting. But since when have librarians been expected to provide a return on investment? Isn't education one of the basic principles in modern America? In D.C., upward of fifty school-librarian positions may be eliminated, even though more than thirty schools are already without site-based librarians. It is tough enough getting students to come to school and pay attention. But how can they continue learning if there is no one in the libraries to guide them? Basic services like school libraries affect not only learning but also students' overall sense of well-being.[39]

Just ask youngster Karla Rivera. "I am 13 years old and I love reading. . . . Without the library, I would DIE," Rivera wrote on the city of New Haven, Connecticut's Web site. It was 2011, and Connecticut's second-largest city was grappling with a $5.5 million budget deficit and debating whether costs should be cut by laying off librarians and reducing library hours. "If I didn't have the library, I probably would not have survived high school," declared another local teen, Shawnese Turner, insisting that it took her four hours to do her homework at home versus just two hours "in a nice quiet place like the library."[40] Few things are more politically unpopular than closing libraries, but New Haven wound up doing it anyway, axing twelve librarians and cutting seventy-five hours from the weekly hours of the city's half dozen libraries—despite the fact that library usage was up nearly 50 percent since 2003. New Haven's mayor, John DeStefano, Jr., insisted he had no choice. Connecticut's real-estate market has been among the hardest hit in the country, and property-tax revenues just weren't keeping up with New Haven's biggest expenses—the cost of public-employee health-insurance and pension plans. Those outlays had soared from $44 million a year to $105 million and now consumed 22 percent of the city budget, up from 12 percent ten years earlier. "They are," DeStefano said of health care and pensions, "the Pac-Man of our city budget, consuming everything in sight."[41]

Parks and Trash Collection

It's one thing to visit a county park one day and find trash near swings or a ball field. But it's quite another to return to that same park week after week and realize that the litter isn't being cleaned up. Not only is this a major eyesore for the community, but it's a red flag for anyone considering purchasing a home there. It effectively says, "We don't care about cleanliness in our community"—even if that is not the full truth. Cities and neighborhoods dealing with mounting budgetary issues have been forced to either privatize waste-collection services (which can eliminate jobs for some residents) or cut services and leave trash disposal up to homeowners. For example, in Roanoke, Virginia, officials needed to cut around $1.4 million from the sanitation department. Of that, $160,000 was saved by removing trash bins from condos and townhomes and by "eliminating free residential garbage disposal at the Roanoke Valley Resource Authority Transfer Station," according to the *Roanoke Times*.[42] Until then, residents had been allowed to drop off their trash a mere twenty times per year at the local transfer station. But really think about that scenario. If you live in a condo or townhome, your trash bins may be removed, meaning you (or your complex) will have to find a way to a regulated trash dump. This increases costs for everyone—gas, service, and equipment. In the past, waste management seemed like a given, one of the benefits of owning your own place. There was a certain pride in rolling your garbage can out to the curb of a home you had worked hard to build and maintain. Who wants to buy a house someplace that makes you pay to take out the trash? Residents will find a way to get by, but they should not have to. Trash removal ought to be a bare-minimum benefit of paying property taxes.

After closing the ten transfer stations where residents hauled their own trash, Hidalgo County in Texas decided to privatize trash collection, a move projected to save the county roughly $6 million annually.[43] There are cost-effective ways like this around poor budgeting by cities and counties. But that raises a question: Where do tax dollars go? After all, it's not as if trash collection were being cut in order to prevent cuts to ostensibly more important services like police and fire departments. Those are being cut too.

Public Safety

With fewer police and firefighters on the streets, response times have gotten longer. In Red Feather Lakes and Upper Poudre, Colorado, residents were warned that they would have to wait between forty and sixty minutes for emergency response, instead of the usual twenty minutes. That's scary given the increased number of hardened criminals who may soon be roaming the streets of budget-strained states. In May 2011 the U.S. Supreme Court ordered the state of California to release thirty thousand prisoners to reduce overcrowding in its prisons. While the issue of overcrowded prisons has been around for years, the solutions once discussed centered on privatizing prisons or granting more lenient sentences to nonviolent offenders—not allowing a mass exodus of convicted felons. In California there's no place to put thirty thousand inmates. "It can be like the Wild West out there if we're not careful," one worried bike-shop owner in Bakersfield told the *Wall Street Journal.* Some prisoners could be relocated from state prisons to municipal jails, but there isn't room for all of them. "I call it 'justice by geography,' depending upon where you get arrested," said UC Berkeley criminal-justice expert Barry Krisberg.[44] California is not alone. Scrambling to find ways to keep prisons open in the face of shrinking budgets, Angola, Louisiana, has resorted to substituting watchdogs for prison guards. After the prison's annual budget was cut back from $135 million five years ago to $115 million today, the warden brought in "wolf dogs" to replace over one hundred prison guards it had to lay off. "You might run," one inmate declared, "but they're going to catch you." According to a *Wall Street Journal* story, the money spent on one prison guard's salary could cover the cost of the full medical care, supplies, and food for thirty of these "wolf dogs." As of August 2012, there have been few protests of the substitution.[45]

In Stockton, California, the murder rate is rising, as the police department has had to lay off several dozen police officers. Others in the department have resigned themselves to asking for their pink slips or accepting lower salaries. Stockton's fire department is in a similar predicament.[46] Shrinking police and fire departments and slower emergency-response times are not what residents sign up for when they scribble their signatures on mortgage documents. This is not the American dream pitched to them by Realtors, politicians, and history books. The dream has been replaced by fears about whether or not their homes will sell or their streets will be safe. Unfortunately, this nightmare is an unavoidable reality for some cities and states struggling to balance budgets. Imagine you live in one of those Colorado communities where police response times have increased from twenty to sixty minutes. Imagine there's an armed robbery or violent assault in progress—with perpetrators seemingly free to commit any crime with the knowledge that they'll be long gone before police ever show up.

In Arizona, a state whose economy is still reeling from the real-estate crash, surviving municipal budget cuts has become a way of life in many communities. Surprise, Arizona, for instance, has been forced to eliminate support roles at its police and fire departments in order to cut costs. While police officers' and firefighters' jobs were saved, their responsibilities have been extended, putting a strain on core police and fire services and the departments' overtime budgets. Other cuts included $50,000 in reductions on spending for training and supplies. In other words, some of these policemen or firefighters don't even have the proper training or equipment to protect their city—all to save $350,000. What is the cost of a lost life or a burglarized home?[47]

With fewer police officers and firefighters, crime rates will inevitably go up, as is already happening in places like San Bernardino, California, and Orlando, Florida. There is no Bruce Wayne or Peter Parker to keep the city's streets safe. Communities will have to get used to lower-quality policing—lower-quality everything, for that matter. "We're going to have to learn to fend for ourselves," Nick Gonzalez, president of a San Bernardino neighborhood group, lamented after his city declared bankruptcy and made such deep cuts to police that property crimes might now go uninvestigated.[48] Clearly these aren't the neighborhoods of yesteryear with tree-lined sidewalks and mail carriers we knew by name extending their greetings to our mothers once we reached home. Rather, the new standard encourages neighborhood watch and vigilante justice, libraries closed on Sundays (and sometimes Mondays too), and shorter hours in the municipal pool—all of which erode quality of life and make the decision to pick up stakes that much easier.

California is going to have a hard time digging out of its fiscal nightmare. Just as excessive leverage gave investment banks like Bear Stearns no margin of error during the financial crisis, there's little budgetary wiggle room for states that carry outsized debt loads. Indeed, it's sadly ironic that a state whose latest boom was so tied to real estate has a law, Proposition 13, that prohibits municipalities from raising property taxes meaningfully enough to keep towns and cities properly funded. California allows a police chief to retire with a pension of over $200,000 after less than a year on the job but doesn't have enough money to buy new books for classrooms or to keep violent felons in jail. No wonder the state is facing an exodus of employers and employees alike.

Things are very different in Indiana, especially when it comes to education. Since 2000 Indiana has increased state spending on K-12 education from $3.9 billion to $7.6 billion and spending on higher education from $1.3 billion to $1.8 billion. Since 1990 the percentage of Indiana's population holding a college degree has increased by almost 50 percent. It still remains too far below the national average, but the metrics are heading in the right direction and the gap is narrowing. The K-12 story is even stronger: Indiana's high-school graduation rate is not only above national average but is also improving faster than the national average.[49] Such things matter. They matter to businesses seeking to relocate or expand. They matter to investors deciding where to put their money. And they matter to families considering where to buy a house. With the housing-bust states showing few signs of pulling out of their economic and budgetary tailspins, these decisions have never been more clear cut.

Chapter 6

■

The New American Poverty

As of this writing, there are more Americans falling into poverty, and they are staying in poverty for longer than at any time in recorded history. The most dangerous deficit in the United States is not the federal deficit but the jobs one. It is truly the Achilles' heel of the U.S. economic recovery. Not only do unemployed people fail to contribute to the carrying costs of public services by paying taxes, but they also demand more of those services. When someone loses their job, they need Medicaid because they no longer are covered by private-plan employer coverage. They collect unemployment insurance. Some need job training and food stamps. Poverty erodes not only the morale of community but also the communities themselves.

Consider Mississippi, a state emblematic of the struggle to reduce poverty in the United States. The days of King Cotton are long, long gone. Today Mississippi is better known for shameful poverty or as the home of Forrest Gump. There was no housing boom in Mississippi, even though proportionally more people owned their own homes than in any state in the United States, save West Virginia. Mississippi residents simply didn't have any money to speculate on real estate. In fact, there hasn't been much money to go around for any big investments. Job growth remains near nonexistent, per-capita income is the lowest in the country, there is not one *Fortune* 500 company headquartered in the entire state, and Mississippi has barely had any population growth over the past ten years.[1] Folks aren't moving to Mississippi for a better way of life. Mississippi has become a welfare state, reliant upon federal aid to support its own people and infrastructure.

With more impoverished and unemployed, there are fewer workers contributing to the tax receipts of the state but more people needing state assistance. With such a large imbalance between those who need services and those who pay for them, the state has sunk deeper into debt, and municipalities have become more dependent on handouts from the state and federal governments. Income and property taxes, designed to underwrite education, infrastructure, and critical social services, don't come close to covering the true costs. While the state has collected an average of $2,300 per capita in tax receipts, per-capita spending is more than twice that at $5,900 per capita. Some of that differential is borrowed money that the state must ultimately pay back. Mississippi has amassed over $17 billion in tax-supported liabilities, which is the equivalent of $6,600 per capita. That's the twelfth highest in the nation—in a state for which average per-capita income was just barely over $31,000 in 2010. Another way to look at it: In 2010 Mississippi's tax-supported liabilities as a percentage of GDP were on par with California and Nevada, two states that until recently had much faster-growing economies.[2] Mississippi has been so bad off for so long that it's hard to even imagine a time when Mississippi's cotton truly was king. It's even harder to imagine how the poor residents of Mississippi can pay off all that debt without a dramatically improved job market.[3]

Sadly, Mississippi's poverty and dependence on federal aid are becoming less unique. Joining the likes of Mississippi, Arkansas, and Louisiana with 15 percent or higher poverty rates are a cadre of *nouveau pauvre* states that not so long ago had about as much in common with Mississippi as a quarterback does with an astronaut. As recently as 2000, Michigan's poverty rate was two percentage points below the national average. Ten years later, the state's poverty rate was nearly two percentage points above average, and federal aid accounted for over 30 percent of Michigan's budget—not even including the auto bailout. Since 2000 Michigan's population has actually shrunk, making it one of only two states in the country to experience net negative migration. From 2000 to 2010 poverty in Michigan jumped by over two-thirds to nearly 16 percent. Other states fared worse. Nevada's poverty rate jumped by almost 90 percent from 2000 to 2010, well over two and a half times the national average. Florida, Nevada, and Ohio all went from poverty levels under 12 percent in 2000 to over 15 percent by 2010. One in five Americans lives in or on the edge of poverty (generally defined as annual income of $23,000 or less for a family of four). By 2020 that number is likely to be closer to one in four.[4]

The reality is that when businesses leave a state, so too do jobs, and there is no single factor more highly correlated with poverty than unemployment. Typically, four years after a recession an economic recovery would already be under way, followed by a meaningful drop in unemployment and poverty. Not this time. The so-called jobless recovery is costing more and more by the day. As of this writing, the poverty rate is 15 percent, up from 11 percent in 2000. In 2010, 24 percent of all federal spending, or $1.2 trillion, was spent on welfare assistance, up from 10 percent in 1980 and 18 percent in 2000.[5] That last number is projected to jump to $1.6 trillion by 2016.[6] States couldn't afford to help all those falling below the poverty line were it not for federal assistance. Federal aid to states is at its highest level ever at over $600 billion, and it's projected to be 17 percent higher, at over $700 billion, by 2016. Put another way, back in 1960 federal fund transfers to states were just 9 percent of total state monies; today they're roughly 25 percent. The percentage of state monies derived from the federal government has bounced from 9 percent to 22 percent in the 1970s, down to the midteens in the 1980s, then back to the high teens in the 1990s, and has consistently been over 20 percent since 2000. The important question is "What has really improved since states began taking more federal aid?"[7]

The two primary segments of federal aid to states are Medicaid and food stamps. Today there are more Americans—forty-three million, or one in seven—living off food stamps than at any point in recorded American history. The federal government allots monies to the states for welfare, and it is the states' responsibility to administer the programs. Some states are more generous than others. California spent over $10 billion in fiscal year 2010 on public assistance—the most it had ever spent on such aid—but in fiscal year 2012 public assistance in California is estimated to have declined, even though the number of those seeking aid actually increased.[8] In 2000 over 7 percent of California's budget was spent on public assistance, but by fiscal year 2010 that percentage was down to 4.9 percent, even though the number of unemployed in the state increased by nearly two million during that time.[9] Michigan is following the same track as California, though states such as Florida and Texas are actually spending more each year on public assistance. Although federal outlays are intended to be doled out according to consistent standards, what's happened lately is that the states whose residents need help most are spending less and less. The problem isn't a lack of compassion but a lack of resources at a time of massive budget deficits.[10]

The cost of caring for the poor has been a burden largely assumed by the federal government, but as these expenses grow larger and larger, how long will this be sustainable? In 2010 total federal payments to individuals totaled $2.1 trillion, and that is expected to rise 29 percent to $2.7 trillion by 2016. Although the federal government pays for 98 percent of all welfare programs, the costs of administering welfare programs are split with the states. A considerable portion of the money distributed has an expiration date, leaving the state to make up any shortfalls. Some of the money distributed even comes in the form of loans, such as extended unemployment benefits. In today's tax-challenged environment, the states are having trouble filling the void or even paying for the increased administrative costs. States with high unemployment, high debt levels, and little money for the job training required to pare welfare rolls are hardly in a position to kick in extra money. The faster the federal government has increased its assistance to the states with "special" assistance, the greater the barriers the federal government puts on the states financially in order to maintain that assistance to their residents. Not only has all this spending done little to get people get back on their feet—with jobs and out of poverty—but it has created a political dependency on aid that is about to get pulled right out from under those most in need. Six programs that began in 2008—and were designed as short-term fixes to help Americans through the cruel recession caused by the housing bust—will expire by November 2013. Five already have. When pundits talk about the "fiscal cliff," they're usually referring to the budget mayhem that would have occurred at the end of 2012—automatic tax hikes and spending cuts affecting everything from defense to Medicare—had Congress and the president not reached a budget deal. But there's a massive fiscal cliff on the state level too, and the states most dependent upon special federal assistance are the ones most vulnerable. Between 2009 and 2011, 37 percent of state budget gaps were closed with ARRA money.[11] Michigan, for example, simply delayed the pain of making necessary changes in its spending, and consequently, when ARRA monies started running out, the state and its municipalities struggled to pay their bills. Cities like Detroit, Flint, Pontiac, and Ecorse and school districts like that of Highland Park have come dangerously close to failure. Highland Park was eventually taken over by a state-appointed emergency manager—who promptly fired all the teachers and outsourced man-

agement of the school system to Leona Group, a for-profit education company. Leona is now charging the state $7,100 per pupil versus
the $16,500 the school district had been paying to educate each stu-
dent.[12]

In 2000 eight states had a poverty rate higher than 15 percent:
Alabama, Arkansas, Kentucky, Louisiana, Mississippi, New Mexico,
Texas, and West Virginia. However, by 2010 twenty-two states (plus
Washington, D.C.) had poverty rates over 15 percent. Four of those
"new" states moving past the 15 percent poverty threshold were California, Florida, Nevada, and Arizona—the four states hardest hit by
the housing crisis. Fewer people were making it out of poverty, and
many more were falling in.[13] Poverty's link to unemployment is unde-
niable, and the states wrecked by the housing bust are experiencing
massive challenges of long-term structural unemployment. By 2010
Florida's unemployment rate had gone from 3.8 percent in 2000 to
14.9 percent. Nevada's unemployment rate had been higher than the
national average in 2000 but still a mere 4.8 percent. By 2010 Nevada's unemployment rate had more than tripled to 14.9 percent.[14] Of
course, the unemployment rate rose everywhere, but unlike in past
recessions, the housing-bust states demonstrated an almost total reversal of fortune as measured by unemployment. High unemployment rates translate not only to lower income-tax revenue but also to
greater demands on social services—a big problem in states struggling to close massive budget gaps. In California, Florida, and Arizona there is a chillingly rational 90 percent correlation between the
number of poor and the number of unemployed.

Poverty Rate (2000)

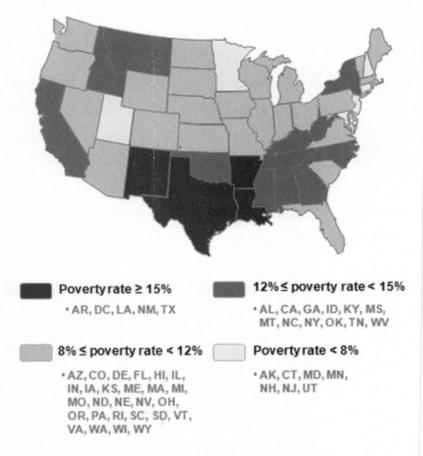

Poverty rate ≥ 15%
• AR, DC, LA, NM, TX

12% ≤ poverty rate < 15%
• AL, CA, GA, ID, KY, MS, MT, NC, NY, OK, TN, WV

8% ≤ poverty rate < 12%
• AZ, CO, DE, FL, HI, IL, IN, IA, KS, ME, MA, MI, MO, ND, NE, NV, OH, OR, PA, RI, SC, SD, VT, VA, WA, WI, WY

Poverty rate < 8%
• AK, CT, MD, MN, NH, NJ, UT

Why is this growth in poverty in the United States occurring at such an astounding pace? The answer: jobs, jobs, and jobs. For decades, the housing boom papered over an undereducated and undertrained workforce with a strong and steady flow of new jobs in construction, real estate, and mortgage finance. Some states, such as Florida and California, had their entire economies transformed by housing. The housing bust exposed a labor force whose skills and

Poverty Rate (2010)

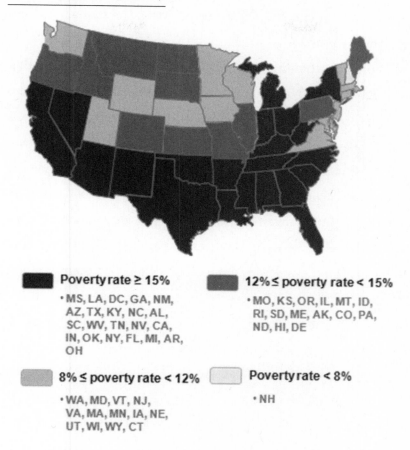

Poverty rate ≥ 15%

• MS, LA, DC, GA, NM,
AZ, TX, KY, NC, AL,
SC, WV, TN, NV, CA,
IN, OK, NY, FL, MI, AR,
OH

12% ≤ poverty rate < 15%

• MO, KS, OR, IL, MT, ID,
RI, SD, ME, AK, CO, PA,
ND, HI, DE

8% ≤ poverty rate < 12%

• WA, MD, VT, NJ,
VA, MA, MN, IA, NE,
UT, WI, WY, CT

Poverty rate < 8%

• NH

training were simply out of date. The states that during the boom boasted the strongest rise in home prices, the biggest booms in new-home building, and the highest number of jobs created from the housing sector are now in the worst position to retrain their unemployed masses. Unemployment in Nevada, California, and Florida tripled between 2000 and 2010. Florida's jump in unemployment was 50 percent higher than the national average. Whereas Alaska,

Washington, D.C., Oregon, and Mississippi had the highest unemployment rates in 2000, by 2010 it was Nevada, California, and Florida topping the list.[15]

Without job training, food stamps and welfare just create another sort of dependency. Nobody wants to live on food stamps. Anyone who has witnessed the shame and embarrassment of someone using food stamps at a local grocery store understands that. What people want are jobs, and it is ultimately the responsibility of the state to provide the training and economic environment required to create jobs. At a minimum it is in the best interest of the states to provide job training to get their residents back to work. However, unless the federal government specifically directs and administers monies for jobs training, most states cannot afford the large-scale job-training programs needed to resuscitate their economies. The Great Recession resulted in states depleting their unemployment-insurance trust funds as high unemployment rates persisted alongside the depressed economy. Many states that relied upon federal assistance to help with unemployment insurance now must pay the federal government back. It's yet another example of how borrowing money against future tax revenues has undercut states' ability to fund key services—such as job training.

We have to break the cycle of poverty in this country. We all know how to do it: Invest in education and create jobs. What's so harrowing about the fiscal condition of many states today is that achieving those goals seems antithetical to the financial realities. But what other option is there? There is no way a society with such a high and growing poverty rate can sustain itself without truly calamitous consequences. It doesn't have to be this way, though. There is a solution right in front of us that U.S. politicians have been embarrassingly slow to embrace: privatization.

Imagine you are in a financial bind. Your choices: Use your kids' college savings fund to make ends meet or miss some mortgage payments, which could mean losing the family home. Put in that situation, you'd look for an alternative. Before draining the college savings fund or ditching your mortgage, you might sell the second car, hawk some valuables on eBay, or cancel the annual Christmas vacation. That's common sense. Yet many states, if put in the same position, would apparently prefer raiding the kids' college savings to monetizing salable assets. States are not supposed to be asset or real-estate managers, but in many cases, that's exactly what they have become. And bad ones at that. States have neglected to perform basic upkeep of roads, bridges, and tunnels yet refuse to sell them to those who would. Imagine a homeowner not tending to the basic upkeep of a house by ignoring a broken stoop, not replacing a failing furnace, or not repairing a leaky roof. The house would ultimately collapse from neglect. That is what states are risking by not servicing existing infrastructure due to lack of funds.

Governor Mitch Daniels of Indiana set a precedent, albeit a controversial one, when he leased a state toll road to a private company for seventy-five years in exchange for almost $4 billion.[16] Some viewed it as a short-term fix, but it gave the state the money to invest in the kind of infrastructure—building highways and making other road improvements—most likely to boost commerce and jobs. The bottom line is that when cash is really needed, the adage "sell what you can, not what you should" truly applies. Just look at the banks around the world after the credit crisis. What did they do as one of several efforts to improve their balance sheets? They sold stuff. And some of the stuff they sold wasn't necessarily stuff they wanted to sell. What choice did they have, after all? They had to downsize in order to survive. Just like consumers, and just like many state and local governments, they thought the good times would never end and they got too big to support themselves. The government has been behind this big-bank downsizing, and it should also be behind states' downsizing through unwinding assets, such as infrastructure, that desperately need investment for overall public safety.

Although selling assets is nothing new for governments in other parts of the world—such deals were especially popular in Europe during the 1990s—even the suggestion of selling assets (otherwise known as privatization) draws ire from some here at home. Proponents of the strategy argue that selling roads, tollways, airports, and other state-owned assets can raise badly needed money, lower operating expenses, and oftentimes result in more efficient, better-operated infrastructure for users. (Singapore's Changi Airport, voted the best airport in the world by *Business Traveler* magazine, has been partially privatized since 2009.)[17] Opponents of such a strategy argue that it is just a short-term fix—that it robs the state of future revenue streams and leads to higher usage fees for state residents.

Certainly in the wrong hands—e.g., those of a governor who wants to use a one-time windfall to, say, give raises to state workers—privatization has some downsides. However, if the alternative to selling state assets is raising taxes or cutting services, then selling assets may well be the least bad option. Backed against a financial wall, states must embrace whatever cash-generating options are at their disposal. In addition to selling assets, a few states are also using public-private partnerships—basically outsourcing assets like toll roads to private companies—to raise money to improve roads, bridges, and airports. Too many American states and cities have been reluctant to embrace such moves. "Why sell the revenues of tomorrow for near-term cash today?" they say. The clear answer: because they have to. Just as strapped families raise money by holding a yard sale, U.S. states and cities will inevitably be forced to go a similar route. It all comes back to kitchen-table economics.

Precedents for governments privatizing or partially privatizing assets—airports especially—exist all across the globe. The United States, however, has been so rich for so long that it is woefully behind the curve—and woefully underinvested in the infrastructure and maintenance of its entire transportation system. In Europe efficiency wasn't considered much of a virtue until the early 1990s, when European countries had to apply for entry to the European Economic and Monetary Union. At the time, in order to qualify for entry to the EU, budget deficits needed to be below 3 percent of a country's GDP. The best way for many countries to clear that hurdle was by raising cash through privatizing telecom networks, utilities, public administration, airports, and other assets. By 1993 most EU countries had launched privatization efforts to help raise money and pay down debt. From 1990 to 2009 nearly $1 trillion was raised by EU countries via privatization. Here at home $1 trillion would go a long way toward solving states' fiscal woes. In Europe the privatization of telecommunication networks that were once state owned raised over $200 billion. Another $200 billion in utilities were also privatized. Sales of financial and real-estate assets raised another $200 billion. And anyone who has visited Europe lately can attest to the beauty and upkeep of European roads, train stations, and airports. In the twenty years from 1990 to 2009, over $100 billion was raised through privatizing transportation assets.[18]

Within the United States, states have the opportunity to privatize or partially privatize toll roads, bridges, airports, and other valuable assets. Some states have already begun by privatizing prisons, roads, and some small regional airports. Chicago mayor Rahm Emanuel, for instance, is pushing to privatize Midway International Airport.[19] But what's being discussed now barely scratches the surface of what's possible. In fact, over the past twenty years the United States has contributed 80 percent less than Europe toward infrastructure public-private partnerships for roads, rail, water, and buildings.[20]

The clear benefits of privatization include quick cash—in the form of either a large upfront payment or ongoing gains in the form of revenue sharing, expense reduction, debt reduction, and the chance to attract outside capital, and importantly jobs, to improve state and local services. Oftentimes the private sector does a better job too. Over the past twenty-five years, the United States has planned and funded less than one-fifth the number of infrastructure projects undertaken by Europe. In fact, by some estimates the United States needs to spend over $1 trillion to improve its infrastructure and become safer, more efficient, and more competitive. These dollars are unlikely to come purely from taxpayers.[21]

What's more, the cost of maintaining decrepit roads, bridges, tunnels, and other transportation infrastructure has become a drain on state budgets. Is it really in citizens' best interests for states to hold on to noncore assets simply because they don't want to sell them or because politically influential public-employee unions oppose the idea? This is a particularly important question for housing-bust states, where the proceeds could be used to pay down debt or to spare education and other programs from deeper cuts. Another consideration: Privately funded infrastructure improvements will bring investment and job creation to states that need it most.

To date Indiana, Florida, Texas, Ohio, and Virginia have been the most open to public-private partnerships and have laws and regulations on the books most conducive to privatization. However, as states' finances grow more strained, expect more states to venture down this path—so long as voters and public-employee unions don't get in the way. California has done privatization and public-private partnerships in the past, but more recently voters shot down one privatization initiative pushed by Governor Brown.

Case Study Indiana

One of the arguments against privatization is that private operators tend to raise tolls and usage fees. It's not as if those tolls and fees had held steady under government stewardship. Take the Holland and Lincoln tunnels connecting New York and New Jersey. In 1992, when I moved to New York, the cost of going through one of those tunnels was $4.00. Today it'll cost you $12.00. Note that from 1975 to 1991 the cost was between $1.50 and $3.00. In Indiana the cost of a toll on the state toll road was $4.65 from 1985 to 2008, when the rate was hiked to $8.00—where it will stay until 2016. This hike was implemented as part of a privatization plan that raised almost $4 billion for the state. It is hard to argue that drivers in Indiana are worse off due to privatization than drivers in New York/New Jersey. The biggest difference is that in Indiana the state had more money to invest in new roads and education.[22]

When Mitch Daniels came into office in 2006, he arrived with a specific agenda: Reduce state debt and rationalize state finances toward a sustainable operating model. Another goal was using current revenues to pay current expenses—which, of course, is what average Americans do every day. When federal dollars became scarcer, Daniels refused to cut into programs like education and infrastructure. He also refused to borrow more or raise taxes. Instead he cut waste and conducted the most successful state auction for a toll road in U.S. history, raising $3.8 billion for the state in exchange for leasing the Indiana Toll Road to Cintas and Macquarie, two private firms, for seventy-five years. Whatever the opposition was to the project at the time, Daniels had almost $4 billion in additional money to reinvest in the state, and he didn't have to raise taxes or cut education.[23]

He did, however, raise taxes on liquor and beverages as well as on rental cars. Raising taxes on all businesses or individuals would have been self-defeating as far as Daniels was concerned. The state needed to attract more businesses and individuals to ultimately raise tax revenues. Raising income- or corporate-tax rates would just discourage businesses and individuals from moving to the state. As Governor Daniels describes it, businesses must believe in the sustainability of the state in order to locate there. Investments in airports, roads, schools, and job training are all part of the equation. Unless states prioritize such investments, they will fall by the wayside—damning their residents to a diminished economic future. With stakes this high, the best thing some states have going for them is the fact that a few good options—unconventional though they may be—are still left on the table. For Mitch Daniels doing nothing was never an option because he understood the velocity of money and realized just how quickly other states could exploit inaction.

■ PART II ■

The Rise

Chapter 7

■

A New Map of Prosperity

It sounded like yet another corporate cutback story.

In March 2009 Tampa Bay–based Sykes Enterprises told city officials in Minot, North Dakota, that the company was going to have to lay off two hundred workers and shutter the call center Sykes had been operating there since 1996. A sign of the bleak economic times—right?

Well, there's a wrinkle to this particular story. Sykes's problem, according to the *Tampa Bay Times,* was not a lack of business. In fact, business was booming. The problem was that Sykes just couldn't find enough employees in Minot to handle all the demand. The company had originally hoped to expand its Minot call center to 450 workers. But in North Dakota's booming economy—one in which fast-food joints are paying high-school kids $20 an hour and young oil workers are pulling in $100,000 a year—hiring has become a huge challenge for employers like Sykes. "They'd been advertising all the time for employees but just couldn't find them," said Minot mayor Curt Zimbelman, noting that true unemployment in North Dakota oil country "probably doesn't exist."[1]

North Dakota may be an extreme case, but believe it or not, the U.S. economy is on the road to recovery. There's just one big problem: The road is unevenly paved. Parts of the country are growing at rates on par with some of the world's fastest-growing emerging markets, while others are being dragged down by high unemployment and mounting debt loads. The dichotomy is obscured by national economic data that show the overall U.S. economy growing at a sluggish 2 percent a year. The strong growth of the central corridor is being obscured by the weakness in the housing-bust states. From 2008 to 2011 Louisiana's economy grew 16 percent, North Dakota's by 27 percent, and Iowa's and Nebraska's by 11 percent. All in all, the seventeen states that I call the central corridor collectively grew their economies by 8 percent from 2008 to 2011. The United States as a whole grew its economy by 6 percent. The housing-bust states grew theirs by 2 percent.[2]

The reality is that the central-corridor states have more resources to attract newcomers because they are not choking on debt and crazy pension obligations and forced into a dependency on higher and higher tax rates. Not coincidentally, these same states are also investing in the right things: jobs, infrastructure, and education. These same states are competing with not just other states but with other countries for businesses that are deciding where to set up shop or expand operations. In an increasingly digital economy unhinged from the demands of geography—corporate titans like Exxon and American Airlines, for instance, no longer need to be headquartered in

New York just to be near Wall Street or Madison Avenue—the states that are in the worst financial shape are struggling to compete.

Where are the businesses and jobs going? Texas, for one. In April 2012 the cost of renting a U-Haul truck for a one-way trip from California to Texas was twice that from Texas to California, according to Mark Perry, an economics professor at University of Michigan's Flint campus. "The price ratios," Perry writes, "suggest that demand for trucks leaving California is roughly double the demand for trucks coming into the Golden State." By 2012 corporate flight from California had become so pervasive that the state legislature sent a team to Texas to learn best-business-practice lessons from state officials.[3] The current population outflow from California to Texas foreshadows a bigger interstate migration to come. Over the next thirty years, businesses and population will migrate from the coasts and Sun Belt to America's central corridor, which extends northward from Texas up though North Dakota and eastward from Colorado to Indiana. Flyover no more, the central corridor will drive the U.S. economy in much the same way the Sun Belt and coastal states powered the nation over the past sixty-plus years. All the while, the coasts and especially the Sun Belt won't be aging gracefully. They'll be slogging through a slow, painful recovery from the housing bust, and they'll likely be more of a drag on the overall economy than a true contributor.

Effectively, the central corridor of the United States will be the new emerging market of the country—the same role Alberta has played for our neighbor to the north, Canada—with outsized growth, greater employment opportunities, and lots of new arrivals from states with higher taxes, shrunken police forces, and declining public schools. You can see it happening already. Texas has one of the lowest unemployment rates in the country, while California has one of the highest. When businesses move out of California to Texas, they take jobs with them. Consumer spending is rising at a faster clip in the Midwest states than in California because they have jobs and less than half the debt of Californians. To be sure, some of the migration under way is tied to booms in agriculture in Iowa or in oil production in North Dakota and Texas. However, Apple didn't choose to open a new campus in Austin because of new oil fields in West Texas, just as cloud-computing company Appirio did not add three hundred jobs in Indianapolis due to strong corn crops in nearby Carroll County.[4] Moreover, not all of the central corridor's advantages are geographical or geological. They're political too. The reality is, California could reap the same shale-oil and shale-gas bounties now benefiting North Dakota. Politicians simply choose not to. California's Monterey shale deposit is considered one of the bigger undrilled hydrocarbon deposits in North America, with an estimated fifteen billion barrels of recoverable oil, about twice the oil remaining on Alaska's North Slope. The economic impact of developing the Monterey shale would be so vast, "it could potentially solve the state's budget deficit," says Katie Potter, an oil-industry recruiter for staffing firm NES Global Talent. Evidently, state pols are not interested.[5] "I asked Jerry Brown about why California cannot come to grips with its huge hydrocarbon reserves. After all, this could turn around the state," John Hofmeister, former president of Royal Dutch Shell's U.S. business, told the *Daily Beast*. "He answered that this is not logic, it's California. This is simply not going to happen here."[6] That's too bad, because communities located near the Monterey shale, like Santa Maria, desperately need the jobs—a point California Lutheran University economist Bill Watkins drove home to an audience in Santa Maria. "If you were in Texas," Watkins said, "you'd be rich."[7]

Unemployment in the central corridor is nearly half of what it is in Nevada and California. In parts of the central corridor, such as North Dakota, there aren't enough people to fill all the available jobs. Along with jobs comes personal-income growth, which is clearly stronger in the central corridor. From 2008 to 2011, for example, personal-income growth in states like Texas, Louisiana, and Tennessee grew by between 5 percent and 10 percent. In both North and South Dakota, personal-income growth grew by over 10 percent. Meanwhile, in California, Nevada, Arizona, and Florida, personal incomes barely grew.[8]

Without doubt, Louisiana and Texas have been clear beneficiaries of rising oil prices. And the natural gas boom in the United States is creating booms in states like North Dakota, Oklahoma, Wyoming, and Pennsylvania too (though not in New York, where political infighting over fracking—a technology that's been around for fifty years—has stymied efforts to develop New York's own natural gas reserves). Cheap natural gas is a huge competitive advantage not just for the producer states but for the whole country. Natural-gas prices are three to four times lower here than in Europe, a price advantage

Unemployment Rate (August 2012)

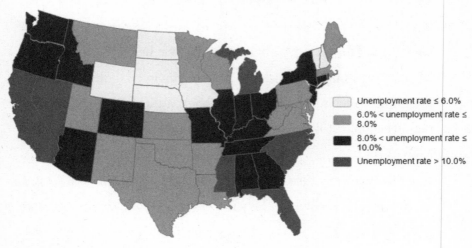

Unemployment rate ≤ 6.0%

6.0% < unemployment rate ≤ 8.0%

8.0% < unemployment rate ≤ 10.0%

Unemployment rate > 10.0%

SOURCES: BLS AND MWAG

Personal Income Growth (2008–2011)

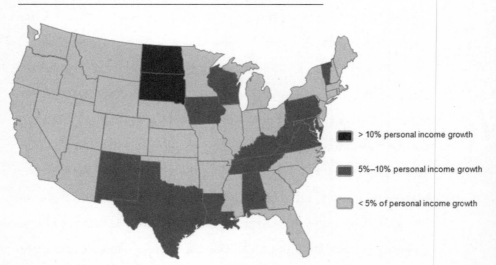

> 10% personal income growth

5%–10% personal income growth

< 5% of personal income growth

SOURCES: BEA AND MWAG

now prompting chemical companies—particularly those that use natural gas as a feedstock—to expand operations here at home. This has Europe worried: "The threat is that the [U.S.] chemical industry attracts more investment and that goes to the expense of the EU industry," Wim Hoste, a chemicals analyst at KBC Securities in Brussels, told the *Wall Street Journal*.[9] Were natural gas to take off as a transportation fuel, the economic impact would be even greater. Natural gas "is the only long-term viable option to diesel," said Michael G. Britt Sr., director of maintenance and engineering at United Parcel Service, which recently added forty-eight CNG trucks and plans to deploy more once more natural-gas fueling infrastructure is in place.[10] This energy boom has literally transformed the financial landscape of the central corridor, creating jobs and rising incomes. In late 2012 North Dakota, Oklahoma, Wyoming, and others had unemployment rates in the lowest quartile in the United States.

Over the past forty years, more and more U.S. jobs have been shipped offshore due to lower labor costs in places like China. However, the differential in production costs between the United States and China is now narrowing, especially when you factor in the cost of shipping large finished goods from China to U.S. markets. In 2000 the average wage in China was 50 cents an hour. Now it's $3.50.[11] Transportation costs in China are soaring. A 2011 article in the *New York Times* cited the cost of trucking goods within China as $2.50 to $3.00 a mile compared with a mere $1.75 in the United States.[12] The point is that the United States is well positioned to compete globally if it can get its fiscal act together locally.

While large corporations are leading the hiring charge in the central-corridor states, small businesses are also creating jobs in those regions. Why? Because they can. Consumers and small-business owners in the central corridor have smaller debt loads than folks on the coasts. The average debt-to-income per capita in California is 170 percent, compared with 80 percent in Texas. The percent of homes with negative equity was 29 percent in California in 2012 versus 9 percent in Texas.[13] The most common way entrepreneurs get their first funding is by tapping into personal credit cards or equity in their homes. If they're too deep in debt, there is obviously nothing to tap. California used to be considered the small-business capital of the world. The world, clearly, has changed.

Chapter 8

■

State Arbitrage

In the business world, any smart up-and-comer will be quick to exploit a competitor's weakness. Under Armour, for example, did not rest on its laurels after it cut in half Nike's lead in sports-apparel market share; no, Under Armour went for the jugular, launching a footwear line that now accounts for 12 percent of the brand's total sales.[1] What do sneakers and gym shorts have to do with jobs and state finances? Well, imagine for a moment that California is Nike and that Texas and North Dakota are Under Armour, and suddenly you get a clear picture of what's at stake. Texas and North Dakota are not resting on their laurels. They want California's jobs. And the reality is that California is far, far more vulnerable than its sneaker-company doppelganger.

By mid-2006 the real cost of homeownership in California was more than twice the national average. The ratio of average home price to per-capita income was 9.7 in California versus 4.2 for the United States nationally. The price-to-income ratio in Texas was a mere 2.6. Was it really worth over three and a half times more to live in California than in Texas? Perhaps the public schools in California were superior. Maybe proximity to the California coastline or the Sierra Nevada ski slopes was worth some sort of a real-estate premium. But just how much? It's not as if the California job market was much of a lure: In the early 2000s California's unemployment rate was 20 percent higher than the national average, and by 2010 it was 33 percent higher. By late 2012 California's home price–to–income ratio—while still above the national average—had narrowed to 6.6.[2] What happened is that people were beginning to vote with their feet. Not only was the cost of living in certain parts of the country no longer justifiable, but also differences between state and local taxes were eroding the desirability of certain locales. At a time when the country has a true structural unemployment epidemic, when recovery from the Great Recession seems painfully slow, and when almost 25 percent of U.S. mortgages are larger than the value of the underlying properties, the fiscal condition of individual states has never been more important. These differences are driving a bigger and bigger wedge between Americans at the most basic levels. Businesses are fleeing housing-bust states for those with relatively low tax rates and more business-friendly policies. Rich people are aggressively choosing their state of residence based on tax rates, the quality and safety of services provided, and the overall fiscal health of a state.

Take New Jersey. The ratio of average home price to per-capita income there was 5.2 in late 2012, 36 percent higher than the national average. But New Jersey residents weren't just paying more for their homes relative to their incomes. They were also paying a lot more in taxes for the privilege of living in the Garden State. In 2009, according to the U.S. Census Bureau, New Jersey had the highest state and local tax burden as a percentage of personal income in the United States at 12.2 percent. To put that into context, the national average was 9.8 percent and New Hampshire, Texas, and Wyoming had burdens of 8.0 percent, 7.9 percent, and 7.8 percent respectively.[3] I was born in New Jersey, and some of the best memories of my childhood are from summers spent at Beaver Lake in Sussex County. Some of my best memories of my midtwenties are summers spent in Bay Head, a small beach town. But is living in New Jersey today, with significantly worse infrastructure and public services, worth five times the national average cost of living? Certainly not for me—I don't live in New Jersey.

Fiscally speaking, states have never been more unequal than they are today. They are unequal in the amount of debt per capita they carry. They are unequal in the tax rates they levy on individuals, corporations, and sales. They are increasingly unequal in terms of public safety and overall quality of life. Government policy has done a lot to contribute to this inequality. Did a state rein in spending and control debt levels, or did a state push tough decisions off until later, piling on more debt and underfunding pension obligations so it could continue to spend beyond its means?

Whatever the federal tax policy, Americans pay the same federal income-tax rates regardless of where they live. However, local and state income taxes vary widely. The most obvious example is that Texas, Nevada, Florida, Wyoming, South Dakota, Washington, and Alaska do not tax individual income, whereas California recently voted to raise income-tax rates on any resident earning over $1,000,000 by nearly a third, to 13.3 percent[4]—the highest state income-tax rate in the country. If you make over $250,000 a year, you will now pay 10.3 percent. Compare that with Texas or Florida, where there is no zero income tax for anyone. That's nearly $26,000 less in after-tax income for a Californian earning $250,000 year.

Companies are paying attention to more than just taxes when deciding on investing in states. Twenty-three states in the United States are "right to work" states, which means workers in those states cannot be required, as a condition of employment, to join a union or pay union dues. Companies argue that this gives them more flexibility to manage their head count and stay competitive. Just last year, Indiana became the latest state to pass a right-to-work law in order to attract more business investment.[5] This isn't about being prounion or antiunion. It's about being proreality.

Like it or not, companies like Boeing want maximum flexibility in their labor forces, and they're choosing to expand in or relocate to states that give them what they want. According to a study by Ohio University economist Richard Vedder, job growth in right-to-work states was almost double that in non-right-to-work states from 1977 to 2008. From 2000 to 2009 domestic migration from non-right-to-work to right-to-work states accounted for a 5 percent population swing.[6] What's more, since 2008 right-to-work states have grown their economies over three times as fast as non-right-to-work states. Specifically, right-to-work states grew their economies by 55 percent from 2001 to 2011, faster than the average for the United States (47 percent) or for non-right-to-work states (41 percent). Average unemployment in July 2012 in right-to-work states was 7.2 percent, versus 8.3 percent in the United States overall. Personal income in right-to-work states grew by 54 percent from 2001 to 2011, 17 percent faster than the U.S. average and 30 percent faster than forced-union states. Average bonded debt in right-to-work states is 3.8 percent of their GDPs, versus 5.8 percent in forced-union states, a difference of over 50 percent. But when you add together bonded debt and unfunded pension and health-care liabilities, the difference is an astonishing 81 percent higher burden in forced-union states. And once again the burden of those obligations goes directly to state residents.[7]

There is an expression on Wall Street, "smart money," that is used to describe fancy hedge-fund and mutual-fund managers who ferret out little-known information about companies, products, or markets. They figure out how to profit from that information via stocks, bonds, or commodities, make their moves early, and, by doing so, make the big bucks. "Dumb money" describes the masses that find out information only after it is too late and act well after the smart money. In some cases the "dumb money" people find out information so late they lose their shirts. They wind up making the absolute wrong investment decision at the wrong time—when the "smart money" is already out the door. Smart-money thinking applies to states too. The smart money (in this case, large corporations and wealthy people) is exiting high-tax, troubled states to low-tax, higher-service states. Companies like Boeing, Google, Intel, Amazon, Toyota, and Facebook are deciding to build their expanded business operations outside their home states in places like Texas, Indiana, Oklahoma, and South Carolina. In Connecticut and Massachusetts, a recent survey conducted by the Connecticut Business & Industry Association found that half of businesses with fifty or more employees in the Hartford-Springfield Knowledge Corridor had considered moving and a quarter had already been approached by other states.[8] The smart money isn't just escaping taxes that are high today but future tax hikes as well. The smart money understands that taxes can only go up given the massive sums of bonded debt and unfunded pension and health-care liabilities coming due in future years. Thanks to reckless fiscal mismanagement by cities and states, individuals and corporations still residing in those states will all be on the hook. The smart money also understands that with those higher taxes will come a lower level of public services—that the states in the deepest fiscal trouble have far fewer resources to invest in roads, bridges, airports, education, public safety, and all the other things relocating businesses look for in a new home.

No wonder smart money is flocking to states with lower tax burdens and less strained budgets. The dumb money is those left behind to pay higher taxes for lesser services. From 2009 to 2010, 12 percent of people moving out of California moved to Texas, almost halfway across the country.[9] The fact is that California's total obligations—obligations that can be escaped by the simple act of moving—increased almost 50 percent in one year alone. During the same time period, 15 percent of the people leaving New York moved to Florida. Some folks don't even have to move that far to get relief. Property taxes in Pennsylvania are almost 50 percent below those of neighboring

New Jersey (which has the highest property taxes in the nation), and Pennsylvania's income-tax rate of 3.07 percent is nearly a third lower than New Jersey's 8.97 percent top rate.[10]

To be sure, there's nothing new about people moving to take advantage of lower taxes or better schools. But today these relocations are increasingly cross country. The states with the best employment growth since 2007 are all non-housing-boom states: North Dakota, Texas, Alaska, Oklahoma, and Louisiana. The worst: Nevada, Arizona, Florida, Alabama, and Rhode Island.[11] In its annual Investment Monitor report, accounting firm Ernst & Young tracks what it calls "mobile capital investments"—essentially business investments that could be made anywhere and are not tied to a specific geographic region (like a copper mine, for instance). According to E&Y, the states landing the most jobs from these investments were Texas (30,100), Pennsylvania (27,100), Ohio (26,200), Virginia (23,100), and North Carolina (20,300). As a side note, little Indiana picked up more jobs from "mobile" business investment (14,500) than did New York (12,300).[12]

State and local governments owe over $6 trillion that we know about. This works out to about $16,600 per capita, but a lot of that money—especially the $2 trillion in debt amassed over the last decade—is not distributed evenly. In New Jersey the total tax-supported debt per capita is a staggering $15,000. In nearby Pennsylvania that number is just $7,000. The contrast is even more dramatic when comparing Illinois and next-door neighbor Indiana. Illinois has a total tax-supported debt per capita of almost $16,000. Indiana: $2,500.[13] The less an individual owes, the more that individual can spend, and the same truism holds for states. Raising taxes and cutting social services is a vicious cycle. The higher the tax rates, the more strained the revenues become as people and businesses flee to avoid higher taxes. The result: less money for social services. Property values continue to decline, wealth declines, and jobs leave. This is exactly what is happening to the most deeply indebted states in the United States.

In prior U.S. economic cycles, industrial revolution and evolution were the catalysts causing regional economies to rise and fall. Geography often played a key role. The lamp oil produced by New England's whaling industry once illuminated the world—until the drilling of the first oil well in Pennsylvania in 1859 put the whale-boat captains out of business. (Yes, oil saved the whales.) Hollywood was created practically overnight in the early twentieth century when filmmakers abandoned New York and New Jersey for California's superior sunlight—and also to escape the East Coast lawyers of Thomas Edison and his motion-picture patents.

This time around geography is almost irrelevant. In today's mobile, digital, overnight-shipping economy, there's no physical reason why Electronic Arts can't design video games in Austin, Texas, instead of Redwood City, California, just as there's no reason Boeing can't build new airplanes in South Carolina instead of Washington State. Government inaction and ineptitude is causing once-vibrant communities to become decrepit and once-sleepy ones to emerge as the new job magnets. Voters and communities are starting to realize just how closely tied their personal economic well-being is to their communities' fiscal well-being. Voters in the mismanaged states, the ones now flushing away jobs, are rising up and putting their feet down. Unemployed workers are packing up their families and relocating to low-tax, non-budget-crunched states like Texas and North Dakota in order to find work.

Moving has become an easier decision for businesses too. Consider, for instance, a corporation headquartered in Silicon Valley. The average corporate tax rate in California is over 8.8 percent and the average sales tax is 7.25 percent. Sure, property taxes are kept in check by Proposition 13, but the cost of living is higher than in most other states and social services are vanishing. Moving a business next door to Nevada, with zero corporate taxes and a lower cost of living, seems reasonable enough, and businesses and individuals have been making such moves. No longer is that competition solely between neighbors. Nowadays a state on one side of the country could be competing with a state thousands of miles away. Indiana, for instance, has actually been running print ads in California that show a coffee-shop napkin with the following handwritten message from Indiana: "Admit it, you find me fiscally attractive."

Indiana governor Mitch Daniels is not the only central-corridor governor mounting a full-on assault on states like California, Illinois, New York, and New Jersey in a bid to lure individuals and businesses. Companies are relocating and channeling investment dollars from struggling states to strong ones like never before. Toyota announced in 2012 its factory-expansion plans in Indiana, investing $400 million to move the production of its Highlander to Indiana from Japan.[14]

COURTESY OF INDIANA ECONOMIC DEVELOPMENT CORPORATION

Boeing plans to close a plant it had operated since 1929 to move all future operations to Oklahoma and Texas.[15] Google spent $700 million to add a new data center in Texas. Amazon and eBay are also investing hundreds of millions to build out facilities in business-friendly Texas.[16]

The simple truth is that moving within the United States has rarely been easier for employers. If all a business needs to operate is a high-speed data network, proximity to an airport and interstate, and a college-educated labor pool, there's not much difference between Portland, Oregon, and Portland, Maine. As a result, businesses are increasingly relocating to or investing in new facilities halfway across the country from where they started. The economics of doing so are that compelling. When a satellite operator like Globalstar moves from California to Louisiana[17] or a food company like Chiquita relocates its headquarters from Ohio to North Carolina, the decision to move often boils down to taxes.[18]

Wisconsin and Indiana Versus Illinois

In a dog-eat-dog economy like this one, the better-off states are more than happy to exploit the economic woes of their neighbors. Mere days after Illinois enacted a 67 percent hike in personal income taxes and a 46 percent increase in corporate taxes, Wisconsin governor Scott Walker responded by publicly urging Illinois companies to "escape to Wisconsin" and by putting up billboards at the Illinois-Wisconsin border announcing, "Wisconsin Is Open for Business."[19] So many big employers wound up threatening to leave Illinois that the state was forced to pay corporations like Sears to stay via special side tax breaks. In other words, Illinois is paying to keep old jobs—money that could have been used to fund job training to create new ones. Insane.[20]

During his tenure as governor of Indiana from 2005 to 2013, Daniels worked to steadily improve Indiana's financial condition and make the state more attractive to businesses and individuals. Formerly the head of the Office of Management and Budget under President George W. Bush, Daniels talks about state competitiveness the same way CEOs talk about sales prowess: "It has become a market share game because America is not growing."[21] While some states offer up-front cash incentives to lure businesses away from other states,

Daniels refused to do so. In direct contrast to Illinois—which has repeatedly resorted to cash or tax incentives just to keep businesses from leaving—Indiana has attracted businesses through its strong balance sheet, lower taxes, and right-to-work law. That didn't come easy. At the end of 2006 Indiana had $19 billion of debt outstanding. In 2010 state debt was worked down to $14 billion. On an individual basis, Indiana had a debt burden per capita—inclusive of unfunded pension and benefit costs—of $2,455 in 2010, the third lowest in the nation.[22]

What made the Daniels administration even more unusual was its commitment to using current revenues to pay for current expenses. By doing so, Indiana steadily reduced its debt and improved its balance sheet so dramatically that the state eventually earned the highest bond rating from all three major credit-rating agencies. Indiana's triple-A rating is actually a notch better than that of the U.S. government. What's most remarkable about the Indiana story is how fast the transformation happened. Knowing he was competing for jobs with other states, Daniels operated with a sense of urgency. "How long does it take to turn around a state?" he said in an interview with me, repeating my question. "I don't know, I was in a hurry."[23]

Florida Versus Connecticut

In 2011 Florida governor Rick Scott phoned his old friend, billionaire investor Eddie Lampert, and asked him a question: Why are you still living in Connecticut? Lampert owned a vacation home in Florida, and Scott wanted to know why Lampert and his hedge-fund firm—ESL Investments, owner of Sears and Kmart and a firm with $10 billion under management—would choose to remain in a state that had corporate taxes 60 percent higher than Florida's and a median personal income tax of 5.75 percent, versus zero in Florida. Soon Lampert was asking himself the same question, and in 2012 he moved his home and his business from Greenwich to Miami. Governor Scott didn't stop with Lampert. Scott continues to make phone calls to other business leaders in Connecticut, New York, New Jersey, and Illinois. What Governor Scott understands is that the more businesses and the more wealth he can attract to Florida, the more jobs will be created and the less pressure he'll face to raise taxes or cut spending.[24]

From the private sector himself—he was a venture capitalist and before that the CEO of the Columbia/HCA hospital chain—Scott understood how important speed of execution is to business. He also appreciated the looming threat of the housing bust to Florida's overall economy. Among the first things he did upon taking office was shrink government agencies, push through a bill that removed the state from local planning and development decisions, and streamline the permitting process for developers and other businesses. "Every rule costs money—just the fact that you have to research to find out if you're in compliance," Scott told the *Tampa Bay Times*.[25] He made jobs his priority and argued that his most important role was to get people back to work. I asked him whether he approached things any differently as chief executive of a state than he did as a chief executive in the private sector. "No difference," he replied, barely even pausing to consider the question.[26]

In contrast to Florida, Connecticut was the only state to raise income taxes in fiscal year 2012. Prior to 1992 the state had no income tax and attracted businesses and individuals from New York and New Jersey specifically because of its advantageous tax environment. And while Connecticut still offers lower taxes than New York and New Jersey today, the gap is narrowing, and all three states rank near the bottom (or near the top, if you like taxes) in terms of state and local tax burdens as a percentage of personal income. Because the tax-arbitrage opportunities within the Tri-state region are so marginal—it just doesn't pay enough nowadays to move from New York City to Greenwich, Connecticut—rich people like Eddie Lampert and businesses like Pilot Pen Corporation of America (which relocated from Trumbull, Connecticut, to Jacksonville, Florida, in 2008) are not moving just regionally.[27] They are moving hundreds or thousands of miles to states like Florida and Texas. The exodus from Connecticut is likely to continue because the state simply cannot afford to cut taxes. At $18,981, Connecticut's per-capita tax burden is now the third highest in the nation—seven times higher than Florida's.[28]

Texas Versus California

Within the high-tech world, there are no bigger California success stories than Apple and eBay. Yet in 2012, when Apple was deciding where to invest $300 million and add 3,600 new sales and accounting jobs, it chose to build in Austin, Texas, instead of near its Cupertino, California, headquarters.[29] When San Jose–based eBay and its PayPal subsidiary were looking to add 1,000 new jobs, eBay also chose Austin, Texas.[30] Where jobs go, taxpayers follow: According to the Manhattan Institute for Policy Research, of the 1.1 million Californians who left the state in the 2000s, 225,000 of them moved to Texas, making it far and away the most popular destination for ex-Californians.[31]

From 2005 to 2009 Texas accounted for just 1.5 percent of migration out of California. By 2010, in just one year, that number had jumped to 12 percent.[32] This attracted so much attention from California politicians that in 2011 they sent a delegation, led by Lieutenant Governor Gavin Newsom, to Texas to learn "best practices" and find out why so many were leaving California for Texas.[33] They should have saved themselves the trip because the answers were fairly obvious. California has the second-highest unemployment rate in the country, among the highest corporate and individual tax rates in the nation, and a regulatory climate businesses consider onerous. In 2012 a survey of CEOs by *Chief Executive* magazine deemed California the worst business climate in the country for the eighth consecutive year.[34] By early 2012 personal income was growing 71 percent faster in Texas than in California. Dallas Federal Reserve president Richard Fisher proudly shows a graph (any and every chance he can) of spectacular job growth in Texas and how it has outpaced that of any other regional Federal Reserve district for the last three decades.[35]

For a young person just graduating from college and now wondering which part of the country offers the best opportunity and quality of life, knowing where the jobs are being created is essential. Governor Scott of Florida often says that what people care about most are education, jobs, and a low cost of living. What state offers the best education programs for children? Which state offers the best job opportunities so people can provide for themselves and their families? A state's commitment to a quality education system matters. Its commitment to well-paying jobs matters. And when it comes to pay, what really counts isn't so much gross salary earned but the after-tax, take-home pay actually deposited in a breadwinner's bank account. The quality and cost of living are also critical variables. Not only is it easier to find a job in Texas than in California, there are no income taxes in Texas, and the average home price is 60 percent less expensive in Texas than in California.[36] In other words, you can get twice as much house for your money in Texas than in California.

Business migration foreshadows economic and employment growth. California's unemployment rate is already twice that of Texas and Oklahoma, and there's a clear connection between their relative unemployment rates and the fact that Texas and Oklahoma have both benefited from California-based companies like Google, Facebook, and eBay building new facilities in their states. Like a young planet whose gravitational pull becomes stronger as it gains mass, states like Texas and Oklahoma will only become more attractive to tech companies and tech workers over time. (Indeed, Priceline.com CEO Jeffery Boyd told *Fortune* that one reason he's kept the online travel company headquartered in Connecticut is the absence of competitors who might pilfer his employees or bid up their pay.)[37]

Job creation, corporate migration, stronger consumer balance sheets, stronger state balance sheets, and a relatively muted impact from the credit crisis are powering the central-corridor states ahead of their coastal counterparts. Sure, there may be nothing in Texas comparable to driving the Pacific Coast Highway with the top down, but when a California home costs three times as much and the taxes are three times higher, a move to Texas starts looking mighty attractive— even if you have to make a yearly trip back to visit family and friends. Indeed, famed economist Arthur Laffer often tells the story of purchasing his home in Tennessee with his first-year tax savings from leaving California.[38]

The United States is already in the process of rebalancing itself demographically based upon opportunity and standard of living. Historically these shifts have taken decades to play out. But in a fast-moving, digital economy like today's, change is happening fast. Central-corridor states don't have the deep scars of the overconsumption, excess spending, and debt racked up over the past twenty-five years. Compared with their coastal rivals, these states now appear nimble and competitive to businesses that need every advantage possible to succeed. No politician wants to raise taxes, but when the mismatch between revenues and expenses hits an inflection point—when simply cutting costs won't close the gaps—raising taxes becomes a last resort. States like California, Illinois, and Connecticut are all raising taxes and cutting programs, while states like Oklahoma and Indiana are cutting taxes and investing in infrastructure and education. Growth rates are just higher and will be for years to come in the central corridor.

The numbers already bear out the regional shift. Since 2008 consumer-spending growth in the Midwest has outpaced that in the

West by 30 percent, and that trend shows no signs of abating. Consumers in Midwest states are more likely to be employed, more likely to have manageable amounts of revolving credit-card debt, and certainly likely to be paying lower taxes. All this leads to higher relative levels of disposable income—a magnet for retailers and service providers. From 2008 to 2010 Wyoming, North Dakota, Texas, Iowa, Indiana, and Colorado all showed strong positive GDP growth, while New Jersey, California, Florida, Arizona, and Nevada all experienced declines. In fact, many of these coastal and Sun Belt economies are reporting lower GDPs today than in 2007, while other parts of the country keep hitting all-time highs. It is exactly due to the economic paralysis of the coasts and the Sun Belt that the overall U.S. economy can't break out of its snail's-pace, sub–2 percent growth. After all, California, Florida, Arizona, and Nevada still account for 21 percent of the total U.S. economy. While that is down from the 2007 peak of 22 percent, the housing-bust states remain a huge drag, diminishing the chances of a vigorous national recovery.[39]

With so many businesses now requiring proximity to little more than a highway, an airport, and a high-speed data network, the nation's business and industrial hubs have never been more vulnerable to poaching by rival states with better services and lower taxes. The history books offer one ominous analogy for the poachees: New York City. Between 1950 and 1980 high taxes, declining schools, rising crime, and political lunacy (culminating in the 1975 fiscal crisis) contributed to a New York City population decline of 800,000—from 7.9

million to 7.1 million people. It took twenty years before New York City recouped those population losses.[40]

In 1950 the city of Detroit boasted a population of 1.8 million people. Just 60 years later its population has been reduced to a mere 600,000. Why? Jobs exodus, political and social instability, and steeply reduced social services create a self-perpetuating downward spiral that many cities find impossible to escape. This is how Detroit, once America's sixth-most-populous city, devolved into a welfare city—another American ghost town.[41] The contexts may be different, but stories like Detroit's are playing out all over the country. Population is declining in the Las Vegas metro area. Even Florida saw its population decline in 2009. The loss of business and jobs always leads to reduced tax revenues, reduced services, and more incentive for residents to leave. What's different today is causation. Governments are no longer helpless victims of business loss but the catalysts for it. Businesses and families are leaving because they cannot afford the taxes now needed to pay out-of-control debt service. It's why America's central corridor—the heartland, the Midwest, the onetime flyover states, the golden triangle within the center of the country—will be the foundation of economic growth for years to come.

Chapter 9

■

David Takes On Goliath:
New Political Precedents

When I first wrote about the threat that state and local budget crises pose to the overall U.S. economy back in September 2010, I assumed the first stories to make headlines would involve heavy pressure on the mayors and governors in housing-bust states to cut expenses and, more important, cut payroll. The outcry would arise from social-contract defaults—in the form of citizens receiving reduced services for higher taxes. This first phase would continue until the pain got so acute that taxpayers and voters stepped in to stop the bleeding. Voter outcry would then initiate phases two and three—cuts to public-employee pensions and refusals to make good on municipal-bond payments. To my surprise, the outcry that deafened all others involved the mere mention of municipal-bond defaults, let alone sizable ones. The loudest complaints were from the municipal-bond dealers, who shouted back that widespread municipal-bond defaults had not happened since the Great Depression and therefore could not and would not happen again. Needless to say, this argument reminded me of those who contended that home prices would never go down because they hadn't since the Great Depression. They also argued that municipal bonds couldn't default because most bonds were backed by the full faith and credit—the guaranteed taxing authority—of the state and local governments that had issued them. Of course, so too did pension obligations. It was never clear to me why muni-bond folks thought there could be defaults on some tax-guaranteed obligations—i.e., pensions—but not on municipal bonds. When a pension contract is renegotiated, isn't that a default? And while not explicitly guaranteed by taxes, how are essential state services like education and infrastructure morally subordinate to bondholders? The issue wouldn't come down to the ability to pay. State and local governments may be technically able to meet their tax-guaranteed obligations, but only if they sacrifice significant services and infrastructure investment. And remember, tax guarantees are only as good as the taxpayers willing to honor them. The bigger and more inflammatory issue would be willingness to pay. So long as willingness to pay was an issue, reform and compromise would be critical.

Reform will be difficult, especially given the outsized political influence wielded by public-employee unions. Ironically, however, many of the early success stories of pension reform come from largely Democratic locales. Voters in San Jose, for example, approved some of the most aggressive pension reform yet in the United States by a margin of nearly 70 percent to 30 percent.[1] San Jose passed reforms that doubled the amount new employees contribute to their pension plans, increased the retirement age, capped the cost-of-living adjustment, and altered the calculation upon which benefits were determined by averaging salaries over the last three years of employment (instead of using just the last year). For existing employees the reforms also re-stricted benefits, either by requiring higher employee contributions or by transferring benefits to a lower-cost plan with reduced benefits.

Why did Mayor Chuck Reed of San Jose get such widespread support for pension reform, which is typically unpopular? How did this come about? The voters of San Jose had reached an inflection point, saying, "Enough is enough." Since taking office in 2007, Reed had done everything within his power to improve the city's finances, yet the city could not escape budget shortfalls. Just like most states, San Jose is required to balance its budget, but doing so required cutting programs and reducing services. So in the summer of 2012, after the city cut more than a thousand jobs and cut salaries by over 10 percent—and all the while not properly funding its heath-care programs—the community took a stand, with 69 percent of voters approving a rollback in pension benefits.[2]

Elected in 2006, Reed says he was not asked one question about pensions in fifty-eight mayoral debates. Today he is the go-to guy across the state of California—and lately across the country—on pension reform. Unwilling to undermine public safety further by reducing the number of police officers and firefighters on the job, Reed focused on the fastest-growing expense in the city's budget: pensions. He began to focus on the importance of bringing down the costs of future accruals. When he took office, Reed's budget staff warned him that annual retirement costs could soar from $155 million to $650 million within five years. Reed kept his message simple: Pension expenses had grown faster than any other single expense in the city, and if they were not addressed, there would literally be no money left for public protection and services. "Taxpayers are paying for services," said Reed. "They should get those services. . . . It's just going to get worse if we don't get control of these costs."[3]

The Bankruptcy Option

Bankruptcy is the last resort for any individual, business, or government. Filing for Chapter 9 bankruptcy is supposed to give a financially distressed government the time and fiscal breathing room required to develop and negotiate plans for reorganizing debt while protecting the government from its creditors. However, while the option may seem enticing, Chapter 9 bankruptcy can be an expensive and time-consuming process with an uncertain outcome. Any municipality choosing to file for Chapter 9 faces a certain negative impact in the credit market, resulting in increased borrowing costs in the future. Indeed, when Orange County declared bankruptcy in 2004, the municipal-bond market punished not just the county but the entire state, demanding higher interest payments from all California issuers of municipal bonds.

The Orange County Precedent

On December 6, 1994, Orange County made history by becoming the largest municipality ever to declare bankruptcy. Before that time, municipal bankruptcies had been rare. Not since the 1920s and '30s had U.S. muni investors faced the prospect of defaults on general-obligation bonds by a major bond issuer like Orange County, the sixth-largest county in the country. At the time, the Orange County bankruptcy was seen as an anomaly. The county was a victim of new-fangled financial instruments known as derivatives and of the reckless behavior of one man—county treasurer Robert Citron—who played the derivatives market in a failed attempt to boost revenues in the midst of recession. Experts in public finance didn't see the Orange County bankruptcy as a precedent or even as a red flag, given that bondholders wound up being repaid in full. This line of thinking had some merit, but the reality is that bondholders would not have been repaid in full had it not been for a bailout by the state of California. Because the municipal-bond market had responded to the Orange County bankruptcy by punishing all California issuers with higher interest rates, it was actually cheaper for California to bail Orange County out than to continue to pay higher borrowing costs. Eighteen years later, California is in no position to bail anyone out.[4]

November 2011: Jefferson County, Alabama

The Jefferson County Commission filed for the largest municipal bankruptcy in U.S. history in 2011[5]—$4.2 billion in unpaid debt, more than double the size of Orange County's once-record bankruptcy filing. Jefferson County's finances were sunk by a water-and-sewer project that, thanks to graft and engineering blunders, never actually got built despite the county's borrowing and spending billions. Following the 2008 housing-market crash and subsequent loss of triple-A ratings by Financial Guaranty Insurance Company (FGIC) and XL Capital Assurance (companies that insured the bonds), the interest on Jefferson County's variable-rate sewer warrants soared. After struggling for years, the county could not support the tentative deal reached with creditors in September 2011 to immediately begin increasing sewer rates by 8.2 percent annually from their current rate for the first three years. The county's bankruptcy filing resulted in a loss to creditors, higher tax rates for local taxpayers, a dramatic cut in services ranging from police to litter cleanup, and a loss of access to the credit markets. "People are desperate to think of anything they can to get the money," local businessman David Sher told the *New York Times*.[6]

The money won't be coming from the state of Alabama, whose legislature is dealing with a $140 million budget deficit of its own and has so far refused pleas for a bailout akin to Orange County's. "In areas outside Jefferson County, the feeling is why should we 'bail them out' for their poor financial management, for their bribery and kickbacks and for what was a seedy, nefarious indebtedness," Alabama state senator Arthur Orr, a Republican from Huntsville, told the Stateline news service.[7] States just have too many budget problems of their own. In New York, for example, Governor Andrew Cuomo has warned municipalities considering bankruptcy not to expect a lifeline from the state. "Some of them are saying, 'Well, we should look to the state for effectively a bailout,'" Cuomo told an upstate New York talk-radio station in September 2012. "We are not in the position of being an underwriter for local governments . . . and I don't believe we should."[8]

June 2012: Stockton, California

The Jefferson County bankruptcy was more rooted in the water-and-sewer fiasco than in any fallout from the recession or the housing crash. The Stockton bankruptcy, on the other hand, is a perfect example of how the housing boom and bust subverted municipal budget making. It also foreshadows more bankruptcies to come. With 292,000 residents, Stockton is the largest U.S. city ever to file for Chapter 9 protection under the bankruptcy code. It's also one of California's grittier cities—the TV biker drama *Sons of Anarchy* is filmed there—which made Stockton a most unlikely beneficiary of the housing boom. Yet between 2001 and 2006 average home prices in Stockton tripled to $400,000, thanks in large part to a surge in subprime mortgage lending. Flush with new tax revenue, city officials increased spending from $160 million in 2003 to over $200 million in 2007.[9] Along the way, the city made some dreadful fiscal decisions—including the back-loading of debt and the granting of overly generous pension deals to city employees. According to the *Wall Street Journal,* even though California state law requires public employees to contribute between 7 percent and 9 percent of their salary to their pension, Stockton actually agreed to pay workers' contributions for them.[10] To top it all off, Stockton rolled the dice in 2007 on pension-obligation bonds, borrowing $125 million in the bond market only to lose $25 million in the stock-market crash. When the real-estate market crashed too—the average Stockton home price fell 58 percent between 2006 and 2011—the city simply could not reduce spending fast enough to pay its bills. By the time it filed for bankruptcy, Stockton had already cut staff 25 percent in its police department and 30 percent in its fire department.[11] Stockton now has the tenth-highest rate of violent crime in the country, according to Stockton city manager Bob Deis. "We have the second-lowest police staffing levels in the country for a large city," Deis wrote in a *Wall Street Journal* op-ed, "and often Stockton Police can respond only to 'in-progress' crimes."[12]

The city is now locked in an expensive legal battle—as of September 2012, Stockton had spent $4.9 million on lawyers—with two bond-insurance companies that want Stockton to suspend all payments into the CalPERS state-employee pension system and redirect those monies toward bond repayment. The city won a court battle with public-employee unions that objected to the city's postbankruptcy decision to cut all health benefits to retirees while it reorganizes. Says Deis: "We are trying to be responsible in dealing with our creditors, but in the process we cannot destroy a community and its hope for the future."[13]

July 2012: Mammoth Lakes, California

The city of Mammoth Lakes decided to seek Chapter 9 bankruptcy protection after losing a $43 million lawsuit against a real-estate developer, Mammoth Lakes Land Acquisition. The tourist town backed out of the agreement once it realized that the development would thwart city plans to lengthen a runway at the local airport in order to accommodate larger commercial jets. The developer sued the town for breaching the development agreement that was supposed to allow the company to build homes, airplane hangars, and other commercial buildings near the Mammoth Yosemite Airport. The judgment totaled nearly three times the Mammoth Lakes annual budget, a budget already $2.8 million in the red for fiscal year 2011–12.[14]

July 2012: San Bernardino, California

A story not unlike Stockton's, San Bernardino's bankruptcy stemmed from budgetary mismanagement coupled with rising pension and debt costs. Despite having trimmed its public workforce by 20 percent since 2008, San Bernardino faced escalating budgetary pressures due to rising costs associated with the city's union contracts. Facing a $46 million budget gap and $157 million in unfunded pension and health-care obligations, San Bernardino filed for Chapter 9 protection in July 2012. City Attorney James Penman defended the mayor and city council, claiming budget officials had falsified fiscal reports, hiding deficits over a sixteen-year period.[15]

In the cases of both Stockton and San Bernardino, the housing boom encouraged politicians to grant excessive pay and benefits to employees and the bust made those pay and benefit increases untenable. Other municipalities in California are flirting with Chapter 9 bankruptcy as rising pension and health-care costs are beginning to push them over the edge. Atwater, a small California city facing a $3 million deficit, recently declared a "fiscal emergency." (Under California law, before cities can declare bankruptcy they must declare a fiscal emergency and agree to mediation with creditors.) Other municipalities facing mammoth budget deficits include Chicago ($298 million), Los Angeles ($216 million), and the School District of Philadelphia ($218 million).[16]

When a municipality such as Stockton or San Bernardino declares bankruptcy, the largest and first-in-line creditors are state pension funds (though pensions' first-in-line status is now being challenged by Stockton's bond insurers). The irony of course is that it is the retiree obligations that forced these communities into bankruptcy. When San Jose residents voted to cut pension benefits in order to preserve basic social services, the city set a precedent that will be closely watched by other municipalities looking for a way out. Stockton is another potential precedent setter, as it is trying to use Chapter 9 to force bondholders to accept not only less interest but also a reduction in principal. Stockton is the first American city to try this since the 1930s, and what's so scary to those in the municipal-bond community is that market insiders said something like this simply just couldn't happen. Well, it's happening.

There's no right or wrong in all this. A government worker rightly feels entitled to the pension and benefits he or she was promised. A taxpayer rightly feels entitled to the essential social services like quality education, safe streets, clean water, and all the other things his tax dollars are supposed to support. The bondholder certainly believes he has the right to be paid back principal and interest in exchange for the municipality's borrowing his investment dollars. It almost doesn't matter whose claim is most worthy. Just as the private sector eventually realized that businesses could not survive unless radical changes were made to their retirement programs, the public sector is now slowly coming to the same conclusion. Once a state chooses to reform its pension plans, great improvements in fiscal health can be achieved. But the longer states wait to make changes, the greater risk there is that states will run out of money to pay their pensioners. There are a few basic ways to reform pensions, many of which have already been tested by states like Rhode Island. In 2012 Rhode Island took its funded-pension ratio from 48 percent to over 60 percent, reduced its unfunded liability by roughly $3 billion, and thereby saved the state over $4 billion over the next twenty years.[17] Reforms were made with bipartisan support because both Democrats and Republicans understood that in order to save funding for public services, the state needed concessions from unions on pensions and cost-of-living adjustments for both current and future retirees. Rhode Island is a great success story, and more cities and states are following its lead.

Chapter 10

■

The Way Forward

Back in December 2010 I was pilloried in the financial press when I went on *60 Minutes* and warned that there would be fifty to a hundred large municipal-bond defaults. A producer for the CBS news show had been hounding me for weeks, begging me to appear in a segment about the looming state and municipal budget crisis. Steve Kroft had already interviewed New Jersey governor Chris Christie and Illinois state comptroller Dan Hynes, and despite some initial misgivings, I agreed to speak with Kroft about all that was at stake economically. It was a wide-ranging interview. When he asked about municipal-bond defaults, I told him that they were coming and that investors would be wise to ignore conventional wisdom. "When individual investors look to people that are supposed to know better," I told Kroft, "they're patted on the head and told, 'It's not something you need to worry about.' It'll be something to worry about within the next twelve months."[1]

Muni bond defaults did increase 400 percent in 2011, to $25 billion from $5 billion in 2010, according to the *Distressed Debt Securities* newsletter.[2] But for the record, I never said those fifty to a hundred defaults would all happen in 2011, which was how my critics spun the story. Kroft had not even asked me for a time frame. He wanted to tell the story of the state and local budget crisis, and what I told him was that the crisis would become a big deal—"something to worry about"—within twelve months.

Twelve months after the *60 Minutes* story aired, I wasn't the only one worrying. A headline from the December 20, 2010, issue of *Businessweek* blared: "New Govs Take Office Amid Historic Budget Crisis."[3] *Time Magazine*, January 20, 2011: "Can Drastic Measures Save the Cash-Strapped States?"[4] Associated Press, January 15, 2011: "Year Ahead Looms as Toughest Yet for State Budgets."[5] *Bloomberg News*, January 19, 2011: "U.S. Mayors Say City Bond Defaults Likely Amid Strain."[6] A January 10, 2011 *National Journal* story asked, "Is [California's] budget crisis even solvable?"[7] In December 2012 Detroit became the latest city to flirt with bankruptcy. Given the scope of Detroit's fiscal problems—a $327 million deficit and $12 billion in accumulated debt[8]—the city's best hope is probably a state takeover and the appointment of an emergency manager. "It is likely the only option to avoid bankruptcy, as the city's expenses continue to outpace revenue," city council president Gary Brown wrote in an e-mail to constituents.[9]

The truth is, more municipalities are debating whether to follow the lead of Stockton, Mammoth Lakes, and San Bernardino and simply walk away from their financial debts in favor of maintaining police, firefighters, low student-to-teacher ratios, and the like. These are tough questions. How bad does it have to get for voters to stand up against the diminished public services they're getting for their hard-earned tax dollars? When do people say "no more" to skyrocketing crime rates because the police force had to be cut in order to afford a retired chief's $200,000-a-year pension? How long before taxpayers refuse to honor their obligations to the bond investors who loaned their communities money? At what point do Americans turn against their own teachers, police officers, and other public servants, arguing that an employee's negotiated right to a generous pension simply cannot take precedence over safe streets or a child's right to a quality education?

For some, defaulting may turn out to be the least bad option. It's not unlike what happened in the housing market, when underwater homeowners dropped mortgage payments from the top to the bottom of their bill-paying priority list. Municipal bankruptcies, writes Michael Corkery of the *Wall Street Journal*, "are reminiscent of the strategic defaults seen during the financial crisis when many homeowners, overwhelmed with spiraling debts, mailed house keys to lenders and stopped paying their mortgages—a trend know as 'jingle mail.'" The stigmas that once surrounded mortgage default and now municipal bankruptcy have faded. Even the rating agencies acknowledge they might have to change how they evaluate default risk for muni bonds. As the chief credit officer for public-sector ratings at Moody's said, "As the stigma around bankruptcy erodes, we are revisiting our long held assumption about the willingness of some cities to repay debt."[10]

Truth be told, that willingness was always in doubt. In 1994 Orange County became the largest municipal bankruptcy in U.S. history, and anyone who followed the Orange County story knew how little obligation voters felt toward general-obligation bondholders. Before the state stepped in with its bailout, James Lebenthal—founder of New York muni-bond firm Lebenthal & Co.—took a film crew with him to Orange County to interview locals about their perceived obligations to investors. Lebenthal said afterward that he was "distressed" to discover that most Orange County residents felt no moral obligation to approve a sales-tax hike in order to repay what was owed on the county's debt. "I don't know who will make up the deficit," one woman told Lebenthal, "but I really don't think it should be the citizens."[11]

Defaults and bankruptcies are important stories, but they remain mere symptoms of and sideshows to something much bigger and more important. A geographic sea change is occurring in the United States, with economic power shifting away from longtime coastal strongholds—states still hung over from the housing bust—and toward the more "fiscally attractive" central corridor. These so-called flyover states contributed 25 percent of U.S. GDP in 2011, up from 23 percent in 1999. A two-percentage-point increase may not sound like a lot, but it's huge—$300 billion in GDP.[12]

With such a large head start in the recovery, the central corridor should continue to drive the U.S. economy for years and even decades to come. Some of this has to do with the commodities boom and the fact that these states are embracing energy production at a time when states like California and New York are saying no. In fact, folks in other parts of the world would be glad if more U.S. states followed New York and California's lead. "We Europeans are currently paying up to four or five times more for natural gas than the Americans," said Harald Schwager, an executive board member for European chemical maker BASF. "Of course, that means increased competition for all the European manufacturing sites." BASF's solution: Invest more in the United States.[13]

Along with cheap energy, the central corridor is benefiting from the boom in agriculture. And while agriculture has historically been quite cyclical, demand for U.S. crops is stronger than ever. And more global too. Urbanization, modernization, and population growth in the third world have dramatically increased global food demand. In order to meet demand, U.S. grain exports are expected to increase 28 percent by 2021, according to the U.S. Department of Agriculture.[14] The economic impact back home is already significant, as corn prices have soared from two dollars to seven dollars a bushel since 2006. A report from the Chicago Federal Reserve in August 2012 showed a 15 percent increase in farmland prices over the prior twelve months across Iowa, Illinois, Indiana, Wisconsin, and Michigan. A similar report from the Kansas City Fed showed a 26 percent gain. While agriculture these days employs a lot fewer people today than it did a hundred or even fifty years ago, higher land values do enrich communities and bolster consumer spending. "I'll probably upgrade a couple tractors myself," Minnesota farmer Gerald Tumbleson said back in 2007, when the corn boom first started to take off. "I'll use a little more fertilizer this year too."[15] No wonder spending growth tracks 30 percent higher in the central corridor versus the coasts. Higher land prices and more consumer spending are good for state and local tax receipts too. It's a virtuous circle: More jobs, more spending, and more housing demand beget a larger tax base and better public services—which attracts new jobs and pushes home prices ever higher.

Many towns and cities throughout the central corridor don't have enough workers to fill all the available jobs. If they do, sometimes there's no place to house them. Home prices in North Dakota are up 17 percent over the past five years, which is one of the highest in the nation but also reflective of the state's severe housing shortage.[16] Housing demand in North Dakota is being driven by the need for living quarters, not by easy credit or get-rich-quick speculation. "Man camps" and "tent camps" are being used as temporary housing for workers from Odessa, Texas, to Williston, North Dakota.[17] Companies like Target Logistics that fill the temporary-housing void are fast becoming big business. The growth of companies like Target Logistics hints at a significant multiplier effect. More jobs and more people mean more demand for stores, movie theaters, restaurants, and, yes, banks. Bank consolidation will be most prolific in this region in coming years, as the growing credit needs of a booming economy create demand for superregional banks—none of which exist in the region today.

The cities and states of the central corridor will step up their investments in the kind of infrastructure most likely to attract business, and they'll have the tax revenues to do it. Duluth, Minnesota, just finished construction on a new $78 million airport.[18] Wichita Falls, Texas, has broken ground on a new $100 million terminal.[19] And Texas recently opened a new $1.3 billion toll road connecting

Austin and San Antonio.[20] These are the kinds of investments likely to attract even more new businesses. The central-corridor states are better able to cut taxes too. As of January 2013 six of these states were considering cuts to state income-tax rates, and a seventh—Kansas—had dropped its top rate from 6.45 percent to 4.9 percent. In neighboring Missouri, Kansas's aggressive tax cutting sparked fears of a westward jobs exodus. "I do think it's hard to be anywhere near Kansas right now," said Amy Blouin, executive director of the Missouri Budget Project, a St. Louis–based nonprofit group that analyzes state spending.[21]

For the housing-bust states there are no easy fixes. Budgets at every level of government are so strained that there can be no repeats of the bailouts Orange County received from the state of California in 1995 or New York City solicited from the federal government in 1975. The damage is done, but hope is not all lost. Since 2010 thirty-six new governors have been elected with broad mandates for change. Many of them probably didn't realize how much of their terms would be shaped by triagelike budget decisions necessary to preserve the solvency of their state finances. Few of them could have imagined that they would have to tackle the politically toxic issues of deep budget cuts and pension reform. Fewer still likely realized that they would have to choose between honoring labor contracts and bond covenants and providing basic services to constituents. The key question all governors face is when to expend political capital for longer-term gains—gains that might not even be fully realized until after they've left office. Willingness or unwillingness to take political risks and make tough decisions increasingly will determine which states dig themselves out of their fiscal holes and which become the twenty-first-century economic heirs of Lowell, Detroit, and Mississippi.

Ultimately no amount of cost cutting or entitlement reform will be enough without a rebound in revenues, and new revenues will have to come from job creation. Job one for any governor or big-city mayor has to be attracting human capital and jobs that contribute to the tax base. Raising taxes to uncompetitive rates is simply not going to work because it's just too easy these days for businesses and taxpayers to pick up stakes. Perhaps twenty years ago paying a big premium to live in California might have been reasonable—there's the great weather, good schools, beaches, mountains, redwood forests, and on and on. But today that premium is just too high. Californians aren't getting enough for their taxes and mortgage payments. With the money they save by moving out of state, they can afford ample vacations to Disneyland and Yosemite.

How can governors create more good jobs in a bad economy? One good example comes from North Carolina and its former governor Beverly Perdue. In 2009 Perdue used $13 million in ARRA money to launch the state's JobsNOW "12 in 6" job-training program. Operated out of the state's fifty-seven community colleges, the program aimed to provide up to six months of training in one of twelve different in-demand fields ranging from health care to manufacturing. A 2011 study by the North Carolina Community College System found that people who completed the course work increased their quarterly income by an average of $415. For those who chose health-care training, the increase was $700.[22] Overall the state added eighty thousand new jobs and $16 billion in new investment during Perdue's tenure. Other initiatives states should consider to restart job growth include opening up oil and gas production, passing right-to-work laws, and, whenever possible, cutting personal and corporate income taxes. There are legitimate political arguments to be made against all of these, but the simple reality is that states are engaged in a bare-knuckle fight for jobs and these happen to be the issues employers care about.

Winning back jobs for states and cities also means finally fixing the fiscal problems and making the tough decisions others had put off for years. There are solutions to the budget woes of the housing-bust states. The challenge is getting voters and unions to accept them. When it comes to state and municipal budgets, compromise has become a game of high-stakes chicken. Most elected officials want to avoid tough choices that in the near term might cost political support. That puts taxpayers at a disadvantage because public-employee unions are disinclined to compromise. Politicians have no explicit obligation to fight for the financial interests of taxpayers, but union leaders do have such a duty to their members. Take a look at the member handbook of the National Education Association, the big teachers' union. One clearly articulated NEA goal is "to preserve and expand collective bargaining rights for education employees and to improve members' compensation and benefits (including pension and health care benefits)."[23]

Teachers and other public-sector employees want what was

promised to them, but suddenly voters are pressuring politicians to fight as hard for their interests as unions fight for their members. And what voters and taxpayers want is good public services with the lowest tax burden possible—a goal incompatible with the mission of public-employee unions. In the private sector the threat of layoffs and business failure has been unions' biggest incentive to compromise. Perhaps a similar dynamic will promote compromise with the public-employee unions. In Central Falls, Rhode Island, the unions would have been better off taking the deal on the table before the city filed for bankruptcy. Since 2010 the ranks of state and local government workers have declined by almost seven hundred thousand; state spending growth is decelerating nationally and declining in many of the populous coastal and Sun Belt states. The issue of willingness to pay bondholders and pensioners is now coming to the forefront of the debate in local politics. Citizens—even prounion ones—are demanding an end to cuts. "In a liberal city, in a blue state, I got a near 70% yes vote," said Reed, the San Jose mayor, of the pension reform vote he thinks will become a national model. "There has to be something here."[24]

Pensions and retirement benefits are the key to fixing state and local finances, but there are smaller steps that can be taken too. Shared services is one such example. Everybody likes the idea of having their own local police department. The town of Mamaroneck, New York, actually has three—one police force for the town, one for the village of Mamaroneck (a district within the town's borders), and one for the village of Larchmont (another district). Of course, having three separate police forces for a town of 19,000 makes little fiscal sense. A Grant Thornton study found that nearby Nassau County, New York, could save millions of dollars a year by streamlining the police force under one reporting structure (down from four), which in turn would lead to better monitoring and lower overtime pay (including scheduling shifts in accordance with actual crime patterns) as well as the consolidation of procurement and other back-office functions. Outsourcing and privatization are other options. In 2008 the town of Molalla, Oregon, spent $507,973 on employee salaries and other expenses to handle building permits, inspections, and other construction-related regulation. After outsourcing most of these duties, the town was spending only $150,000 a year for the same work. All of this requires political will, but these are the low-hanging fruit available to governors, mayors, and other local lawmakers.[25]

Despite so many dreary economic headlines, the potential still exists for a powerful recovery in the United States. Manufacturing is bouncing back, adding some five hundred thousand new jobs since 2010. The growth rate of our biggest economic rival, China, continues to slow, and Europe seems stuck in a Japan-in-the-2000s-style malaise. Domestic oil and gas production is increasing for the first time in over twenty years. We now boast the lowest natural-gas prices in the world, which is a giant magnet to global manufacturers. Clearly there's a lot to like. However, if states don't have the money to build business-friendly infrastructure and to educate and train their people, their communities will suffer because of it. The real-estate industry that transformed the nation over the past thirty-plus years has now left much of it weakened, sparing only those states that it ignored during the bubble. The damage can be fixed, so long as states get serious about digging themselves out of debt. Good leaders acting quickly is the only hope for the worst-off states, for they've been left with the smallest margins of error. As my grandfather used to say, you can't expect to make a lot of money if you owe a lot too.

Acknowledgments

This book was born out of my love of history and my deep appreciation for all of the advantages that living in America has given me. Although I have written prolifically for years, I never had any intention of writing a book. All of that changed one night over dinner in New York with Michael Ovitz and Andy Walter. I credit Michael not only with convincing me to write a book but also with introducing me to Adrian Zackheim, the publisher of this book. He, Niki Papadopoulos, and the team at Portfolio were excellent partners throughout the process and I thank them for that. For a first-time author, patience is a scarce commodity. Adrian had enough patience for both of us. Thank you also to Bob Barnett at Williams & Connolly.

On the research side, Angela Cantu, Marc Lombardo, Brittani Caetano, and the rest of the MWAG team have been invaluable. Brittani, you are wise well beyond your years. Thank you.

This book benefited greatly from the cooperation and contribution of the people on the front line of state issues. Thanks go to the governors, mayors, and other representatives who were so gracious with their time: Mitch Daniels, Rick Scott, Mary Fallin, Terry

Branstad, as well as Gina Raimondo, Chuck Reed, Edward P. Mangano, Susan Combs, and so many more.

Thank you to Jon Birger, the excellent writer who helped get me over the finish line.

Mom, I cannot thank you enough for all of the wonderful encouragement you have always given me.

Lavelle Layfield was both supportive and constructive with his feedback.

Leigh Gallagher and Shawn Tully, thank you for all of your smart, sage, and extremely generous feedback. You are dear friends. Maria Bartiromo, one of the hardest-working people I know, thank you for both your support and friendship.

I am so very grateful for the consistent support and example of Ken Wilson, Diane Taylor, Ed Herlihy, Tom Hoenig, Rich Handler, Molly Ashby, Jim Robinson III, Ken Langone, Rodgin Cohen, and Michael Lewis.

Finally, to my husband, John Layfield, who is exhaustively curious and makes me smarter every day.

Notes

Introduction

1. Michiyo Nakamoto and David Wighton, "Citigroup Chief Stays Bullish on Buy-outs," *Financial Times*, July 9, 2007, http://www.ft.com/intl/cms/s/0/80e2987a-2e50-11dc-821c-0000779fd2ac.html#axzz2JwvzZCZO.
2. Steve Rosenbush, "Citi: That Sinking Feeling," *Bloomberg Businessweek*, November 1, 2007, http://www.businessweek.com/stories/2007-11-01/citi-that-sinking-feelingbusinessweek-business-news-stock-market-and-financial-advice.
3. Corey Hajim and Adam Lashinsky, "How Bear Stearns Lost Its Way," *CNNMoney*, August 21, 2007, http://money.cnn.com/2007/08/20/magazines/fortune/bear_stearns.fortune/index.htm.
4. Credit Writedowns and Global Macro Advisors LLC, "Credit Crisis Timeline," *Credit Writedowns*, 2009, http://www.creditwritedowns.com/credit-crisis-timeline/.
5. Susan Burhouse and Yazmin Osaki, Federal Deposit Insurance Corporation, "2011 FDIC National Survey of Unbanked and Underbanked Households," September 2012, http://www.fdic.gov/householdsurvey/2012_unbankedreport.pdf.
6. Federal Housing Finance Agency, "City HPI Data, MSA HPI Comparisons," 2012, http://www.fhfa.gov/Default.aspx?Page=216&Type=compare&Area1=11180&Area2=27260&Area3=38060.

7. U.S. Department of Labor, Bureau of Labor Statistics, "Historical State Unemployment Rate Maps," http://www.bls.gov/lau/maps/stseries.pdf; U.S. Census Bureau, "Quarterly Summary of State and Local Taxes," table 3: "Historical State Tax Collections by State," http://www.census .gov/govs/qtax/table_3.html.

8. William La Jeunesse, "California Residents, Businesses Consider Bailing on Golden State over Taxes," *FoxNews.com*, January 23, 2013, http://www .foxnews.com/politics/2013/01/23/california-residents-businesses -consider-bailing-on-golden-state-over-taxes/.

9. Monica Davey, "Questions Persisting as Illinois Raises Taxes," *New York Times*, January 12, 2011, http://www.nytimes.com/2011/01/13/us/ 13illinois.html?_r=0.

10. U.S. Department of Labor, Bureau of Labor Statistics, "Historical State Unemployment Rate Maps," http://www.bls.gov/lau/maps/stseries.pdf.

11. Steven Greenhouse, "Tentative Pact for City Teachers Increases Pay, and Workweek," *New York Times*, June 11, 2002, http://www.nytimes.com/ 2002/06/11/nyregion/tentative-pact-for-city-teachers-increases-pay-and -workweek.html.

12. Kenneth C. Wolensky, "Barbara T. Zolli on 'A Drop of Oil,'" *Pennsylvania Heritage*, 35, no. 2 (spring 2009), http://www.portal.state.pa.us/portal/ server.pt/community/history/4569/drake_well__oil150/471308.

Chapter 1: It Starts at Home

1. World Trade Organization, "International Trade and Market Access Data," http://www.wto.org/english/res_e/statis_e/statis_e.htm; U.S. Energy Information Administration, "Countries: Overview," http://www.eia .gov/countries/; United States Department of Agriculture, Foreign Agricultural Service, "Frequently Asked Questions About Agricultural Trade," http://www.fas.usda.gov/itp/Policy/tradeFAQ.asp.

2. Michelle V. Rafter, "Manufacturing Jobs Making a Comeback in Southern U.S.," *NBC News*, December 20, 2012, http://www.nbcnews.com/

business/manufacturing-jobs-making-comeback-southern-u-s-
1C7660234.

3. Eugene R. Dattel, "Cotton in a Global Economy: Mississippi (1800–
1860)," *Mississippi History Now*, October 2006, http://mshistorynow
.mdah.state.ms.us/articles/161/cotton-in-a-global-economy-mississippi
-1800-1860.

4. "America the History of Us, Episode 4: Division," *History.com*, http://
www.history.com/shows/america-the-story-of-us/articles/episode-4-divi
sion; Heidi Ridgley, "An Industrial Revolution," *National Parks*, Spring
2009 Issue, http://www.npca.org/news/magazine/all-issues/2009/spring/
an-industrial-revolution.html.

5. Amanda Ripley, "Kerry's Massachusetts: The Not So Favorite Son," *Time*,
August 2, 2004, http://www.time.com/time/printout/0,8816,994770,00
.html; History of Lowell, Massachusetts, Wikipedia, http://en.wikipedia
.org/wiki/History_of_Lowell,_Massachusetts.

6. Chris Isidore, "GM Bankruptcy: End of an Era," *CNNMoney.com*,
June 2, 2009, http://money.cnn.com/2009/06/01/news/companies/gm_
bankruptcy/.

7. U.S. Census Bureau, State Government Tax Collections, "2011 Annual
Survey of State Government Tax Collections," http://www2.census.gov/
govs/statetax/2011stcreport.pdf; U.S. Department of Commerce, Bureau of Economic Analysis, Regional Data: GDP and Personal Income,
Gross Domestic Product by State, http://www.bea.gov/iTable/iTable
.cfm?reqid=70&step=1&isuri=1&acrdn=1#reqid=70&step=1&isuri=1.

8. Meredith Whitney Advisory Group, "Tragedy of the Commons Third
Edition: 2012 Update"; U.S. Department of Commerce, U.S. Census
Bureau, "Quarterly Summary of State and Local Taxes," table 3: "Historical State Tax Collections by State," http://www.census.gov/govs/qtax/
table_3.html.

9. William H. Frey, "The Great American Migration Slowdown: Regional
and Metropolitan Dimensions," Brookings Institution, Metropolitan
Policy Program, December 2009, http://www.brookings.edu/~/media/

research/files/opinions/2011/1/12%20migration%20frey/1209_migra
tion_frey.pdf.

10. Wendell Cox, "The Export Business in California (People and Jobs),"
Fox & Hounds, May 11, 2012, http://www.foxandhoundsdaily.com/2012/
05/the-export-business-in-california-people-and-jobs/.

Chapter 2: Housing Revisited

1. Library of Congress, Primary Documents in American History, "Homestead Act," http://www.loc.gov/rr/program/bib/ourdocs/Homestead.html.

2. Mary Evans, "Better Homes in America/Making Bricks with 1st Grad-
ers," *National Archives, Hoover Blackboard*, October 15, 2010, http://
blogs.archives.gov/hoover-blackboard/2010/10/15/better-homes-in
-america/; Wenli Li and Fang Yang, "American Dream or American Ob-
session?: The Economic Benefits and Costs of Homeownership," Federal Reserve Bank of Philadelphia, 2010, http://www.philadelphiafed.org/
research-and-data/publications/business-review/2010/q3/brq310_benefits-
and-costs-of-homeownership.pdf; Eduardo Porter, "Buy a Home, and
Drag Society Down," *New York Times*, November 13, 2005, http://www
.nytimes.com/2005/11/13/weekinreview/13port.html.

3. Dennis Cauchon, "Why Home Values May Take Decades to Recover,"
USA Today, December 15, 2008, http://usatoday30.usatoday.com/money/
economy/housing/2008-12-12-homeprices_N.htm.

4. U.S. Department of Commerce, U.S. Census Bureau, "Historical Census of Housing Tables," 2011, http://www.census.gov/hhes/www/housing/
census/historic/owner.html.; U.S. Department of Commerce, U.S. Census Bureau, *U.S. Census Bureau News*, January 29, 2013, http://www.cen
sus.gov/housing/hvs/files/qtr412/q412press.pdf.

5. Paul Sullivan, "Despite Critics, Mortgage Deduction Resists Change,"
New York Times, November 8, 2011, http://www.nytimes.com/2011/11/
09/your-money/despite-critics-mortgage-interest-deduction-persists
.html?pagewanted=all&_r=0.

6. Dan Andrews and Aida Caldera Sanchez, OECD, "The Evolution of Homeownership Rates in Selected OECD Countries: Demographic and Public Policy Influences," *OECD Journal: Economic Studies*, http://www.oecd.org/eco/growth/evolution%20of%20homeownership%20rates.pdf; Nation Master, People Statistics: Home Ownership by Country, http://www.nationmaster.com/graph/peo_hom_own-people-home-ownership.

7. Mark J. Perry, "Due North: Canada's Marvelous Mortgage and Banking System," *American*, February 26, 2010, http://www.american.com/archive/2010/february/due-north-canadas-marvelous-mortgage-and-banking-system.

8. Federal Housing Finance Agency, Office of the Inspector General, "History of the Government Sponsored Enterprises," http://fhfaoig.gov/LearnMore/History.

9. U.S. Department of Commerce, U.S. Census Bureau, "Housing Vacancies and Homeownership (CPS/HVS): 2012," table 5: "Homeownership Rates for the United States: 1968 to 2012," http://www.census.gov/housing/hvs/files/qtr312/tab5.xls.

10. Federal Housing Finance Agency, Office of the Inspector General, "History of the Government Sponsored Enterprises," http://fhfaoig.gov/Content/Files/History%20of%20the%20Government%20Sponsored%20Enterprises.pdf.

11. Alan S. Blinder and Ricardo Reis, "Understanding the Greenspan Standard," prepared for the Federal Reserve Bank of Kansas City symposium, The Greenspan Era: Lessons for the Future, August 4, 2005, http://www.kc.frb.org/publicat/sympos/2005/pdf/blinderreis.paper.0804.pdf.

12. Alan Greenspan, "Understanding Household Debt Obligations," remarks at the Credit Union National Association 2004 Governmental Affairs Conference, Washington, D.C., February 23, 2004, http://www.federalreserve.gov/boarddocs/speeches/2004/20040223/.

13. Christopher Mayer, Karen Pence, and Shane M. Sherlund, "The Rise in Mortgage Defaults," *Journal of Economic Perspectives* 23, no. 1 (Winter

2009): 27–50, http://dss.ucsd.edu/~grondina/pdfs/week2_mayer_risemort gagedefaults.pdf; Kelly Edmiston, "Foreclosures: A Closer Look at Nebraska and the Region" (paper presented at the Banker's Roundtable on Community Development, University of Nebraska, Lincoln, NE, September 18, 2007), http://www.kansascityfed.org/speechbio/speeches/Fore closuresNE.pdf.

14. Sue Kirchhoff and Barbara Hagenbaugh, "Greenspan Says ARMs Might Be Better Deal," *USA Today*, February 24, 2004, http://usato day30.usatoday.com/money/economy/fed/2004-02-23-greenspan-debt_ x.htm.

15. Sheila Bair, interview by members of *Fortune* editorial staff, New York, January 17, 2008.

16. Data from CoreLogic Loan Performance Database and Federal Housing Finance Board, "Monthly Interest Rate Survey"; Yuliya Demyanyk and Otto Van Hemert, "Understanding the Subprime Mortgage Crisis," Federal Reserve Bank of St. Louis (Supervisory Policy Analysis Working Paper 2007-05, August 2008), http://www.stlouisfed.org/banking/pdf/SPA/ SPA_2007_05.pdf.

17. James R. Barth, Tong Li, Wenling Lu, Triphon Phumiwasana, and Glenn Yago, Milken Institute, "The Rise and Fall of the U.S. Mortgage and Credit Markets," January 2009, http://www.milkeninstitute.org/pdf/Rise andfallexcerpt.pdf; "Top Residential Originators in Q2 07," *National Mortgage News*, September 10, 2007, http://www.nationalmortgagenews .com/nmn_issues/31_49/-448295-1.html.

18. Associated Press, "Wachovia Acquires Golden West Financial," *NBC News.com*, May 8, 2006, http://www.nbcnews.com/id/12680868/#.UQ_ 5kR3Ac9U.

19. Christopher Palmeri, "JPMorgan Chase to Buy Washington Mutual," *Bloomberg Businessweek*, September 26, 2008, http://www.business week.com/stories/2008-09-26/jpmorgan-chase-to-buy-washington -mutualbusinessweek-business-news-stock-market-and-financial-advice.

20. Eric Dash, "BB&T Takes Over Failing Colonial BancGroup," *New York Times*, August 14, 2009, http://www.nytimes.com/2009/08/15/business/15bank.html.

21. Dan Fitzpatrick, "BofA's Blunder: $40 Billion-Plus," *Wall Street Journal*, July 1, 2012, http://online.wsj.com/article/SB1000142405270230356 1504577495332947870736.html.

22. U.S. Department of Housing and Urban Development, "The National Homeownership Strategy: Partners in the American Dream," May 1995, http://www.globalurban.org/National_Homeownership_Strategy.pdf; Peter Coy, "Bill Clinton's Drive to Increase Homeownership Went Way Too Far," *Bloomberg Businessweek*, February 27, 2008, http://www.businessweek.com/the_thread/hotproperty/archives/2008/02/clintons_drive.html.

23. Dean Baker, "The Housing Bubble and What Greenspan Should Have Done," Center for Economic and Policy Research, January 11, 2012, http://www.cepr.net/index.php/op-eds-&-columns/op-eds-&-columns/the-housing-bubble-and-what-greenspan-should-have-done.

24. Kathryn J. Byun, "The U.S. Housing Bubble and Bust: Impacts on Employment," *Monthly Labor Review*, December 2010, http://www.bls.gov/opub/mlr/2010/12/art1full.pdf.

25. U.S. Department of Commerce, U.S. Census Bureau, Housing Vacancies and Homeownership: Historical Tables, table 14: Homeownership Rates for the U.S. and Regions: 1965 to Present, http://www.census.gov/housing/hvs/data/histtabs.html, http://www.census.gov/housing/hvs/data/histtab14.xls.

26. Federal Housing Finance Agency, House Price Indexes, State HPI Comparisons, http://www.fhfa.gov/Default.aspx?Page=215&Type=compare&Area1=CA&Area2=FL&Area3=; Federal Housing Finance Agency, Downloadable Data, Purchase Only Indexes: U.S. Summary through 2012Q4, http://www.fhfa.gov/Default.aspx?Page=87, http://www.fhfa.gov/webfiles/24974/4q12POSummary.xls.

27. Homeownership rates data from U.S. Department of Commerce, U.S. Census Bureau, The 2012 Statistical Abstract, Construction and Housing: Homeownership and Housing Costs, http://www.census.gov/com pendia/statab/2012/tables/12s0993.pdf; unemployment data from U.S. Department of Labor, Bureau of Labor Statistics, Archived News Releases|Regional and State Employment and Unemployment, year 1994 and 2006, http://www.bls.gov/schedule/archives/laus_nr.htm; GDP data from U.S. Department of Commerce, Bureau of Economic Analysis, Regional Data: GDP and Personal Income, Gross Domestic Product by State, http://www.bea.gov/iTable/iTable.cfm?reqid=70&step=1&isuri=1& acrdn=1#reqid=70&step=1&isuri=1.

28. Meredith Whitney Advisory Group; Federal Reserve Bank of New York, "Household Debt and Credit Report: Historical Reports," http://www .newyorkfed.org/research/national_economy/householdcredit/county_ report_by_year.xlsx.

29. Rachel Baye, "MontCo Lawmakers Criticize Schools for Using Surplus on Pay, Not Classes," *Examiner,* May 16, 2012, http://washingtonexam-iner.com/montco-lawmakers-criticize-schools-for-using-surplus-on-pay -not-classes/article/619171#.UFiw96SXQxI.

30. U.S. Department of Commerce, U.S. Census Bureau, State Government Finances, Historical Data: 2000, "Summary Table," http://www .census.gov//govs/state/historical_data_2000.html; U.S. Department of Commerce, U.S. Census Bureau, State Government Finances, Historical Data: 2010, "Summary Table," http://www.census.gov//govs/state/his torical_data_2010.html.

31. U.S. Department of Commerce, Bureau of Economic Analysis, "Regional Economic Accounts: GDP and Personal Income," http:// www.bea.gov/iTable/iTable.cfm?reqid=70&step=1&isuri=1&acrdn= 1#reqid=70&step=1&isuri=1/; U.S. Department of Labor, Bureau of Labor Statistics, Archived News Releases|Regional and State Employment and Unemployment, http://www.bls.gov/schedule/archives/laus_ nr.htm.

32. Katalina M. Bianco, "The Subprime Lending Crisis: Causes and Effects of the Mortgage Meltdown," *CCH*, 2008, http://www.business.cch.com/bankingfinance/focus/news/Subprime_WP_rev.pdf.

33. Federal Housing Finance Agency, news release, February 26, 2013, http://www.fhfa.gov/webfiles/25010/2012Q4HPI.pdf; Federal Housing Finance Agency, Historical HPI:Cities, http://www.fhfa.gov/webfiles/24979/4q12hpicbsapo.txt.

34. Federal Housing Finance Agency, Downloadable Data, Purchase Only Indexes: U.S. Summary through 2012Q4, http://www.fhfa.gov/Default.aspx?Page=87, http://www.fhfa.gov/webfiles/24974/4q12POSummary.xls.

35. Ben S. Bernanke, "Challenges in Housing and Mortgage Markets," Operation HOPE Global Financial Dignity Summit, November 15, 2012, http://www.federalreserve.gov/newsevents/speech/bernanke20121115a.htm.

36. Kevin Landrigan, "Recession Hit NH, NE Hardest in '90s," *Nashua Telegraph*, December 27, 2010, http://www.nhpolicy.org/news/recession_hit_nh_ne_hardest.pdf; Federal Housing Finance Agency, "House Price Index: State HPI Comparisons," http://www.fhfa.gov/Default.aspx?Page=215&Type=compare&Area1=NH&Area2=&Area3=; U.S. Department of Labor, Bureau of Labor Statistics, Archived News Releases|Regional and State Employment and Unemployment, http://www.bls.gov/schedule/archives/laus_nr.htm.

37. Christopher Chantrill, "Compare State and Local Spending," *USGovernmentSpending.com*, http://www.usgovernmentspending.com/compare_state_spending_2012bF0a.

38. Federal Deposit Insurance Corporation, Statistics on Banking, http://www2.fdic.gov/SDI/SOB/.

Chapter 3: States Gone Wild

1. Governmental Accounting Standards Board of the Financial Accounting Foundation, "GASB Reconciles Disclosure Requirements for

Governmental Pension and OPEB Reporting," June 2007, http://www
.gasb.org/cs/BlobServer?blobkey=id&blobwhere=1175820457306&blob
header=application%2Fpdf&blobcol=urldata&blobtable=MungoBlobs.

2. John Cornyn, "Sen. John Cornyn Says 49 States Have a Balanced Budget Amendment in Their State Constituitions," December 1, 2010,
http://www.politifact.com/texas/statements/2010/dec/25/john-cornyn/
sen-john-cornyn-says-49-states-have-balanced-budge/; National Governors Association and National Association of State Budget Officers,
"The Fiscal Survey of States," Fall 2012, http://www.nasbo.org/sites/de
fault/files/Fall%202012%20Fiscal%20Survey%20of%20States.pdf.

3. Laura Myers, "Legislation Aims to Aid Mentally Ill in Nevada," *Las Vegas Review-Journal*, January 27, 2013, http://www.lvrj.com/news/legisla
tion-aims-to-aid-mentally-ill-in-nevada-188558511.html; Scott Waldman,
"SUNY Fee Idea Off the Table," *Times Union*, January 11, 2013, http://
www.timesunion.com/local/article/SUNY-fee-idea-off-the-table
-4187351.php; "Washington's Per-Student Investment Continues to Decline Compared to Other States," *Lake Stevens Journal*, January 14, 2013,
http://www.lakestevensjournal.com/county-state/article.exm/
2013-01-14_washington_s_per_student_investment_continues_to_de
cline_compared_to_other_states.

4. Elizabeth McNichol, "Out of Balance: Cuts in Services Have Been
States' Primary Response to Budget Gaps, Harming the Nation's Economy," Center on Budget and Policy Priorities, April 18, 2012, http://
www.cbpp.org/cms/index.cfm?fa=view&id=3747.

5. U.S. Department of Commerce, U.S. Census Bureau, State and Local
Government Finances, "State and Local Government Finance Summary Report," http://www.census.gov/govs/estimate/.

6. U.S. Department of Commerce, U.S. Census Bureau, "State Government Finances: Historical Data: 2010," http://www.census.gov/govs/state/
historical_data_2010.html; U.S. Department of Commerce, U.S. Census Bureau, "State Government Finances: Historical Data: 2000," http://
www.census.gov/govs/state/historical_data_2000.html.

7. Laura Kinsler, "State Budget Provides $1 Million for Lacoochee Club," *Tampa Tribune*, April 18, 2012, http://www2.tbo.com/news/politics/2012/apr/18/1/panewso1-state-funding-for-county-survives-ar-393605/.

8. U.S. Department of Commerce, U.S. Census Bureau, "State Government Tax Collections: 2008 Annual Survey of State Government Tax Collections," http://www.census.gov/govs/statetax/historical_data_2008.html.

9. Dan Atkinson, "Dollars Don't Measure New Newton North High School's Full Cost," *Wicked Local Newton*, June 2, 2010, http://www.wickedlocal.com/newton/news/x709124874/Dollars-dont-measure-new-Newton-North-High-Schools-true-cost?zc_p= 0#axzz2Kq0GCUpw.

10. U.S. Department of Commerce, U.S. Census Bureau, "State Government Tax Collections: 2009 Annual Survey of State Government Tax Collections," http://www.census.gov/govs/statetax/historical_data_2009.html; U.S. Department of Commerce, Bureau of Economic Analysis..

11. Michael Cooper, "Recession Tightens Grip on State Tax Revenues," *New York Times*, February 22, 2010, http://www.nytimes.com/2010/02/23/us/23states.html.

12. Reuters, "State Budgets Spring New, Smaller Holes," May 24, 2012; Phil Oliff, Chris Mai, and Vincent Palacios, "States Continue to Feel Recession's Impact," Center on Budget and Policy Priorities, June 27, 2012; U.S. Department of Education, "Condition of Education 2012."

13. *Public School Forum's Friday Report* 14, no. 40 (April 5, 2012), http://www.ncforum.org/doclib/2012_0405.pdf.

14. Allysia Finley, "California Prison Academy: Better Than a Harvard Degree," *Wall Street Journal*, April 30, 2011, http://online.wsj.com/article/SB10001424052748704132204576285471510530398.html.

15. "Income for Life," *CNNMoney*, http://cgi.money.cnn.com/tools/annuities/.

16. Steven Malanga, "How Stockton, California Went Broke in Plain Sight," *Wall Street Journal*, March 30, 2012, http://online.wsj.com/article/SB10001424052702303404704577309231747497906.html.

17. Mary Williams Walsh, "How Plan to Help City Pay Pensions Backfired," *New York Times,* September 3, 2012, http://www.nytimes.com/2012/09/04/business/how-a-plan-to-help-stockton-calif-pay-pensions-backfired.html?pagewanted=all.

18. California Constitution Article 13A [Tax Limitation], http://www.leginfo.ca.gov/.const/.article_13A.

19. Associated Press, "N.J. Tax Amnesty Program Totals Record $725M," *Star-Ledger,* July 8, 2009, http://www.nj.com/news/index.ssf/2009/07/nj_tax_amnesty_program_totals.html.

20. U.S. Census Bureau, "State Government Finances: Historical Data: 2009," http://www.census.gov/govs/state/historical_data_2009.html.

21. U.S. Department of Commerce, Bureau of Economic Analysis, "Regional Accounts Archive for June 5, 2008," http://www.bea.gov/histdata/RMyearAPFfiles.asp?docDir=/2007/GDP/state/advance_June-05-2008.

22. Alan M. Wolf, "Biogen Will Build Bigger Space," *Newsobserver.com,* April 26, 2011, http://www.newsobserver.com/2011/04/26/1154147/biogen-will-build-bigger-space.html; Joseph Vranich, "Calif. Business Departures Increasing—Now Five Times Higher Than in 2009," *Business Relocation Coach,* Monday, June 20, 2011, http://www.thebusinessrelocationcoach.blogspot.com/2011/06/calif-business-departures-increasing.html.

23. Meredith Whitney Advisory Group, "Tragedy of the Commons Third Edition: 2012 Update," p. 22.

24. U.S. Department of Commerce, U.S. Census Bureau, "State Government Finances: Historical Data: 2010," http://www.census.gov/govs/state/historical_data_2010.html; U.S. Department of Commerce, U.S. Census Bureau, "State Government Finances: Historical Data: 2000," http://www.census.gov/govs/state/historical_data_2000.html.

25. Meredith Whitney Advisory Group, "3Q12 Municipal Analytics," p. 13.

26. Mary Williams Walsh, "JPMorgan Faces New Suit in Alabama County's Woes," *New York Times,* November 13, 2009, http://www.nytimes.com/2009/11/14/business/14muni.html; Romy Varghese, "Harrisburg

Incinerator, Source of Fiscal Woes, May Save Its City," *Bloomberg*, May 10, 2011, http://www.bloomberg.com/news/2011-05-11/harrisburg -incinerator-may-save-the-city.html.

27. Jeffery Bell, "THE BIG LIE: Rich People Create Jobs," *Yahoo Finance*, February 3, 2012, http://finance.yahoo.com/blogs/daily-ticker/meredith -whitney-along-jefferson-county-ala-files-largest-174407736.html.

28. U.S. Department of Commerce, U.S. Census Bureau, State and Local Government Finances, "State and Local Government Finance Summary Report," http://www.census.gov/govs/estimate/.

29. Christina Romer, "The Impact of the American Recovery Reinvestment Act," January 10, 2009, http://www.ampo.org/assets/library/184_obama .pdf; Mark S. Ludwick and Benjamin A. Mandel, "Analyzing Federal Programs Using BEA Statistics," U.S. Department of Commerce, Bureau of Economic Analysis, http://www.bea.gov/scb/pdf/2011/09%20Sep tember/0911_unemploy.pdf.

30. Pennsylvania Budget and Policy Center, "Budget Points: Stimulus Transition Fund Reduces Future Deficits, Preserves Education and Health Care," March 9, 2010, http://pennbpc.org/budget-points-stimulus-transition-fund.

31. Mac Taylor, "Federal Economic Stimulus Package: Fiscal Effect on California," Legislative Analyst's Office, 2009–2010 Budget Analysis Series, March 10, 2009, http://www.lao.ca.gov/2009/bud/fed_stimulus/fed_ stimulus_031009.pdf.

32. Max Taves, "Private Fix for Public Parks," *Wall Street Journal*, June 17, 2012, http://online.wsj.com/article/SB10001424052702303410404577464 724255828622.html; *Arizona Heritage Alliance*, "Arizona State Parks Keeps 9 Parks Open; 13 Will Close," January 17, 2010, http://azheritage .wordpress.com/2010/01/17/arizona-state-parks-keeps-9-parks-open -13-will-close/.

33. National Association of State Budget Officers, "State Expenditure Report: Examining Fiscal 2010–2012 State Spending," 2012, http://www .nasbo.org/sites/default/files/State%20Expenditure%20Report_1.pdf;

Meredith Whitney Advisory Group, "State Comprehensive Annual Financial Reports"; U.S. Department of Commerce, U.S. Census Bureau, "State Government Finances Summary: 2010," http://www.census.gov/prod/2011pubs/g10-asfin.pdf.

34. The Bond Buyer, Market Data, Monthly, Primary Market Statistics: A Decade of Bond Finance, http://www.bondbuyer.com/marketstatistics/decade_1/?data-type=monthly#dataTable; Meredith Whitney Advisory Group, "The 50 Dirtiest Little Secrets: New Analysis on States' Underfunded Pensions, Healthcare, and Other Off Balance Sheet Obligations," p. 8, Exhibit 1; U.S. Department of Commerce, U.S. Census Bureau, "State Government Finances," year 2000 and 2010, http://www.census.gov/govs/state/historical_data_2000.html, http://www.census.gov/govs/state/historical_data_2010.html.

35. Nicholas Johnson, Phil Oliff, and Erica Williams, "An Update on State Budget Cuts: At Least 46 States Have Imposed Cuts That Hurt Vulnerable Residents and the Economy," Center on Budget and Policy Priorities, February 9, 2011, http://www.cbpp.org/cms/index.cfm?fa=view&id=1214.

36. U.S. Department of Commerce, U.S. Census Bureau, "Housing Vacancies and Homeownership (CPS/HVS): 2012," table 5: "Homeownership Rates for the United States: 1968 to 2012," http://www.census.gov/housing/hvs/files/qtr312/tab5.xls.

37. Board of Governors of the Federal Reserve System, "Mortgage Debt Outstanding," December 2012, http://www.federalreserve.gov/econresdata/releases/mortoutstand/current.htm.

38. Meredith Whitney Advisory Group, "Tragedy of the Commons Third Edition: 2012 Update," p. 50, September 21, 2012.

39. Federal Reserve Bank of New York, "Quarterly Report on Household Debt and Credit," August 2010, http://www.newyorkfed.org/research/national_economy/householdcredit/DistrictReport_Q22010.pdf, "Historical Reports: Statistics by year," http://www.newyorkfed.org/research/national_economy/householdcredit/area_report_by_year.xlsx; U.S. Department of

Commerce, Bureau of Economic Analysis, Regional Data, GDP and Personal Income, Quarterly State Personal Income, http://www.bea.gov/iTable/iTable.cfm?reqid=70&step=1&isuri=1&acrdn=3#reqid=70&step=1&isuri=1.

40. Dan Fitzpatrick, "Need a Loan? Where Do You Live?" *Wall Street Journal*, September 26, 2012, http://online.wsj.com/article/SB10000872396390443328404578020501373436128.html.

41. Federal Reserve Bank of New York, Quarterly Report on Household Debt and Credit, November 2012, http://www.newyorkfed.org/research/national_economy/householdcredit/DistrictReport_Q32012.pdf.

42. Federal Reserve Bank of New York, "Historical Reports: Statistics by area and year," http://www.newyorkfed.org/research/national_economy/householdcredit/area_report_by_year.xlsx.

43. U.S. Small Business Administration, Frequently Asked Questions, http://web.sba.gov/faqs/faqIndexAll.cfm?areaid=24.

44. Michael J. Carr, Dun and Bradstreet Credibility Corp., "Real Statistics Show That 70 Percent of Small Businesses Succeed at First," August 6, 2012, http://business.dnb.com/small-business-information/real-statistics-show-that-70-percent-of-small-businesses-succeed-at-first/; Federal Housing Finance Agency, Downloadable Data, Purchase Only Indexes: U.S. Summary through 2012Q4, http://www.fhfa.gov/Default.aspx?Page=87, http://www.fhfa.gov/webfiles/24974/4q12POSummary.xls.

45. CNBC, "America's Top States for Business 2012: #40 California," http://www.cnbc.com/id/100013714.

46. Federal Housing Finance Agency, Downloadable Data, Purchase Only Indexes: U.S. Summary through 2012Q4, http://www.fhfa.gov/Default.aspx?Page=87, http://www.fhfa.gov/webfiles/24974/4q12POSummary.xls; U.S. Department of Labor, Bureau of Labor Statistics, Local Area Unemployment Statistics, http://www.bls.gov/lau/lastrk11.htm, http://www.bls.gov/lau/lastrk10.htm, http://www.bls.gov/lau/lastrk09.htm, http://www.bls.gov/lau/lastrk08.htm, http://www.bls.gov/lau/lastrk07.htm; U.S. Department of Labor, Bureau of Labor Statistics, Labor Force Statistics

from the Current Population Survey, http://data.bls.gov/pdq/Survey OutputServlet.

47. Federal Reserve Bank of New York, "Quarterly Report on Household Debt and Credit," November 2012, http://www.newyorkfed.org/research/ national_economy/householdcredit/DistrictReport_Q32012.pdf; Meredith Whitney Advisory Group, "U.S. Consumer Spending Outlook 2012."

48. U.S. Bureau of Economic Analysis, Regional Data, GDP and Personal Income, http://www.bea.gov/iTable/iTable.cfm?ReqID=70&step=1#reqid= 70&step=1&isuri=1; Meredith Whitney Advisory Group, "Rebalancing of the U.S. Economy: State Analysis."

49. U.S. Department of Commerce, U.S. Census Bureau, "Population Estimates: Historical Data: 2000s," http://www.census.gov/popest/data/his torical/2000s/index.html.

50. Federal Reserve Bank of New York; CoreLogic LoanPerformance Data; Meredith Whitney Advisory Group; Wikipedia, "Subprime Mortgage Crisis," http://en.wikipedia.org/wiki/Subprime_mortgage_crisis.

51. Federal Reserve Bank of New York, "Quarterly Report on Household Debt and Credit," November 2012, http://www.newyorkfed.org/research/ national_economy/householdcredit/DistrictReport_Q32012.pdf; U.S. Department of Commerce, U.S. Census Bureau, Population Estimates, 2012 State Total Population Estimates, http://www.census.gov/popest/; U.S. Department of Commerce, Bureau of Economic Analysis, Regional Data, GDP & Personal Income, Quarterly State Personal Income, http://www.bea.gov/iTable/iTable.cfm?reqid=70&step=1&isuri=1& acrdn=3#reqid=70&step=1&isuri=1.

52. Meredith Whitney Advisory Group, "Tragedy of the Commons Third Edition: 2012 Update," p. 50, September 21, 2012.

53. Gary Rivlin, "It's a Hot Time to Be a Pawn Star," *Daily Beast*, June 19, 2011, http://www.thedailybeast.com/newsweek/2011/06/19/it-s-a-hot-time -to-be-a-pawn-star.html.

54. Jennifer Oldham, "Nevada Desert Drowning in Sea of Underwater Loans," *Bloomberg Businessweek*, September 13, 2012, http://www.busi

nessweek.com/news/2012-09-13/nevada-desert-drowning-as-underwater-loans-hurt-schools-police.

55. Federal Reserve Bank of New York, Household Debt and Credit Report, Historical Reports: Statistics by area and year, http://www.newyorkfed.org/householdcredit/.

56. Dan Chapman and Jeffry Scott, "Boom Goes Bust in Atlanta's Exurbs," *Atlanta Journal-Constituition*, September 7, 2010, http://www.ajc.com/news/business/boom-goes-bust-in-atlantas-exurbs/nQj2w/.

57. Jenifer Shockley, Georgia State University, "Economy to Grind Out Reasonable Growth in 2012," February 23, 2012, http://robinson.gsu.edu/news/6221.html.

Chapter 4: Pensions: The Debt Bomb Nobody's Talking About

1. Caitlin Kenney, "Firefighters Deal with Community Backlash," *National Public Radio*, December 26, 2012, http://m.npr.org/news/Business/168059128; National Public Radio, Planet Money, "Episode 424: How Much Is a Firefighter Worth?" December 18, 2012, http://www.npr.org/blogs/money/2012/12/18/167265874/episode-424-how-much-is-a-firefighter-worth.

2. Meredith Whitney Advisory Group, "Our Annual Pension and OPEB Analysis: Deterioration Continues and Meaningful Accounting Reform Looms."

3. Pew Center, "The Widening Gap Update," June 18, 2012, http://www.pewstates.org/research/reports/the-widening-gap-update-85899398241; Meredith Whitney Advisory Group, "The 50 Dirtiest Little Secrets: New Analysis on States' Underfunded Pensions, Healthcare, and Other Off Balance Sheet Obligations," May 2, 2011, p. 17; State Comprehensive Annual Financial Reports; Meredith Whitney Advisory Group, "Tragedy of Commons Third Edition: 2012 Update," p. 26.

4. Gina Raimondo, in conversation with Meredith Whitney, September 10, 2012.

5. Jess Jiang, "The Deadliest Jobs in America, in One Graphic," *National Public Radio,* January 23, 2013, http://www.npr.org/blogs/money/2013/01/08/168897140/the-deadliest-jobs-in-america-in-one-graphic.

6. Governmental Accounting Standards Board, "GASB Moves to Improve Pension Disclosures," February 2007, http://www.gasb.org/cs/Blob Server?blobkey=id&blobwhere=1175820457268&blobheader=applica tion%2Fpdf&blobcol=urldata&blobtable=MungoBlobs.

7. Robert Novy-Marx and Joshua D. Rauh, "Public Pension Promises: How Big Are They and What Are They Worth?" December 18, 2009, http://econ.as.nyu.edu/docs/IO/14310/Rauh_20100310.pdf.

8. U.S. Department of Commerce, U.S. Census Bureau, Population Estimates, 2012 State Total Population Estimates, http://www.census.gov/popest/; Federal Reserve Bank of New York; Bureau of Economic Analysis; Moody's Investors Service, "2011 State Debt Medians Report," http://www.vermonttreasurer.gov/sites/treasurer/files/pdf/bonds/Moody's%20State%20Debt%20Medians%202011-corrected.pdf.

9. NARSA Issue Brief, Employee Contributions to Public Pension Funds, January 2013, http://wikipension.com/images/8/8e/Issuebrief130102.pdf.

10. U.S. Social Security Administration, Social Security Cost-of-Living Adjustments, http://www.ssa.gov/oact/cola/colaseries.html; U.S. Social Security Administration, Measure of Central Tendency for Wage Data, http://www.ssa.gov/oact/cola/central.html.

11. Jilian Mincer, "Public Pension Funds to Face Calls to Set Realistic Targets," *Reuters,* July 23, 2012, http://www.reuters.com/article/2012/07/23/us-usa-pensions-finreturns-idUSBRE86M1AA20120723.

12. Terrence Dopp, "N.J. Towns Borrow $200,000 Farewells Christie Abhors," Bloomberg, August 10, 2012, http://www.bloomberg.com/news/2012-08-10/n-j-towns-borrow-for-200-000-farewells-christie-abhors.html.

13. Edward Mangano, interview by Meredith Whitney, July 3, 2012.

14. NARSA Issue Brief: Public Pension Plan Investment Return Assumptions, January 2013, http://www.nasra.org/resources/issuebrief120626.pdf; State Comprehensive Annual Financial Reports; Gina M. Raimondo, "Truth in

Numbers: The Security and Sustainability of Rhode Island's Retirement System," Office of the General Treasurer of Rhode Island, June 2011, http://www.treasury.ri.gov/documents/SPRI/TIN-WEB-06-1-11.pdf; Meredith Whitney Advisory Group, "Our Annual Pension and OPEB Analysis: Deterioration Continues and Meaningful Accounting Reform Looms," pp. 16 and 27.

15. U.S. Department of Commerce, U.S. Census Bureau, "Annual Survey of Public Pensions: State and Local Data," 2011, http://www.census.gov/govs/retire/; U.S. Department of Commerce, U.S. Census Bureau, State and Local Government Finance, 2010 State and Local Government: Missouri—Wyoming, http://www.census.gov/govs/estimate/.

16. Meredith Whitney Advisory Group, "Tragedy of Commons: Comprehensive Update and Expansion of Coverage to 25 States," p. 33.

17. The Pew Center on the States, Issue Brief: The Widening Gap Update, June 2012, http://www.pewstates.org/uploadedFiles/PCS_Assets/2012/Pew_Pensions_Update.pdf; "Governor Cuomo Announces Passage of Major Pension Reform," Governor's Press Office, March 15, 2012, http://www.governor.ny.gov/press/03152012pensionagreement.

18. Mary Williams Walsh, "Illinois Debt Takes Toll, Study Finds," *New York Times,* October 24, 2012, http://www.nytimes.com/2012/10/25/business/illinois-debt-takes-toll-on-services-study-finds.html.

19. "Stop the Pension Bond Rush," *Chicago Tribune,* March 25, 2003, http://articles.chicagotribune.com/2003-03-25/news/0303250298_1_pension-bond-borrowing-plan-bond-plan.

20. Meredith Whitney Advisory Group, "50 Dirtiest Little Secrets: New Analysis on States' Underfunded Pensions, Healthcare, and Other Off Balance Sheet Obligations"; Pew Center on the States, Issue Brief: The Widening Gap Update, June 2012, http://www.pewstates.org/uploaded-Files/PCS_Assets/2012/Pew_Pensions_Update.pdf; U.S. Department of Commerce, U.S. Census Bureau, State and Local Government Finance, Historical Data: 2002, "US Summary & Alabama-Mississippi," http://www2.census.gov/govs/estimate/02slsstab2a.xls; *Bloomberg.*

21. "Not So Fast, Legislators," *Chicago Tribune*, January 3, 2011, http://arti
cles.chicagotribune.com/2011-01-03/news/ct-edit-legis-20110103_1_legis
lative-session-state-capital-illinois; Jonathan Ingram, "Illinois' $44 Bil-
lion Retiree Health Pricetag," Illinois Policy Institute, March 6, 2012,
http://illinoispolicy.org/blog/blog.asp?ArticleSource=4719.

22. National Center for Education Statistics, "Fast Facts," http://nces.ed
.gov/fastfacts/display.asp?id=28.

23. Michael Pearson and Holly Yan, "Official: No Deal Yet Between Chicago Teachers and School System," CNN, September 10, 2012, http://
www.cnn.com/2012/09/10/us/illinois-chicago-teachers-strike/index
.html.

24. "How San Diego's Pension Problems Compare," *NBC 7 San Diego*, January 3, 2013, http://www.nbcsandiego.com/news/local/How-San-Diegos
-Pension-Problems-Compare-185480942.html.

25. Alison Vekshin and James Nash, "California Pension Victories Could
Catch On Nationwide," *Bloomberg*, June 6, 2012, http://www.bloomberg
.com/news/2012-06-06/san-diego-san-jose-voters-approve-pension-cost
-limits.html.

26. Elliot Spagat, "2 California Cities Vote on Public Pension Cuts," *Bloomberg Businessweek*, June 5, 2012, http://www.businessweek.com/ap/
2012-06/D9V75GP00.htm.

27. Stephen Goldsmith, "A Mayor's Roadmap for Reforming Pensions,"
Governing, July 16, 2012, http://www.governing.com/blogs/bfc/col-san
-diego-mayor-jerry-sanders-pension-reform.html.

Chapter 5: The Negative Feedback Loop from Hell

1. Elliot Spagat, "2 California Cities Vote on Public Pension Cuts," *Bloomberg
Businessweek*, June 5, 2012, http://www.businessweek.com/ap/2012-06/
D9V75GP00.htm; U.S. Department of Commerce, Bureau of Economic
Analysis, News Release: Personal Income for Metropolitan Areas, 2005,
http://www.bea.gov/newsreleases/regional/lapi/2006/mpi0906.htm.

2. Colleen May, "Strategic Planning for the Future of Las Vegas," 8 *News NOW*, KLAS-TV Las Vegas, September 19, 2005, http://www.8news now.com/story/3870884/strategic-planning-for-the-future-of-las-vegas? clienttype=printable.

3. Federal Housing Finance Agency, "City HPI Data, MSA HPI Comparisons," 2012, http://www.fhfa.gov/Default.aspx?Page=216&Type=com pare&Area1=29820&Area2=&Area3=; Federal Housing Finance Agency, Downloadable Data, Purchase Only Indexes: U.S. Summary through 2012Q4, http://www.fhfa.gov/Default.aspx?Page=87, http:// www.fhfa.gov/webfiles/24974/4q12POSummary.xls; CoreLogic, "CoreLogic Third Quarter 2011 Negative Equity Data Shows Slight Decline But Remains Elevated," November 29, 2011, http://www.corelogic.com/ about-us/news/corelogic-third-quarter-2011-negative-equity-data-shows -slight-decline-but-remains-elevated.aspx; Michael Leachman, Erica Williams, and Nicholas Johnson, "Governors Are Proposing Further Deep Cuts in Services, Likely Harming Their Economics," Center on Budget and Policy Priorities, March 21, 2011, http://www.cbpp.org/cms/ index.cfm?fa=view&id=3389.

4. Paul Takahashi, "School District to Lay Off 1,015 Teachers, Literacy Specialists," *Las Vegas Sun*, May 16, 2012, http://www.lasvegassun .com/news/2012/may/16/school-district-lay-1015-teachers-and-literacy -spe/.

5. Paul Takahashi, "School District Sends Pink Slips to 419 Teachers," *Las Vegas Sun*, June 11, 2012, http://www.lasvegassun.com/news/2012/ jun/11/school-district-sends-pink-slips-400-teachers/.

6. Clark County School District, "Comprehensive Annual Budget Report: Statistical Data," p. 164, July 1, 2012, http://ccsd.net/resources/budget -finance-department/pdf/publications/cabr/2013/statistical-data.pdf.

7. Annie E. Casey Foundation, "Data Across States: Per-Pupil Educational Expenditures Adjusted for Regional Cost Differences (Currency): 2009," March 2012, http://datacenter.kidscount.org/data/acrossstates/Rankings .aspx?loct=2&by=a&order=a&ind=5199&dtm=11678&tf=38.

8. National Governors Association and National Association of State Budget Officers, "The Fiscal Survey of States," Fall 2012, http://www.nasbo.org/sites/default/files/Fall%202012%20Fiscal%20Survey_Final%20Version.pdf ; National Governors Association and National Association of State Budget Officers, "The Fiscal Survey of States," Spring 2012, http://www.nasbo.org/sites/default/files/Spring%202012%20Fiscal%20Survey_1.pdf.

9. U.S. Census Bureau, "Quarterly Summary of State and Local Taxes," table 2: "Historical National Totals of State Tax Revenue," http://www.census.gov/govs/qtax/table_2.html; U.S. Census Bureau, State Government Finances, Historical Data: 2000 Annual Survey of State Government Finances, http://www.census.gov/govs/state/historical_data_2000.html; U.S. Census Bureau, State Government Finances, Historical Data: 2010 Annual Survey of State Government Finances, http://www.census.gov/govs/state/historical_data_2010.html.

10. National Association of State Budget Officers, "State Expenditure Report: Examining Fiscal 2010–2012 State Spending," 2012, http://www.nasbo.org/sites/default/files/State%20Expenditure%20Report_1.pdf; U.S. Census Bureau, State Government Finances, Historical Data: 2009 Annual Survey of State Government Finances, Summary Table, http://www.census.gov/govs/state/historical_data_2009.html; U.S. Census Bureau, State Government Finances, 2011 Annual Survey of State Government Finances, Summary Table, http://www.census.gov/govs/state/.

11. Ryan Hagen, "San Bernardino City Attorney: Evidence of Budget Falsification Given to Other Agencies," *Sun* (San Bernardino County), July 11, 2012, http://www.sbsun.com/ci_21052495/breaking-news-san-bernardino-mayor-morris-addresses-citys.

12. Fitch Ratings, "U.S. Local Government Downgrades to Persist," August 20, 2012, http://voiceofdetroit.net/wp-content/uploads/2012/11/Fitch-Ratings-Local-Govt-Downgrades-to-Persist.pdf.

13. Reuters, "San Bernardino Bankruptcy May Start Trend for California Cities: Moody's," August 9, 2012, http://www.reuters.com/article/2012/08/10/us-municipals-sanbernardino-idUSBRE87902L20120810.

14. Federal Reserve Bank of St. Louis, FRED Economic Data, Graph: State and Local Bonds—Bond Buyer Go 20-Bond Municipal Bond Index (WSLB20), http://research.stlouisfed.org/fred2/graph/?s[1][id]= WSLB20.

15. Organisation for Economic Co-operation and Development, "Special Feature: Trends in Personal Income Tax and Employee Social Security Contribution Schedules," 2012, http://www.oecd.org/tax/taxpolicyanal ysis/50131824.pdf.

16. Trading Economics, Greece Unemployment Rate, http://www.trading economics.com/greece/unemployment-rate; Trading Economics, Greece GDP Annual Growth Rate, http://www.tradingeconomics.com/greece/ gdp-growth-annual.

17. Ioanna Fotiadi, "Smaller Companies Heading to Bulgaria in Droves," *Ekathimerini.com*, June 11, 2012, http://www.ekathimerini.com/4dcgi/_ w_articles_wsite2_1_11/06/2012_446468.

18. Li-mei Hoang and Renee Maltezou, "Families Leaving Greece in Droves to Stay Afloat Financially," April 28, 2012, http://business.finan cialpost.com/2012/04/28/families-leaving-greece-in-droves-to-stay -afloat-financially/.

19. Elizabeth McNichol, "Out of Balance: Cuts in Services Have Been States' Primary Response to Budget Gaps, Harming the Nation's Econ-omy," Center on Budget and Policy Priorities, April 18, 2012, http://www .cbpp.org/cms/index.cfm?fa=view&id=3747.

20. State Budget Solutions, "K-12 Education," http://www.statebudgetsolu tions.org/issues/detail/k-12-education.

21. Phil Oliff and Michael Leachman, "New School Year Brings Steep Cuts in State Funding for Schools," Center on Budget and Policy Priorities, October 7, 2011, http://www.cbpp.org/cms/?fa=view&id=3569.

22. Motoko Rich, "Enrollment Off in Big Districts, Forcing Layoffs," *New York Times*, July 23, 2012, http://www.nytimes.com/2012/07/24/education/ largest-school-districts-see-steady-drop-in-enrollment.html?page wanted=all&_r=0.

23. Mokoto Rich, "Enrollment in Charter Schools Is Increasing," *New York Times*, November 14, 2012, http://www.nytimes.com/2012/11/14/us/charter-schools-growing-fast-new-report-finds.html?_r=0.

24. Benjamin Herold, "This Year, It's Philly Charter Schools' Turn to Wrestle with Budget Cuts," *NewsWorks*, August 30, 2012, http://www.newsworks.org/index.php/local//region/43574-this-year-its-philly-charter-schools-turn-to-wrestle-with-budget-cuts.

25. U.S. Department of Commerce, Bureau of Economic Analysis, Regional Data: GDP and Personal Income, Gross Domestic Product by State, California, http://www.bea.gov/iTable/iTable.cfm?reqid=70&step=1&isuri=1&acrdn=1#reqid=70&step=10&isuri=1&7007=-1&7093=Levels&7090=70&7035=-1&7036=-1&7001=1200&7002=1&7003=200&7004=NAICS&7005=-1&7006=06000; U.S. Census Bureau, State Government Finances, Historical Data: 2007 Annual Survey of State Government Finances, http://www.census.gov/govs/state/historical_data_2007.html; U.S. Census Bureau, State Government Finances, 2011 Annual Survey of State Government Finances, http://www.census.gov/govs/state/historical_data_2011.html.

26. "California Budget Crisis," *New York Times*, January 11, 2013, http://topics.nytimes.com/topics/news/national/usstatesterritoriesandpossessions/california/budget_crisis_2008_09/index.html.

27. Hailey Persinger, "School Music, Arts Programs on Chopping Block," *U-T San Diego*, March 6, 2011, http://www.utsandiego.com/news/2011/mar/06/unifieds-music-arts-programs-chopping-block/.

28. Toni McAllister, "School Bus Service Eliminated for LEUSD Kids," *Lake Elsinore-Wildomar Patch*, February 10, 2012, http://lakeelsinore-wildomar.patch.com/articles/school-bus-service-eliminated-for-leusd-kids.

29. Jesse McKinley, "California Students Protest Education Cuts," *New York Times*, March 4, 2010, http://www.nytimes.com/2010/03/05/education/05protests.html.

30. "Student Data: Tuition and Fees, 1999–2000 to 2012–13," *Chronicle of Higher Education*, October 24, 2012, http://chronicle.com/article/Searchable-Database-Tuition/48879/.

31. Joint Legislative Audit and Review Commission, "National Rankings on Taxes, Budgetary Components, and Other Indicators, 2011 Edition," Table 31: Average Annual In-State Tuition and Fees at Public 40 Year Institutions (2010–2011), http://jlarc.state.va.us/mobile/states/t31.htm.

32. Hans Johnson, Public Policy Institute of California, "Defunding Higher Education," May 2012, http://www.ppic.org/content/pubs/report/R_512HJR.pdf.

33. Carla Rivera, "Californians' Enrollment in UC, CSU Declines, Study Finds," *Los Angeles Times*, May 10, 2012, http://articles.latimes.com/2012/may/10/local/la-me-0510-college-report-20120510.

34. David F. Shaffer and David J. Wright, "A New Paradigm for Economic Development," Nelson A. Rockefeller Institute of Government, State University of New York, University at Albany, March 2010. http://www.immagic.com/eLibrary/ARCHIVES/GENERAL/NARIG_US/R100311S.pdf.

35. John Pelletier, "Why Go to College If I Can't Get a Job?" *Wall Street Journal Market Watch*, August 23, 2012, http://articles.marketwatch.com/2012-08-23/finance/33323518_1_student-loan-debt-nonprofit-four-year-colleges-college-grads (data originally from Economic Policy Institute's research).

36. Scott Thurm and Pui-Wing Tam "California's Boom Masks State's Uneven Recovery," *Wall Street Journal*, August 15, 2012, http://online.wsj.com/article/SB10001424052702303505504577405221289491972.html.

37. Roberta Stevens, president of the American Library Association, "Library Technology: Helping Job Seekers," *Huffington Post*, June 28, 2011, http://www.huffingtonpost.com/roberta-stevens/library-technology_b_885980.html.

38. Shannon Jones, "Democrats Seek to Defuse Opposition to Detroit Library Cuts," *World Socialist Web Site*, January 2012, http://www.wsws.org/en/articles/2012/01/libr-j27.html.

39. Beverly Goldberg, "D.C. Officials Feel the Heat over Planned School Library Cuts," *American Libraries*, May 4, 2012, http://americanlibraries-magazine.org/news/05042012/dc-officials-feel-heat-over-planned-school-library-cuts.

40. "Why Is New Haven Public Library Important to You?" http://www.cityofnewhaven.com/uploads/Why%20is%20New%20Haven%20Public%20Library%20important%20to%20you%202(1).pdf.

41. Paul Bass, "No Tax Hike in Mayor's New Budget," *New Haven Independent*, March 1, 2011, http://www.newhavenindependent.org/index.php/archives/entry/despite_pension_health_spikes_no_tax_hike/; John DeStefano, Jr., Elsie Chapman, et al., "Chief Administrative Officer's 2012 Annual Report: New Haven Free Public Library," http://www.cityofnewhaven.com/ChiefAdministrator/pdf/2012%20NHFPL%20review.pdf; Keith M. Phaneuf, "Connecticut Home Sale Prices Show Biggest Decline in Nation," *CT Mirror*, August 28, 2012, http://ctmirror.org/story/17329/connecticut-tops-nation-declining-home-sale-prices.

42. Mason Adams, "Roanoke County Officials Eye Waste Disposal Cuts," *Roanoke Times*, March 14, 2012, http://www.roanoke.com/news/roanoke/wb/306174.

43. Jared Janes, "County Wants High Participation in Rural Trash Collection," *Monitor*, 2013, http://m.themonitor.com/news/local/article_6dfdfaa8-470c-11e2-bd97-0019bb30f31a.html?mode=jqm.

44. Vauhini Vara, "Jail Shift Makes Waves in California," *Wall Street Journal*, July 8, 2012, http://online.wsj.com/article/SB10001424052702304458604577491100435436414.html.

45. Gary Fields, "Prison's Guards Are Part Wolf, All Business," *Wall Street Journal*, July 31, 2012, http://online.wsj.com/article/SB10000872396390444130304577561273226636482.html.

46. John Rudolf, "Stockton's Poor Mired in Violence After Police Cuts, Recession," *Huffington Post*, March 19, 2012, http://www.huffingtonpost .com/2012/03/18/stockton-poor-poverty-crime-california_n_1346096 .html.

47. D. S. Woodfill, "Surprise Police, Fire Departments Not Spared Spending Cuts," *azcentral.com*, May 14, 2012, http://www.azcentral.com/community/westvalley/articles/2012/05/08/20120508surprise-police-fire -departments-not-spared-spending-cuts.html.

48. Imran Ghori, "San Bernardino: Budget Plan Criticized," *Press-Enterprise*, August 30, 2012, http://www.pe.com/local-news/politics/imran -ghori-headlines/20120830-san-bernardino-budget-plan-criticized.ece; Ryan Hagen, "Volunteers Try to Fill Growing Hole in San Bernardino's Service Levels," *Contra Costa Times*, September 9, 2012, http://www .contracostatimes.com/california/ci_21503330/volunteers-try-fill -growing-hole-san-bernardinos-service.

49. Purdue University Department of Agriculture, "An Overview of the Indiana State Budget," Indiana Local Government Information Web site, January 2011, http://www.agecon.purdue.edu/crd/localgov/topics/essays/ State_Budget.htm].

Chapter 6: The New American Poverty

1. U.S. Department of Commerce, U.S. Census Bureau, Population Estimates: State Intercensal Estimates (2000–2010), Annual Population Estimates,http://www.census.gov/popest/data/intercensal/state/state2010 .html; U.S. Department of Labor, Bureau of Labor Statistics, Archived News Releases|Regional and State Employment and Unemployment, http://www.bls.gov/schedule/archives/laus_nr.htm.

2. Meredith Whitney Advisory Group, "Tragedy of Commons Third Edition: 2012 Update," pp. 5, 7, 25.

3. U.S. Department of Commerce, U.S. Census Bureau, "Quarterly Summary of State and Local Tax Revenue," table 1: "Historical National Totals

of State and Local Tax Revenue," http://www.census.gov/govs/qtax/, http://www2.census.gov/govs/qtax/2012/q3t1.xls; Moody's Investors Service, "2011 State Debt Medians Report," http://www.vermonttreasurer.gov/sites/treasurer/files/pdf/bonds/Moody's%20State%20Debt%20Medians%202011-corrected.pdf; Meredith Whitney Advisory Group, "Poverty Report," p. 25.

4. U.S. Department of Commerce, U.S. Census Bureau, Poverty, Historical Poverty Tables—People: table 21. Number of Poor and Poverty Rate, by State, http://www.census.gov/hhes/www/poverty/data/historical/people.html.

5. Ibid.

6. Office of Management and Budget, "Fiscal Year 2012: Historical Tables: Budget of the U.S. Government," http://www.whitehouse.gov/sites/default/files/omb/budget/fy2012/assets/hist.pdf.

7. U.S. Department of Commerce, U.S. Census Bureau, Census Bureau Reports About Governments, http://www.census.gov/govs/pubs/topic.html#federal_programs; Meredith Whitney Advisory Group.

8. National Association of State Budget Officers, "State Expenditure Report: Examining Fiscal 2010–2012 State Spending," 2012, http://www.nasbo.org/sites/default/files/State%20Expenditure%20Report_1.pdf.

9. National Association of State Budget Officers, "State Expenditure Report: 2001," Summer 2002, http://www.nasbo.org/sites/default/files/ER_2001.pdf.

10. Meredith Whitney Advisory Group, "Poverty Report," p. 6; Meredith Whitney Advisory Group, "Poverty in America," Appendix, p. 4.

11. Elizabeth McNichol, Center on Budget and Policy Priorities, "Out of Balance: Cuts in Services Have Been State's Primary Response to Budget Gaps, Harming the Nation's Economy," April 18, 2012, http://www.cbpp.org/cms/index.cfm?fa=view&id=3747.

12. Gary Jason, "Governments Finally Outsourcing," *Liberty*, September 1, 2012, http://www.libertyunbound.com/node/889.

13. U.S. Department of Commerce, U.S. Census Bureau, "Current Population Survey."

14. U.S. Department of Labor, Bureau of Labor Statistics, Local Area Unemployment Statistics, Annual Average: Statewide Data: Tables: Unemployment Rates for States: 2000 and 2010, http://www.bls.gov/lau/lastrk00 .htm, http://www.bls.gov/lau/lastrk10.htm.

15. U.S. Department of Labor, Bureau of Labor Statistics, Local Area Unemployment Statistics, Annual Average: Statewide Data: Tables: Unemployment Rates for States: 2000 and 2010, http://www.bls.gov/lau/lastrk00 .htm, http://www.bls.gov/lau/lastrk10.htm.

16. Ryan Holeywell, "The Indiana Toll Road: A Model for Privatization?" *Governing*, October 2011, http://www.governing.com/topics/mgmt/in diana-toll-road-model-privatization.html.

17. "Business Traveller Awards 2012," *Business Traveller*, September 17, 2012, http://www.businesstraveller.com/awards2012.

18. Public Works Financing, Vol. 253, October 2010 Issue, http://www.pwfi nance.net/pwf_major_projects.pdf; Privatization Barometer, http://www .privatizationbarometer.net/database.php.

19. Scott McCartney, "The World's Best Airport?" *Wall Street Journal*, December 1, 2011, http://online.wsj.com/article/SB10001424052970204397 704577070502443425304.html; Associated Press, "Chicago Mayor Wants to Lease Out Midway Airport," *nwitimes.com*, December 21, 2012, http:// www.nwitimes.com/news/local/illinois/chicago/chicago-mayor -wants-to-lease-out-midway-airport/article_b082df59-108f-5c2d-933b -27c0f4a9e397.html.

20. Public Works Financing, Vol. 253, October 2010 Issue, http://www.pw finance.net/pwf_major_projects.pdf; Privatization Barometer, http:// www.privatizationbarometer.net/database.php.

21. Ryan Holeywell, "Engineers: U.S. Needs to Invest $1 Trillion More in Infrastructure," *Governing*, January 16, 2013, http://www.governing.com/ blogs/fedwatch/gov-report-details-under-investment-in-infrastructure .html.

22. Keith Benman, "Indiana Toll Road Rate Increase Hits Sunday," *nwitimes.com*, June 27, 2012, http://www.nwitimes.com/business/local/

indiana-toll-road-rate-increase-hits-sunday/article_8df15891-b27b
-579a-b3af-36f158b43b1d.html.

23. Ryan Holeywell, "The Indiana Toll Road."

Chapter 7: A New Map of Prosperity

1. Jeff Harrington, "Unable to Find Workers, Tampa's Sykes Will Close North Dakota Call Center," *Tampa Bay Times*, March 13, 2009, http://www.tampabay.com/news/business/unable-to-find-workers-tampas-sykes-will-close-north-dakota-call-center/983528.

2. U.S. Department of Commerce, Bureau of Economic Analysis, Regional Data: GDP and Personal Income Growth, http://www.bea.gov/iTable/iTable.cfm?reqid=70&step=1&isuri=1&acrdn=1#reqid=70&step=4&isuri=1&7001=1200&7002=1&7003=200&7090=70; Meredith Whitney Advisory Group.

3. Mark J. Perry, "U-Haul Rates Confirm the Great California Exodus," *Carpe Diem*, April 21, 2012, http://mjperry.blogspot.com/2012/04/u-haul-rates-confirm-california-exodus.html.

4. Sarah Wolfe, "New $304 Million Apple Campus Planned in Austin, Texas," *Global Post*, March 9, 2012, http://www.globalpost.com/dispatch/news/regions/americas/united-states/120309/new-304-million-apple-campus-planned-austin-texas; "Web Services Firm Plans Downtown Office, 300 Jobs," *Indianapolis Business Journal*, August 22, 2012, http://www.ibj.com/web-services-firm-plan-downtown-office--300-jobs/PARAMS/article/36239.

5. Steve Hargreaves, "California Could Be Next Oil Boom State," *CNNMoney*, January 15, 2013, http://money.cnn.com/2013/01/14/news/economy/california-oil-boom/.

6. Joel Kotkin, "Is Energy the Last Good Issue for Republicans?" *Daily Beast*, March 1, 2012, http://www.thedailybeast.com/articles/2012/03/01/is-energy-the-last-good-issue-for-republicans.html.

7. Joel Kotkin, "Silicon Valley Can No Longer Save California—or the U.S.," *Forbes*, October 12, 2011, http://www.forbes.com/sites/joelkotkin/2011/10/12/silicon-valley-no-longer-save-california-or-america/2/.

8. U.S. Department of Commerce, Bureau of Economic Analysis, Regional Data: GDP and Personal Income, http://www.bea.gov/iTable/iTable.cfm?reqid=70&step=1&isuri=1&acrdn=1#reqid=70&step=1&isuri=1; Meredith Whitney Advisory Group, "Tragedy of Commons Third Edition: 2012 Update," p. 44.

9. Alessandro Torello, "Cheap U.S. Gas Is Europe's Loss," *Wall Street Journal*, October 24, 2012, http://online.wsj.com/article/SB1000142405 29702038974045780765639797611862.html.

10. Matthew L. Wald, "U.P.S. Finds a Substitute for Diesel: Natural Gas, at 260 Degrees Below Zero," *Green, New York Times*, February 22, 2011, http://green.blogs.nytimes.com/2011/02/22/u-p-s-finds-a-substitute-for-diesel-natural-gas-at-260-degrees-below-zero/.

11. Ian M. Taplin, *Sociation Today*, Vol. 10, No. 1, "The Changing North Carolina Workplace," 2012, http://www.ncsociology.org/sociationtoday/v101/ncjobs.htm.

12. David Barboza, "China's Exports Perch on Uncertain Truck System," *New York Times*, April 28, 2011, http://www.nytimes.com/2011/04/29/business/global/29truckers.html?pagewanted=all&_r=0.

13. Federal Reserve Bank of New York, "Quarterly Report on Household Debt and Credit," November 2012, http://www.newyorkfed.org/research/national_economy/householdcredit/DistrictReport_Q32012.pdf; U.S. Department of Commerce, U.S. Census Bureau, Population Estimates, 2012 State Total Population Estimates, http://www.census.gov/popest/; U.S. Department of Commerce, Bureau of Economic Analysis, Regional Data, GDP & Personal Income, Quarterly State Personal Income, http://www.bea.gov/iTable/iTable.cfm?reqid=70&step=1&isuri=1&acrdn=3#reqid=70&step=1&isuri=1; Meredith Whitney Advisory Group.

Chapter 8: State Arbitrage

1. Matt Townsend, "Under Armour Plans to Dethrone Nike, Jordan in Basketball Shoes," *Bloomberg*, October 22, 2010, http://www.bloom berg.com/news/2010-10-22/under-armour-ceo-plank-plots-to -dethrone-nike-jordan-in-basketball-shoes.html.

2. U.S. Department of Commerce, U.S. Census Bureau, "Housing Vacancies and Homeownership: Historical Tables," http://www.census.gov/ housing/hvs/data/histtabs.html; U.S. Department of Labor, Bureau of Labor Statistics, Archived News Releases|Regional and State Employment and Unemployment, http://www.bls.gov/schedule/archives/laus_ nr.htm; Federal Housing Finance Agency, Downloadable Data, Purchase Only Indexes: U.S. Summary through 2012Q4, http://www.fhfa .gov/Default.aspx?Page=87, http://www.fhfa.gov/webfiles/24974/4q12PO-Summary.xls.

3. Tax Foundation, "State and Local Tax Burdens: All States, One Year, 1977–2010," http://taxfoundation.org/article/state-and-local-tax-burdens -all-states-one-year-1977-2010, data retrieved from: http://interactive.tax foundation.org/burdens/burdensdata.php?state=all&mode=all_states_ one_year&format=csv; Federal Housing Finance Agency, Downloadable Data, Purchase Only Indexes: U.S. Summary Through 2012Q4, http://www.fhfa.gov/Default.aspx?Page=87, http://www.fhfa.gov/webfiles/ 24974/4q12POSummary.xls.

4. California Taxpayers Association, "Proposition 30: Retroactive Income Tax Increase with Penalty Relief; No Relief for Government on Sales Tax Hike," November 16, 2012, http://www.caltax.org/homepage/111612_ prop_30.html.

5. Susan Guyett, "Indiana Becomes 23rd 'Right-to-Work' State," Reuters, February 1, 2012, http://www.reuters.com/article/2012/02/01/us-unions -indiana-righttowork-idUSTRE81018920120201.

6. Richard Vedder, Matthew Denhart, and Jonathan Robe, "Ohio Right-To-Work: How the Economic Freedom of Workers Enhances

Prosperity," Buckeye Institute for Public Policy Solutions, March 2012. http://www.buckeyeinstitute.org/uploads/files/BUCKEYE-ohio-right-to-work-rev2012-3.pdf.

7. Meredith Whitney Advisory Group, "Tragedy of Commons Third Edition: 2012 Update," p. 9, Right-to-Work States; U.S. Department of Labor, Bureau of Labor Statistics, Archived News Releases|Regional and State Employment and Unemployment, http://www.bls.gov/schedule/archives/laus_nr.htm; National Right to Work; U.S. Bureau of Economic Analysis, Regional Data, GDP and Personal Income, Gross Domestic Product by State, http://www.bea.gov/iTable/iTable.cfm?ReqID=70&step=1#reqid=70&step=1&isuri=1.

8. Jim Kinney, "Connecticut and Massachusetts Businesses Have Considered Moving: Survey," *MassLive.com*, June 26, 2011, http://www.masslive.com/business-news/index.ssf/2011/06/connecticut_and_massachusetts_businesses.html.

9. U.S. Department of Commerce, U.S. Census Bureau, "Geographical Mobility/Migration: State-to-State Migration Flows, Tables: State-to-State Migration Flows 2009 and 2010," http://www.census.gov/hhes/migration/data/acs/state-to-state.html.

10. Federation of Tax Administrators, "State Individual Income Taxes (Tax Rates for Tax Year 2013—as of January 1, 2013)," January 2013, http://www.taxadmin.org/fta/rate/ind_inc.pdf.

11. U.S. Department of Labor, Bureau of Labor Statistics, Archived News Releases|Regional and State Employment and Unemployment, 2007 and 2012, http://www.bls.gov/schedule/archives/laus_nr.htm.

12. Ernst & Young LLP, "Ernst & Young LLP's 2012 US Investment Monitor Shows Increased Investment in New Facilities and Jobs," May 24, 2012, http://www.ey.com/US/en/Newsroom/News-releases/Ernst---Young-LLPs-2012-US-Investment-Monitor-shows-increased-investment-in-new-facilities-and-jobs.

13. Moody's Investors Service, 2011 State Debt Medians Report, http://www.governing.com/gov-data/economy-finance/state-debt-per-capita-figures

.html; Governing, State Debt per Capita, http://www.governing.com/
gov-data/economy-finance/state-debt-per-capita-figures.html.

14. Micki Maynard, "Indiana Gets a $400 Million Infusion from Toyota,"
    Changing Gears, February 8, 2012, http://www.changinggears.info/2012/
    02/08/indiana-gets-a-400-million-infusion-from-toyota/.

15. Roxana Hegeman, "Boeing to Close Historic Wichita Plant by End of
    2013," *USA Today*, January 4, 2012, http://usatoday30.usatoday.com/
    money/industries/manufacturing/story/2012-01-04/boeing-plant
    -closing-wichita-kansas/52377688/1.

16. Louise Story, "Lines Blur as Texas Gives Industries a Bonanza," *New
    York Times*, December 2, 2012, http://www.nytimes.com/2012/12/03/
    us/winners-and-losers-in-texas.html?pagewanted=all.

17. "Globalstar Announces Relocation of Its Corporate Headquarters to
    Louisiana from California," *Louisiana Economic Development*, July 13,
    2010, http://www.louisianaeconomicdevelopment.com/led-news/news
    -releases/globalstar-announces-relocation-of-its-corporate
    -headquarters-to-louisiana-from-california.aspx.

18. Rick Rothacker, "Chiquita Moving HQ to North Carolina from Ohio,"
    Reuters, November 29, 2011, http://www.reuters.com/article/2011/11/
    30/chiquita-hq-idUSN1E7AS1N820111130.

19. Monica Davey, "Questions Persisting as Illinois Raises Taxes," *New
    York Times*, January 12, 2011, http://www.nytimes.com/2011/01/13/us/
    13illinois.html?.

20. Markos Moulitsas, "Democratic Illinois Economically Outpaces Scott
    Walker's Wisconsin," *Daily Kos*, April 20, 2012, http://www.dailykos
    .com/story/2012/04/20/1085039/-Democratic-Illinois-economically
    -outpaces-Scott-Walker-s-Wisconsin.

21. Mitch Daniels, in conversation with Meredith Whitney, May 18, 2012.

22. U.S. Department of Commerce, U.S. Census Bureau, "State Govern-
    ment Finances: Historical Data: 2010," http://www.census.gov/govs/
    state/historical_data_2010.html; U.S. Department of Commerce, U.S.
    Census Bureau, "State Government Finances: Historical Data: 2006,"

http://www.census.gov/govs/state/historical_data_2006.html; Governing, State Debt per Capita, http://www.governing.com/gov-data/economy-finance/state-debt-per-capita-figures.html; Moody's Investors Service, 2011 State Debt Medians Report, http://www.governing.com/gov-data/economy-finance/state-debt-per-capita-figures.html; Meredith Whitney Advisory Group, "Tragedy of the Commons Third Edition: 2012 Update," p. 7.

23. Mitch Daniels, in conversation with Meredith Whitney, May 18, 2012.

24. Michelle Celarier, "Home Is Where . . . ," *New York Post*, July 27, 2012, http://www.nypost.com/p/news/business/home_is_where_KMF2T2RLPYc2KRvkXHNyyK.

25. Janet Zink, "Gov. Rick Scott on a Mission to Repeal 1,000 State Rules," *Tampa Bay Times*, September 5, 2011, http://www.tampabay.com/news/politics/gubernatorial/gov-rick-scott-on-a-mission-to-repeal-1000-state-rules/1189933.

26. Rick Scott, in conversation with Meredith Whitney, August 7, 2012.

27. "Pilot Pen Moving Headquarters to Jacksonville," *Jacksonville Business Journal*, September 8, 2008, http://www.bizjournals.com/jacksonville/stories/2008/09/08/daily5.html.

28. Tax Foundation, "State and Local Tax Burdens: All States, One Year, 1977–2010," http://taxfoundation.org/article/state-and-local-tax-burdens-all-states-one-year-1977-2010, data retrieved from: http://interactive.taxfoundation.org/burdens/burdensdata.php?state=all&mode=all_states_one_year&format=csv.

29. Colin Pope, "Apple to Build $304M Campus, Hire 3,600 in Austin," *Austin Business Journal*, March 9, 2012, http://www.bizjournals.com/austin/news/2012/03/09/apple-to-build-304m-campus-hire.html.

30. Jeff Adkins, "eBay Creating 1,000 Jobs in Austin, TX," *BusinessClimate.com*, October 10, 2012, http://businessclimate.com/texas-economic-development/ebay-creating-1000-jobs-austin-tx.

31. Tom Gray and Robert Scardamalia, "The Great California Exodus: A Closer Look," Manhattan Institute for Policy Research, September

2012, http://www.manhattan-institute.org/html/cr_71.htm#.URBBN-h3Ac9U.

32. U.S. Department of Commerce, U.S. Census Bureau, Geographical Mobility/Migration: State-to-State Migration Flows, Tables: State-to-State Migration Flows 2005–2009 and 2010,http://www.census.gov/hhes/migration/data/acs/state-to-state.html.

33. Tami Luhby, "California Companies Fleeing the Golden State," *CNNMoney*, July 12, 2011, http://money.cnn.com/2011/06/28/news/economy/California_companies/index.htm.

34. J. P. Donlon, "Another Triumph for Texas: Best/Worst States for Business 2012," *Chief Executive*, May 2, 2012, http://chiefexecutive.net/best-worst-states-for-business-2012.

35. Sheryl Jean, "Dallas Fed President Richard Fisher: Texas Jobs Have Grown Across All Income Categories, Outpacing U.S. Job Growth," *Dallas Morning News*, December 18, 2012, http://bizbeatblog.dallasnews.com/2012/12/dallas-fed-president-richard-fisher-texas-jobs-growing-across-all-income-categories-outpacing-u-s-job-growth.html/.

36. Federal Housing Finance Agency, House Price Indexes, State HPI Comparisons, California and Texas, http://www.fhfa.gov/Default.aspx?Page=215&Type=compare&Area1=CA&Area2=TX&Area3=.

37. Jon Birger, "How Jeffery Boyd Took Priceline from Dot-bomb to High-flier," *CNNMoney*, September 11, 2012, http://tech.fortune.cnn.com/2012/09/11/priceline-jeffery-boyd/.

38. Arthur Laffer, interview by Meredith Whitney, June 14, 2012.

39. U.S. Department of Commerce, Bureau of Economic Analysis, Regional Data, GDP and Personal Income, http://www.bea.gov/iTable/iTable.cfm?reqid=70&step=1&isuri=1&acrdn=1#reqid=70&step=10&isuri=1&7007=2011,2007&7093=Levels&7090=70&7035=-1&7036=-1&7001=1200&7002=1&7003=200&7004=NAICS&7005=-1&7006=00000,04000,06000,12000,32000.

40. Campbell Gibson, U.S. Department of Commerce, U.S. Census Bureau, "Population of the 100 Largest Cities and Other Urban Places in

the United States: 1790 to 1990," June 1998, http://www.census.gov/
population/www/documentation/twps0027/twps0027.html#citypop.

41. Curt Guyette, "Detroit's Vision and Revision," *Metrotimes*, January 16,
2013, http://metrotimes.com/detroit-s-vision-and-revision-1.1430411.

Chapter 9: David Takes On Goliath: New Political Precedents

1. Catherine Saillant and Tony Perry, "2 Big Cities OK Cuts to Worker
Pension Costs," *Los Angeles Times*, June 7, 2012, http://articles.latimes
.com/2012/jun/07/local/la-me-pensions-20120607.

2. Michael Corkery, "San Jose Voters Back Pension Overhaul," *Wall
Street Journal*, June 6, 2012, http://online.wsj.com/article/SB100014240
52702303918204577449410119033138.html.

3. "Elected Official of the Year," *PublicCEO.com*, 2011, http://www.pub
licceo.com/elected-official-of-the-year/; Ben Tracy, "Calif. City Seeks
to Escape Soaring Pension Costs," *CBS News*, March 7, 2012, http://
www.cbsnews.com/8301-18563_162-57392812/calif-city-seeks
-to-escape-soaring-pension-costs/.

4. Floyd Norris, "Orange County's Bankruptcy: The Overview; Orange
County Crisis Jolts Bond Market," *New York Times*, December 8, 1994,
http://www.nytimes.com/1994/12/08/business/orange-county
-s-bankruptcy-the-overview-orange-county-crisis-jolts-bond
-market.html.

5. James O'Toole, "Jefferson County, Alabama to File for Largest Municipal
Bankruptcy," *CNNMoney*, November 9, 2011, http://money.cnn.com/
2011/11/09/news/economy/jefferson_county_bankruptcy/index.htm.

6. Mary William Walsh, "In Alabama, a County That Fell Off the Financial Cliff," *New York Times*, February 18, 2012, http://www.nytimes
.com/2012/02/19/business/jefferson-county-ala-falls-off-the
-bankruptcy-cliff.html?pagewanted=all.

7. Stephen C. Fehr, "Alabama's Largest County Faces Bankruptcy Without State Help," *Stateline*, August 22, 2012, http://www.pewstates.org/

projects/stateline/headlines/alabamas-largest-county-faces-bankruptcy
-without-state-help-8589941276.

8. "NY's Cuomo Warns Localities Not to Expect State Bailout," *Reuters*,
   September 11, 2012, http://in.reuters.com/article/2012/09/10/usa-newyork
   -cuomo-idINL1E8KAFRM20120910.

9. U.S. Department of Commerce, U.S. Census Bureau; Federal Housing Finance Agency, House Price Index, MSA HPI Comparisons,
   Stockton, CA, http://www.fhfa.gov/Default.aspx?Page=216&Type=
   compare&Area1=44700&Area2=&Area3=.

10. Steven Malanga, "How Stockton, California Went Broke in Plain Sight,"
    Wall Street Journal, March 30, 2012, http://online.wsj.com/article/SB100
    01424052702303404704577309231747497906.html.

11. Sydney Evans, Bohdan Kosenko, and Mike Polyakov, "How Stockton
    Went Bust: A California City's Decade of Policies and the Financial
    Crisis That Followed," California Common Sense, http://www.record
    net.com/assets/pdf/SR1474619.PDF.

12. Bob Deis, "A Message from the City That Went Bankrupt," *Wall Street
    Journal*, September 27, 2012, http://online.wsj.com/article/SB10000872
    396390443995604578002200588578188.html.

13. Mary Williams Walsh, "How Plan to Help City Pay Pensions Backfired,"
    New York Times, September 3, 2012, http://www.nytimes.com/2012/09/
    04/business/how-a-plan-to-help-stockton-calif-pay-pensions-backfired
    .html?pagewanted=all; EconStats, "OFHEO House Price Index," http://
    www.econstats.com/ofheo/ofheo_q70.htm; "Why Stockton, California is
    a Sister City to Buffalo, NY," *Get Real Buffalo*, March 31, 2012, http://
    getrealbuffalo.blogspot.com/.

14. Louis Sahagun, "Mammoth Lakes Files for Bankruptcy," L.A. Now,
    Los Angeles Times, July 2, 2012, http://latimesblogs.latimes.com/lanow/
    2012/07/mammoth-lakes-bankruptcy.html.

15. Ryan Hagen, "San Bernardino City Attorney: Evidence of Budget Falsi-
    fication Given to Other Agencies," *Daily News Los Angeles*, July 12,

2012, http://www.dailynews.com/news/ci_21052495/breaking-news-san -bernardino-mayor-morris-addresses-citys.

16. "City Budget Deficit Falls to $300 Million," *CBS Chicago*, September 24, 2012, http://chicago.cbslocal.com/2012/09/24/city-budget-deficit -falls-to-300-million/; Kristen A. Graham, "Phila. School Budget Gap Grows by at Least $37M," *Philly.com*, July 8, 2012, http://articles.philly .com/2012-07-08/news/32578414_1_tax-collection-plan-property-tax -appeals-delinquent-taxes; Alice Walton, "Los Angeles Maintains Credit Ratings Despite Fiscal Concerns," *89.3 KPCC Southern California Public Radio*, June 18, 2012, http://www.scpr.org/blogs/news/2012/06/18/ 6673/la-maintains-credit-ratings-despite-concerns/.

17. Institute for Illinois' Fiscal Sustainability, "What Are the Rhode Island Pension Reforms?" April 19, 2012, http://www.civicfed.org/iifs/blog/what -are-rhode-island-pension-reforms.

Chapter 10: The Way Forward

1. Meredith Whitney and Steve Kroft, *60 Minutes*, CBS News, aired on December 19, 2010; James Jacoby, "State Budgets: The Day of Reckoning," CBS News, December 19, 2010, http://www.cbsnews.com/8301 -18560_162-7166220.html?pageNum=4.

2. Robert Slavin, "Muni Defaults Up 111% and Down 38%, Depending on Data," as quoted in *Bond Buyer*, April 2, 2012, http://www.bondbuyer .com/issues/121_64/muni-defaults-2012-up-and-down-1038128-1.html.

3. Beth Fouhy, "New Govs Take Office Amid Historic Budget Crisis," *Bloomberg Businessweek*, December 20, 2010, http://www.businessweek .com/ap/financialnews/D9K7QCI01.htm.

4. Steven Gray, "Can Drastic Measures Save the Cash-Strapped States?" *Time*, January 20, 2011, http://www.time.com/time/nation/article/ 0,8599,2043086,00.html.

5. Judy Lin and Shannon McCaffrey, "State Budgets: Year Ahead Looms as Toughest Yet," *Huffington Post*, January 15, 2011, http://www

.huffingtonpost.com/2011/01/15/state-budgets-year-ahead-_n_809521.html.

6. William Selway, "U.S. Mayors Say Bond Defaults Likely Amid Strain," *Bloomberg*, January 19, 2011, http://www.bloomberg.com/news/2011-01-19/cities-may-default-on-borrowings-amid-financial-strains-u-s-mayors-say.html.

7. Ray Gustini, "Will Jerry Brown's Budget Save California?" *National Journal*, January 11, 2011, http://www.nationaljournal.com/dailyfray/will-jerry-brown-s-budget-save-california--20110110?mrefid=site_search.

8. Paul Egan and Steve Neavling, "Detroit's Debt Crisis Even Worse Than Thought, State's Review Reveals," *Detroit Free Press*, December 22, 2011, http://www.freep.com/article/20111222/NEWS01/112220519/Detroit-s-debt-crisis-even-worse-than-thought-state-s-review-reveals.

9. Jack Lessenberry, "Missing Headline: Detroit Jumps Off Fiscal Cliff," *Dome*, December 14, 2012, http://domemagazine.com/lessenberry/jl121412.

10. Michael Corkery, "Muni Blues Worry Investors," *Wall Street Journal*, July 25, 2012, http://online.wsj.com/article/SB10000872396390443295404577545362747435078.html.

11. Jon Birger, "Word on Orange County Streets Is No New Sales Tax, Lebenthal Finds (Jim Lebenthal of Lebenthal and Co.)," *Bond Buyer*, June 26, 1995, http://www.highbeam.com/doc/1G1-17138068.html.

12. U.S. Department of Commerce, Bureau of Economic Analysis, Regional Economic Accounts, GDP and Personal Income Gross Domestic Product by State, http://www.bea.gov/iTable/iTable.cfm?reqid=70&step=1&isuri=1&acrdn=1#reqid=70&step=1&isuri=1.

13. Stanley Reed, "High Energy Costs Plaguing Europe," *New York Times*, December 26, 2012, http://www.nytimes.com/2012/12/27/business/energy-environment/27iht-green27.html?_r=0.

14. United States Department of Agriculture, "USDA Agricultural Projections to 2021," February 2012, http://www.usda.gov/oce/commodity/archive_projections/USDAAgriculturalProjections2021.pdf.

15. Jon Birger, "The Great Corn Gold Rush," *CNNMoney*, March 30, 2007, http://money.cnn.com/2007/03/29/magazines/fortune/corn_gold_rush .fortune/index.htm.

16. Federal Housing Finance Agency, "News Release: U.S. House Prices Rose 1.8 Percent from First Quarter to Second Quarter 2012," news release, August 2012, http://www.fhfa.gov/webfiles/24216/q22012hpi.pdf.

17. Moana Howard, "The Booming Business of Worker Accommodations," *Permian Basin Petroleum Association*, August 3, 2012, http://pbog.zac pubs.com/the-booming-business-of-worker-accommodations/.

18. Dan Kraker, "$78M Airport Terminal Opens in Duluth," *MPR News*, January 13, 2013, http://minnesota.publicradio.org/display/web/2013/ 01/12/regional/airpot-terminal-opens-duluth.

19. John Stearns, "Demolition Begins at Site of New Airport Terminal," *Wichita Business Journal*, October 9, 2012, http://www.bizjournals .com/wichita/blog/2012/10/demolition-begins-at-site-of-new.html.

20. Linda Cunningham, "Texas' New P3 Toll Road Project Open to Traffic," *Infra Insight*, October, 24, 2012, http://www.infrainsightblog.com/ 2012/10/articles/tollroadsturnpikesmanaged-lane/texas-new-p3-toll -road-project-open-to-traffic/.

21. Tim Jones, "Bleeding Kansas Shows Peril of GOP Bid to End Income Tax," *Bloomberg*, January 24, 2013, http://www.bloomberg.com/news/2013-01-25/ kansas-bonds-left-behind-highlight-risks-of-levy-cuts-taxes.html.

22. North Carolina Community College System, "Final Summary Report: JobsNOW: '12 in 6' Project," September 2011, http://www.aging.unc .edu/programs/readiness/liaisons/2012_0127/documents/JobsNOW% 20Report.pdf.

23. National Education Association, "2012 Handbook," 2012, http://www .nea.org/assets/docs/nea-handbook.pdf.

24. Chuck Reed, in conversation with Meredith Whitney, July 24, 2012.

25. Joel Millman, "Towns Cut Costs by Sending Work Next Door," *Wall Street Journal*, July 25, 2012, http://online.wsj.com/article/SB1000142405 2702303612804577531543876815920.html.

Index

Adjustable-rate mortgages (ARMs),
    39–41
    Greenspan as proponent of, 38–39
    types of, 41
Agriculture
    boom in central corridor states, 199
    U.S. historical view, 20
Alabama
    Jefferson County bankruptcy, 65,
        187–89
    poverty level in, 141
    unemployment, 169
Alaska
    employment growth, 169
    zero state income tax, 165–66
American Dream, components of,
    31–32
American Recovery and Reinvestment
    Act (ARRA) (2011), 67–69, 140,
    202
Arizona
    home price decline, 47–48
    housing boom in, 45–47
    population inflow to, 82
    poverty level in, 141
    privatization of services, 69–70
    public safety–related cuts, 131
    unemployment, 169
    unfunded pension fund, 102
Arkansas, poverty level in, 137, 141
Asset sales. See Privatization
Atlanta, housing bust impacts, 87–88
Automobile industry

boom-and-bust cycle, 23–25
natural gas as fuel, 161
postrecession rise of, 17, 171

Balloon payment loans, 33
Bank of America, 41–42
Bankruptcy. See Municipal
    bankruptcy
Bear Stearns, 4–5, 47
Bernanke, Ben, on restrictive lending,
    49
Bonds. See General-obligation bonds;
    Municipal bonds;Pension-
    obligation bonds
Boom towns, to ghost town transition,
    19–20, 25

California
    ARRA money, inappropriate use of,
        68
    bankrupt municipalities, 60–61,
        113–14, 186–87, 189–93
    boom-time spending excess, 46, 56,
        60–61
    consumer credit collapse, 75, 80, 86
    consumer debt problem, 74, 80,
        83–85
    debt per capita in, 162
    education cuts, 121–24
    home price decline, 47–48, 80, 87,
        190
    home price escalation, 163, 189
    housing boom in, 44–46, 79, 82–83

California (cont.)
  hydrocarbon reserves, potential for,
    158–59
  negative business environment,
    158–59, 177
  negative equity in, 79, 162
  population flight from, 9, 27–29,
    63–64, 157, 163–64, 168, 177
  poverty level in, 141
  privatization of services, 69
  property-tax capping in, 61–62,
    132, 171
  public employees, excess payments
    to, 60–61, 89–91, 105, 132, 189
  public safety–related cuts, 129–30,
    190
  small businesses collapse, 79–80
  state government indebtedness, 80
  subprime mortgage excess in,
    82–83
  tax rate hike, 9, 166
  tax receipt declines, 27–28
  tax receipts outpaced by spending,
    62
  tax revenues, drop in (2008–), 27
  technical/scientific fields decline,
    28, 176–77
  unemployment, 28, 47, 63–64, 68,
    80, 143–44, 164, 177
  unfunded pension fund, 102
  welfare assistance spending,
    138–39
California Public Employees
    Retirement System (CalPERS),
    61, 190
Canada, mortgage loans in, 35–36
Central corridor states, 155–62. *See
    also specific states*
  agriculture boom in, 199
  bids to lure business/people to,
    171–81
  consumer credit gains in, 76
  consumer debt, lack of, 84
  corporations moving to, 63–64,
    156–57, 166–68, 170–80
  debt-to-income per capita (2011),
    81, 162

  economic boom in, 63–64, 109–11,
    155–62, 198–201
  education spending increase,
    132–33
  financial stability of, 7–8, 29,
    75–76, 109–10, 178–80
  as future economic leaders, 157–58,
    198–201
  jobs/employment growth in, 8,
    63–64, 155–62, 167–73
  manufacturing revival in, 8, 17–18,
    25, 109
  oil and gas production, 158–61
  population inflow to, 27–29, 63–64,
    110, 157, 163–64
  small business growth in, 162
  tax rate cuts in, 201
Chicago, consumer credit collapse, 75
Citigroup, 4
Coal industry, 23
Coastal states. *See also* Housing-bust
    states
  population flight from, 27–29
  real estate asset inflation in, 26
Community Reinvestment Act (1994),
    43
Connecticut
  library cuts, 126–27
  population flight from, 176
  tax rate hike, 69, 176
  unfunded pension fund, 102
Construction companies,
    unemployment problem, 80,
    142–43
Consumer credit
  creditworthiness and
    homeownership, 73–74
  new lenders, types of, 85–86
  unused lines as safety net, 76–77,
    83
Consumer credit cuts, 76–80
  economic disruption from, 7,
    76–77, 79
  limit on access to (2007–), 5–7, 10,
    50, 75–77
  small businesses, impact on, 45,
    79–80

Consumer debt
  in central corridor states, 84
  credit cards, amount on (2008),
    75
  debt per capita in states, 81,
    83–85
  home-based debt. SeeHome-equity
    loans; Mortgage loans
  and homeowners, 45, 74–75
  most overburdened states, 6–7, 74,
    80, 83–85
Corporations, move to central
  corridor states, 63–64, 156–57,
  166–68, 170–80
Cotton production, 20
Countrywide, 40, 41–42
Credit, consumer. *See* Consumer
  credit;Home-equity loans;
  Mortgage loans

Debt, consumer. *See* Consumer
  debt
Demographics. *See* Population
  shifts
Detroit
  boom-and-bust cycle, 23–25
  population flight from, 181
Dot-com crash, 37–38, 59
Down payments, 33
Downsizing, as financial rescue,
  145–46, 150
Dumb money, 167

Economic multiplier effect, 43–44,
  50, 80
Education cuts, 119–24. *See also*
  specific states
  extent in U.S., 73, 119–20
  forms of, 58, 121–22
  higher education, as discretionary
    expense, 119–20, 122
  parental choices, 120
  and tuition cost increase, 123
Employment. *See also* Job creation
  in central corridor states, 8, 63–64,
    155–62, 167–73
  during housing boom, 43–44

losses after crash. *See*
  Unemployment
  inright-to-work states, 166–67
European Union (EU), privatization
  in, 147–48

Fannie Mae, 36–37, 43
Federal Deposit Insurance
  Corporation (FDIC), 36
Federal government
  federal-to-state money transfers,
    67–69, 70
  fiscal cliff, 140
  homeownership, promotion of,
    33–39, 42–43, 50–51
  poverty-related assistance, 138–40
Federal Housing Authority (FHA), 34,
  35, 36
Financial collapse (2007–). *See also*
  specific topics
  and consumer credit collapse, 5–7,
    10, 50, 75–77
  financial industry losses, 4–5
  and irresponsible lending practices.
    See Housing bust;Mortgage-
    backed securities; Subprime
    loans
  loan originators, collapse of, 41–42
  and poverty, 135–45
  recovery, regional differences, 8,
    156, 165–73
  retirement plan losses, 94, 97
  and state/local governments. *See*
    Central corridor states;Housing-
    bust states; Local governments;
    State governments
  stock market losses (2008), 94
  and unemployment, 7, 9, 141–44
Fire department cuts, 131
Fiscal cliff, 68, 140
Florida
  bid to lure business/people to,
    174–76
  boom-time spending excess, 57
  consumer credit collapse, 75
  education cuts, 59
  financial recovery tactics, 175

Florida (cont.)
home price decline, 47–48
housing boom in, 44–47
population inflow to, 168
poverty level in, 137, 141
tax receipts outpaced by spending,
63
unemployment, 141, 143–44, 169
welfare assistance spending, 139
zero state income tax, 165–66, 175
Flyover states. *See* Central corridor
states
Food stamps, 138, 144
Freddie Mac, 37

Gambling, 69
General-obligation bonds. *See also*
Municipal bonds
new issues (2010–), 70–71
Geographic mobility. *See* Population
shifts
Georgia, housing bust impacts, 87–88
Ghost towns, 19–20, 25
Global view
homeownership/mortgages, 35–36
privatization of services, 146,
147–48
U.S. as global competitor, 17, 161
Golden West Financial, 40, 41
Governmental Accounting Standards
Board (GASB) rules, 53, 91, 95
Government-sponsored enterprise
(GSE), 36–37
Great Depression, 6, 33
Great Recession. *See* Financial
collapse (2007–)
Greenspan, Alan
connection to securitization, 39
interest rate cuts by, 38
as proponent of ARMs, 38–39

Home-equity loans
during boom, 74
inappropriate use of, 43, 46
limited access, post–2007, 76–77
small business use of, 7, 79
Homeownership

during boom, 43, 44, 45, 73
and creditworthiness, 73–74
economic multiplier effect, 43–44,
50, 80
federal government promotion of,
32–43, 50–51
global view, 35–36
Home Owners' Loan Corporation,
34
Home price decline
negative equity created by, 7, 79,
86, 108, 162
and property taxes, 78–79, 88
reverse wealth effect, 88
states with highest rate, 47–48, 80,
87
Homestead Act (1862), 32
Housing boom, 43–47
booming states, 26, 44, 82
consumer debt during, 45
economic era of, 25–26, 44–47
economic ripple effect of, 43–44,
81–83, 143
homeowner misperception during,
46
home price escalation, 44–45
irresponsible lending during. *See*
Subprime loans
new homeowners, statistics on, 43,
44, 45, 73
property tax increase during, 81–82
and retirement age buyers, 18–19,
26
state spending excess during, 9–11,
46, 49, 56–63, 81–82
Housing bust, 47–51
and consumer credit collapse, 5–7,
10, 50, 75–77
home price decline, 47, 75, 78–79,
88
loan originators, collapse of,
41–42
negative equity created by, 7, 79,
108, 162
progression of, 47, 82
states, overall impacts on, 6–11, 49,
57–59, 88

states negatively impacted.
*See*Housing-bust states
states not affected by. *See* Central
corridor states
and unemployment, 7, 9, 142–44
Housing-bust states. See also specific
states
bankrupt cities/municipalities,
186–93
debt per capita in, 81, 83–85, 162
Greek crisis compared with, 116
list of, 6–7, 26, 44
population flight from, 27–29,
63–64, 157
public services decline in, 9, 10–11,
26–27, 110
states with contraction versus
collapse, 87
assubprime-loan targets, 7
total liabilities (2011), 111–13

Illinois
consumer debt, average in, 169
debt per capita in, 96
education cuts, 123
pension-obligation bond debt,
103–4
tax rate hike, 9, 69, 173
Indiana
bid to lure business/people to,
172–74
consumer debt, average in, 169
corporations moving to, 171
debt per capita in, 96
education spending increase,
132–33
financial recovery tactics, 145–46,
149–50, 174
mobile capital investment in, 169
privatization of services in, 145–46,
149–50
Industrial Revolution, 20–22
Infrastructure
new, in central corridor states,
200–201
privatization of services for, 145–46,
147–48

Iowa
consumer credit gains in, 76
economic boom in, 109, 156, 180

Jefferson County (Alabama)
bankruptcy, 65, 187–89
Job creation
in bad economy, 202–3
and job training, 144–45, 202–3
and privatization, 145, 149
Job training
cuts to programs, 124, 140
necessity for, 144–45, 202–3
JPMorgan Chase, 41

Kentucky, poverty level in, 141

Las Vegas
home price decline, 108
housing boom in, 107–8
population flight from, 181
subprime mortgage excess in, 86
Lehman Brothers, 47
Libraries, cuts and closings, 124–27
Local governments
programs/services cutbacks, 55
property tax hikes, 66, 69
public service delivery by, 66
revenue, sources of, 64, 66
state government transfers to (2010),
67
state revenue cuts to, 55, 64, 72, 110
Lottery laws, 69
Louisiana
corporations moving to, 173
economic boom in, 156
employment growth, 169
oil and gas production, 159
personal income growth in, 159
poverty level in, 137, 141

Mammoth Lakes (California)
bankruptcy, 114, 190–91
Manufacturing jobs
decline of, 5
rise in central corridor states, 8,
17–18, 25, 109

Maryland, tax rate hike, 69
Massachusetts
    boom-and-bust cycle, 20–23, 25
    boom-time spending excess, 58
    education cuts, 58
Medicaid
    federal aid to states for, 138
    increase in enrollees/expense, 59,
        65, 119
Michigan
    education cuts, 123
    emergency management measures,
        114, 140–41
    library closings, 125–26
    poverty level in, 137
    welfare assistance spending, 139
Mississippi
    boom-and-bust cycle, 20, 32
    poverty level in, 135–36, 141
    tax-supported liabilities of, 136
Mobile capital investment, 169
Mortgage-backed securities
    collapse of market, 3–6, 48
    creation and sale of, 2–3, 40, 82
    Greenspan connection to, 39
Mortgage loans
    adjustable-rate. *See*Adjustable-rate
        mortgages (ARMs)
    Canadian system, 35–36
    interest tax deduction, 35
    irresponsible lending. *See*
        Subprime loans
    loan modification programs, 34
    postcollapse conditions for,
        48–49
    in U.S., historical view, 33–43
Municipal bankruptcy
    bankrupt cities/municipalities,
        60–61, 113–14, 186–93
    priority payments after, 106, 186,
        187, 192
Municipal bonds
    bankruptcy and payouts, 106, 186,
        187, 190
    defaults on, 114–15, 183–84,
        195–97
    new issues (2010–), 70–71

    payouts by state residents, 77–78,
        198
    as revenue source, 65, 71

Nebraska, economic boom in, 156
Negative equity
    defined, 7, 108
    states with, 79, 86, 108, 162
Nevada
    boom-time spending excess, 56
    consumer debt problem, 74
    education cuts, 108–9, 117
    home price decline, 87, 108
    home price escalation, 108
    housing boom in, 45–47, 107–8
    housing bust impacts, 108–9
    mortgage credit, limits on, 86
    negative equity in, 86, 108
    poverty level in, 137, 141
    state budget cuts, 55
    state budget deficit, 108
    subprime mortgage excess in, 86
    tax rate hike, 69
    unemployment, 47, 141, 143–44,
        169
    unfunded pension fund, 102
    zero state income tax, 165–66
New Hampshire, S&L crisis, 49
New Jersey
    consumer debt, 80, 169
    education cuts, 123
    housing boom in, 45
    pension fund borrowing by, 62, 101
    property tax, highest in U.S.,
        164–65, 169
    state government indebtedness, 80
    unfunded pension fund, 98–99,
        104
New Mexico, poverty level in, 141
New York
    fracking debate, 159
    housing boom in, 45
    pension fund health of, 102
    state budget cuts, 55
    tax receipts outpaced by spending,
        62–63
New York City

consumer credit collapse, 75
population flight from (1950–1980), 180–81
public employees, excess payments to, 11
NINJA loans, 41
North Carolina
corporations moving to, 173
education cuts, 59
job creation in, 202–3
mobile capital investment in, 169
North Dakota
economic boom in, 109–10, 155–56, 180
employment growth, 159, 161, 169, 199
housing shortage in, 199
oil and gas production, 155, 158, 159, 161
personal income growth in, 159

Ohio
mobile capital investment in, 169
poverty level in, 137
unfunded pension fund, 104
Oil and gas production, in central corridor states, 158–61
Oklahoma
corporations moving to, 171
employment growth, 161, 169
oil and gas production, 159, 161
Orange County (California)
bankruptcy, 186–87, 197–98, 201

Pawn shops, 85–86
Pennsylvania
boom-and-bust cycle, 23, 170
consumer debt, average in, 169
mobile capital investment in, 169
oil and gas production, 159
taxes, low in, 168–69
Pension funds. *See* Public employee pension funds
Pension-obligation bonds, 103–4, 184, 189–90
Personal income growth, states with, 159–60

Plath, Tony, 42
Police department cuts, 129, 131–32, 190
Population shifts
andboom-and-bust cycles, 19–20, 25, 169–70
to lower taxation regions, 168–69, 171
migration to central corridor states, 27–29, 63–64, 110, 157, 163–64, 177
to Sand States, during boom, 82
state tax receipts, impact on, 27–29, 63
Poverty, 135–45
breaking cycle, actions for, 144–45
high-poverty states, 135–37, 141
rate comparison (2000 and 2010), 142–43
and unemployment, 137–38, 141–44
Poverty assistance
dependency created by, 140, 144
federal aid/costs related to, 138–40
program expirations (2013), 140
states with highest, 138–39
Prison system cuts, 129–30
Privatization, 145–51
arguments against, 149–50
assets to privatize, 145–48
economic advantages of, 145–49
of education, 140–41
global examples, 146, 147–48
Indiana example, 145–46, 149–150
job creation through, 145, 149
of state park operations, 69–70
of waste collection, 128–29
Property taxes
cap on, California, 61–62, 132, 171
as factor in home purchase, 79, 168–69
highest in U.S., 164–65, 169
hikes after housing bust, 66, 69
and home price decline, 78–79, 88
increase during boom, 81–82
as local government revenue, 64, 66
and public services, 7, 27, 66, 128

Public employee pension funds,
    89–106
  arguments against high payouts,
    91–93, 190, 192–93
  cost-of-living adjustments (COLAs)
    on, 96, 97–98
  crowding out of state budget by,
    92–93, 104–5, 115
  disclosure on unfunded debt
    (2008–2011), 91, 95, 101–5
  financing of, 97–100
  future scenario for, 115
  investment returns, accounting
    tricks for, 100–101
  pension-obligation bonds, 103–4,
    184
  priority over other spending, 92,
    115, 192
  reforms, types of, 102, 105–6,
    184–86, 193
  responsible states, 102
  running out of money prediction,
    96
  state borrowing from, 62, 65,
    95–96, 101, 102–3
  taxpayer responsibility for, 95, 97–98
  unfunded state obligations, 53, 70,
    91–92, 98–99, 101–2
Public employees. See also specific
    states
  excessive benefits to, 11, 60–61,
    81–82, 89–91, 116–17, 132
  incentives for workers, 94–95
  pensions to. See Public employee
    pension funds
  reform of system, 203–5. See also
    Privatization
Public safety problem, and budget
    cuts, 129–32, 190

Real-estate boom. See Housing boom
Relocation. See Population shifts
Retirement plans
  growth, factors in, 97
  losses and financial collapse, 94, 97
  of public employees. See Public
    employee pension funds

Reverse wealth effect, 88
Rhode Island
  pension fund reform, 106, 193
  pension investment return
    assumption, 100–101
  unemployment, 169
Right-to-work laws, 166
Romer, Christina, 67
Roosevelt, Franklin D., 33

San Bernadino (California)
    bankruptcy, 113, 131–32, 191–93
Savings-and-loan (S&L) banks, 34–35,
    37
Securitization. SeeMortgage-backed
    securities
Slavery, 20
Small businesses
  credit, sources for, 7, 79
  credit cuts, impact of, 45, 79–80
  growth, central corridor states, 162
Smart money, 167–68
South Dakota
  personal income growth in, 159
  zero state income tax, 165–66
State budgets. See also individual
    states
  boom-time spending excess, 9–11,
    46, 49, 56–63
  closing gaps, methods used, 62,
    109, 112, 117
  debt caps of, 77–78
  debts, taxpayer responsibility for,
    11–12, 77–78
  discretionary budget items, 117, 119
  downsizing, necessity of, 145–46
  economically stable states. See
    Central corridor states
  economically unstable states.
    SeeHousing-bust states
  education cuts, 58, 119–24
  emergency money, lack of, 117
  expenditure changes (2000–2010),
    56–57
  fiscal cliff, 140
  geographic mobility, impact on,
    26–29, 63–64

largest expenses, 119
legal disclosure requirements for, 53, 91, 95
libraries, cuts to, 124–27
Medicaid costs, increase in, 59, 65, 119
miscellaneous tax hikes, 69
mismanagement, lack of transparency about, 113–17
pension fund debt. *See* Public employee pension funds
pet projects, financing of, 11, 57
public health cuts, 73
public safety–related cuts, 129–32
revenue sources for, 53–55, 65, 70–71
tax rate hikes, 69, 78–79
tax receipt declines, 27–28, 57–58, 63
tax receipt rebound (2010–), 63, 69
tax receipts outpaced by debt service, 72–73
tax receipts outpaced by spending, 58–59, 64–65, 72, 111, 118, 136
total liabilities (2011), 111–13
waste-collection cuts, 127–29
welfare monies from fed to, 138–40
State governments. See also specific states
ARRA money, use of, 67–69, 140
borrowing and loans by, 11, 65–66, 71–72, 77–78, 116, 118
federal government transfers to, 67–69, 70, 112–13
gambling, considering, 69
housing bust, overall impacts, 6–11, 49, 57–59
municipal bond debt issued by, 65, 70–71, 77–78
privatization of services, 69–70, 128–29, 145–51
public service delivery by, 54, 66
and unemployment cycle, 10, 63
Steel industry, 23
Stockton (California) bankruptcy, 60–61, 114, 130, 189–90
Subprime loans, 7–8

advantages for banks, 2, 5
ARMs as, 39–41
bank-targeted states, 7
birthplace of, 82–83
creation and sale of, 39–40
irresponsible lending practices, 3, 5, 7, 39, 41, 43
securitization of. *See*Mortgage-backed securities
Suburbanization, 21
Sun Belt states. *See also specific states*
real estate inflation in, 26

Taxation. *See also* Property taxes
mortgage interest deduction, 35
state tax hikes. *See specific states*
zero tax states, 165–66
Tennessee, personal income growth in, 159
Texas
boom-time spending excess, 56, 57
corporations moving to, 171, 176–78
debt per capita in, 83
employment growth, 169, 177
infrastructure projects, 200–201
mobile capital investment in, 169
oil and gas production, 158, 159
personal income growth in, 159
population inflow to, 63–64, 157–58
poverty level in, 141
revenue, sources of, 57
tax receipts outpaced by spending, 63
waste-collection cuts, 128
welfare assistance spending, 139
zero state income tax, 165–66, 178
Textile industry, 20–22

Unemployment
breaking cycle, actions for, 144–45
economic costs of, 135–36, 141
insurance, state depletion of, 144
and poverty, 137–38, 141–44
states with highest rate, 7, 9, 47, 68, 160
states with lowest rate, 8, 160

Unions
  contracts/compensation. *See* Public
    employees
  right-to-work laws versus, 166–67
U.S. economy, 19–29
  agrarian economy era, 20
  boom-and-bust cycles, 19–20,
    22–26, 170
  economic crash/recession (2007–).
    See Financial collapse (2007–)
  housing/leverage revolution, 25–26,
    44
  Industrial Revolution, 20–22
  manufacturing era, 23–25, 44
  manufacturing revival, 17–18, 25
  power revolution era, 22–23
  state and local level. *See* Local
    governments; State budgets;
    State governments
U.S. government. *See* Federal
    government

Veteran's Administration (VA)
  mortgages, 36

Virginia
  mobile capital investment in,
    169
  waste-collection cuts, 128

Wachovia, 41
Washington, D.C., poverty level in,
  141
Washington Mutual, 41
Washington State
  state budget cuts, 55
  zero state income tax, 165–66
Waste-collection cuts, 127–29
Welfare programs. *See* Poverty
    assistance
West Virginia, poverty level in,
  141
Wisconsin, bid to lure business/people
  to, 173
Wyoming
  high per capita income of, 123
  oil and gas production, 159, 161
  tuition costs in, 123
  zero state income tax, 165–66